LEVEL 3 PRACTICE EXAMS – VOLUME 1

Online Answers and Explanations 3

How to Use The Level 3 Practice Exams 5

Practice Exam 1

    Morning Session ....

    Afternoon Session ....

Practice Exam 2

    Morning Session 71

    Afternoon Session 97

Practice Exam 3

    Morning Session 127

    Afternoon Session 155

Practice Exam 1 Answers

    Morning Session 183

    Afternoon Session 215

Practice Exam 2 Answers

    Morning Session 232

    Afternoon Session 261

Practice Exam 3 Answers

    Morning Session 281

    Afternoon Session 311

CFA® LEVEL 3 PRACTICE EXAMS – VOLUME 1

©2009 Kaplan, Inc. All rights reserved.

Published in September 2009 by Kaplan Schweser.

Printed in the United States of America.

ISBN: 1-4277-9471-5

PPN: 4550-0124

2010 Practice Exam Answers and Explanations are Online at www.schweser.com

Answers and explanations for self-grading all questions, essays as well as item sets, are available at the end of this book. For the essay questions, you will find both "For the Exam" and "Discussion" answers. "For the Exam" answers are short, to-the-point answers that would earn 100% of the available points for the question. They are presented to help you practice cutting down your actual exam answers to the bare minimum to conserve valuable time. "Discussion" answers explain the related concepts and help you to understand why the answer is what it is. In the process of taking the practice exams, the discussion answers will actually serve as a review.

Answers to item set questions are also available online at *www.schweser.com*. They contain embedded links to supporting curriculum material for the relevant Learning Outcome Statements. You also have online access to Performance Tracker, a tool that will provide you with exam diagnostics to target your study and review effort and allow you to compare your scores on Practice Exams to those of other candidates.

Just Use Your Schweser *Online Access* Account

All purchasers of SchweserNotes™ receive an e-mail with login information for Online Access. This is your login to view the video volumes in the Schweser Library, to use the Schweser Study Planner, to get Practice Exam item set answer explanations, to use Performance Tracker, and (if you purchased the Essential, Premium, or PremiumPlus Solutions) to get your questions answered during Office Hours. Simply log in at *www.schweser.com* and select Online Access to use any of these features. Access Practice Exam answers and explanations with the Practice Exams Vol. 1 left-hand menu item. If you need password help, go to *www.schweser.com/password* or use the Password Help link that appears if your login is unsuccessful.

Practice Exam Online Features at a Glance

Item Set Answer Explanations
Our format contains expanded Practice Exam answer explanations to help candidates understand why one answer is the best of all the choices. When using Performance Tracker, you can choose to get detailed explanations for only those questions you missed or for all questions.

Links to Curriculum
Within the answer explanations, we have embedded links to the relevant content for review. This can include multiple Learning Outcome Statements, concepts, definitions, or formulas.

Exam Diagnostics

When you enter your answers in our Performance Tracker utility, you can request a breakdown of your overall score on the afternoon session of any exam. You can even get the Learning Outcome Statement references for questions you answered incorrectly to help you focus your review efforts.

HOW TO USE THE LEVEL 3 PRACTICE EXAMS

Save the Practice Exams for last. A good strategy is to take one exam in each of the three weeks prior to the exam. Plan ahead (e.g., actually schedule each practice exam and take it on the scheduled day) and do your best to mimic actual exam conditions: take the entire exam in one sitting, time yourself, have someone work on a computer in the same room; for distractions, have that person leave the room occasionally, turn the temperature in the room up and down, and talk to himself. Remember, no matter how challenging we make our Practice Exams, the actual exam experience will be different, because you and everyone else in the room will be nervous and fidgety with the pressures of the day. Also, your perception will probably be that the actual exam was much more difficult than our Practice Exams or even old CFA Exam questions you may have seen.

At times it can even appear that the material on the exam wasn't covered anywhere in our study products or the curriculum. This is because the Level 3 curriculum is far broader than it seems, and no one can anticipate everything that will be asked on the exam. It could also simply be that the material is asked in a form or language that is different from what you expect. Regardless, the important thing is to be able to think clearly and draw on your store of knowledge. As I have described my doctoral program experience, they teach you a lot of finance, but they can't teach you everything. They do, however, teach you to think on your feet and piece together your knowledge in several areas to arrive at a reasonable explanation.

Be ready for essay and multiple-choice questions. The morning session (3 hours and 50% the exam) is entirely constructed response essay format. The afternoon session (3 hours and 50%) is 10 selected response item sets, each worth 18 points. For the 2010 exam, expect any topic (e.g., portfolio management, derivatives, GIPS®) in either format. The Level 3 topic area weights, as presented by CFA Institute®, are shown in Figure 1.

Figure 1: Topic Area Weights for the Level 3 CFA Exam

Topic Area	Level 3 Weight
Ethical and Professional Standards (total)	10%
Quantitative Methods, Economics, Financial Reporting and Analysis, and Corporate Finance	0%
Equity Investments	5–15%
Fixed Income	10–20%
Derivatives	5–15%
Alternative Investments	5–15%
Portfolio Management and Wealth Planning (total)	45–55%

* Note: These weights are intended to guide the curriculum and exam development processes. Actual exam weights may vary slightly from year to year. Please note that some topics are combined for testing purposes.

Figure 2 below shows the topic areas by study session. When you compare Figure 2 to Figure 1, the topic area weights in Figure 1 are a little confusing. For example, you will notice in Figure 2 that Study Session 7 is titled *Economic Concepts for Asset Valuation in Portfolio Management*. Then you will notice that the weight for Economics in Figure 1 is zero. As explained to me by a representative of CFA Institute, this is because Economics is tested as part of Portfolio Management. In fact, Study Sessions 3 through 18 fall under the umbrella of Portfolio Management. Just how the individual topics will be tested is somewhat of an unknown, so your focus is exactly the same as that for prior years' candidates; you must learn the entire Level 3 curriculum.

Figure 2: 2010 Level 3 Topic Areas by Study Session

Study Session	Topic Area	Title
1	Ethics and Standards	Code of Ethics and Professional Standards
2	Ethics and Standards	Ethical and Professional Standards in Practice
3	Portfolio Management	Behavioral Finance
4	Portfolio Management	Private Wealth Management
5	Portfolio Management	Portfolio Management for Institutional Investors
6	Portfolio Management	Capital Market Expectations
7	Portfolio Management	Economic Concepts
8	Portfolio Management	Asset Allocation
9	Portfolio Management	Management of Fixed Income Portfolios
10	Portfolio Management	Global Bonds and Fixed Income Derivatives
11	Portfolio Management	Equity Portfolio Management
12	Portfolio Management	Equity Portfolio Management
13	Portfolio Management	Alternative Investments
14	Portfolio Management	Risk Management
15	Portfolio Management	Risk Management Application of Derivatives
16	Portfolio Management	Execution; Monitoring and Rebalancing
17	Portfolio Management	Performance Evaluation and Attribution
18	Portfolio Management	Global Investment Performance Standards

Don't underestimate Level 3. Many candidates believe that the Level 2 curriculum and exam are the hardest and Level 3 is the most enjoyable. However, do not take Level 3 lightly. Your best strategy is to come to the exam as prepared and confident as you can be. There is a lot of new material every year at Level 3, and the Level 3 pass rate has been below 55% the last three years, so relying on the comments of those who took the exam last year, or even relying on last year's study materials, could be a prescription for disaster.

Write effective answers to the essay questions. CFA Institute's guideline answers for old exam questions are "perfect answers" (i.e., the one you would write if you had enough time). Also, CFA Institute typically gives you much more answer space than you need (often several pages for a one-paragraph answer), so don't think you are expected to fill all the answer space provided. Just like our "For the Exam" answers, your responses should be concise and, most importantly, address the command words. This way, there can be no doubt that you are addressing the question.

Give the CFA answer. Graders use an answer key and don't give points for creative thought, either yours or theirs! That is, they are not allowed to read anything into your answer, so you must be precise. Also, organize your work and think before you write. If the graders can't find or decipher your work, you will receive no credit. Although not strictly required, make sure to use the template for your answer, if one is provided.

Be prepared. It should go without saying that you should get plenty of sleep the night before the exam. Bring all necessary items (including snacks) with you, and arrive early enough at the test site to get a decent parking space. In fact, I recommend thoroughly checking out the site before exam day. *Important!* Be sure to read the CFA Institute guidelines for test day, which can be found on the CFA Institute website. Also, remember to answer *every* question, even if it means guessing. Graders can only award points; they cannot deduct points for wrong answers.

My thanks to the Schweser team. I would like to thank all of my colleagues at Schweser, especially Kurt Schuldes, CFA; Kristen Hutchins, Lead Editor; and Jessica Benrud, Editorial Assistant, for their incredible work ethic and commitment to quality. Schweser would not be the company it is, nor could it provide the quality products you see, without all the Schweser content and editing professionals.

Best regards,

Bruce Kuhlman

Dr. Bruce Kuhlman, CFA, CAIA
Vice President and Level 3 Manager
Kaplan Schweser

Exam 1
Score Sheet

MORNING SESSION		
Question	Maximum Points	Your Estimated Score
1A	12	
1B	10	
1C	6	
1D	4	
2A	12	
2B	18	
3	9	
4	12	
5A	9	
5B	12	
5C	6	
6A	6	
6B	6	
6C	6	
7A	6	
7B	6	
7C	6	
8	12	
9A	4	
9B	8	
9C	10	
Total	180	

AFTERNOON SESSION		
Question	Maximum Points	Your Score
10	18	
11	18	
12	18	
13	18	
14	18	
15	18	
16	18	
17	18	
18	18	
19	18	
Total	180	

Certain Passing Score: 252 of 360 (70%)
Probable Passing Score: 234 (65%)

Please note that we write these exams to be as challenging and representative as possible. However, due to the relaxed conditions that most candidates apply when they "take" these exams (e.g., "I need a break; I think I'll go to the refrigerator and get a snack"), you should adjust your score downward by 10–15 percentage points to get a more accurate measure of the score you would have actually received on exam day. Also, you must be honest with yourself for your score on this exam to have any meaning. Don't assume, for example, that if your essay answer is close, the graders will be generous with points.

Exam 1 Morning Session
Topic Breakdown

Question	Topic	Minutes
1	Portfolio Management—Individual	32
2	Portfolio Management—Institutional	30
3	Behavioral Finance	12
4	Global Investment Performance Standards	12
5	Equity Portfolio Management	27
6	Performance Evaluation and Attribution	18
7	Fixed Income/Derivatives	15
8	Portfolio Management—Individual	12
9	Economic Concepts	22
	Total	180

EXAM 1
MORNING SESSION

QUESTION 1 HAS FOUR PARTS FOR A TOTAL OF 32 MINUTES

Ernie Marks, 62, is the owner of a regional construction company. Marks started the company when he was 20 years old, after receiving his grandfather's old pick-up truck as a birthday gift. Through conservative management and judicious use of bank debt, Marks was able to build the company to over 150 employees. The company is debt-free and generates all required operating funds from internal operations.

Marks' wife, Ellie, does not work and they have two children. Their daughter Allison, 28, suffers from a debilitating illness and requires constant attention. Their son Ernie Jr., 26, is in good health and graduated in the top 5% of his class at a prestigious New England liberal arts university. Marks wants to retire at 65 and wants Ernie Jr. to succeed him in running the company, but all efforts to train his son for succession have failed.

Marks has just sold the company to a national construction concern for cash. The after-tax proceeds from the sale plus the Marks' current investment portfolio total $5 million. The only requirement of the sale agreement is that Marks remain at the firm until he reaches 65, at which time he will retire and have no further obligations to the company.

Marks is seeking financial advice from Christopher Weber, CFA. In their first meeting, Marks makes the following statements:

- "Ellie and I owe nothing on the home in which we have lived for the past 30 years and we do not plan to move. The new owners of the company will pay me $150,000 next year, and that amount will grow at the general rate of inflation until I retire. They will provide medical benefits for Ellie and me for life, but I will not participate in their retirement plan."

- "I would prefer that the portfolio not lose more than 2% of its value in any one year. Since my bank account is earning only 1.5%, however, I realize that my portfolio may require some risk exposure."

- "Ellie and I estimate our personal living expenses will be $100,000 in the coming year, and I agree with you that they will probably grow at the general rate of inflation of 2% per year thereafter. My accountant indicates I will have a 33% average tax rate."

- "We have decided that Ellie can no longer care for Allison as in the past. Had Ellie not helped care for Allison over the past year, we estimate the total cost would have been $100,000, and there would have been no associated tax breaks. Given that a large portion of this cost was medical, I would expect the cost of her care to increase at a rate of approximately 5% annually. It is our intention to provide for Allison's care as long as she lives."

- "Ernie Jr.'s 'free spirit' has essentially made him unemployable, so I want to provide him with a stipend of $50,000 per year with the first $50,000 paid in the coming year. I would also like the stipend to increase annually at the general rate of inflation. When Ellie and I have both passed away, the stipend will stop and Ernie Jr. is to receive a lump-sum payment equal to 50% of our estate. The remainder of the estate will go to charities that I will designate later."

A. **Formulate** the Marks' risk objective. **Calculate** the after-tax nominal rate of return that is required to meet all expenses for the coming year. **Show** your calculations.

Answer Question 1-A in the template provided.

(12 minutes)

Template for Question 1-A

Investment Policy Statement for the Marks	
Risk Objective	
Return Objective	

B. **Construct** the constraints portion of an investment policy statement for the Marks. **Justify** each response with one reason.

Answer Question 1-B in the template provided.

(10 minutes)

Template for Question 1-B

Time Horizon	
Liquidity	
Legal/ Regulatory	
Tax	
Unique Circumstances	

A recent analysis of market expectations has crossed Knight's desk, and she has formulated alternatives for allocating the assets from the sale proceeds. T-bill rates are 2%, and the characteristics of four alternative portfolio allocations are provided in the following table.

Asset Classes	Portfolios			
	A	B	C	D
U.S. stocks	50%	40%	20%	30%
Non-U.S. stocks	25%	20%	10%	0%
U.S. corporate bonds	10%	20%	30%	35%
Cash and equivalents	5%	10%	20%	10%
Real estate (REITs)	0%	5%	10%	10%
U.S. Treasury bills	10%	5%	10%	15%
After-tax income yield	2.0%	2.85%	4.30%	3.90%
Expected Sharpe ratio	0.46	0.60	0.75	0.88
After-tax expected return	8%	7.2%	6.3%	5.2%

C. **Calculate** Roy's Safety-First ratio for the above portfolios and **explain** the information provided by the ratio.

(6 minutes)

D. **Recommend** and **justify** one of the portfolios in the table.

(4 minutes)

QUESTION 2 HAS TWO PARTS FOR A TOTAL OF 30 MINUTES

Universal Insurance Company is an insurance mega-store selling life, property, and casualty insurance policies in all fifty states. The life insurance subsidiary sells products under the UniLife label, and the property and casualty subsidiary sells policies under the UniPC label.

UniLife's total assets are approximately $10 billion, which results in a surplus of $1 billion. As with most life insurance companies, UniLife's asset portfolio is segmented to cover the products sold and to achieve surplus growth to expand business. The segmentation of portfolio assets is a direct result of the increased competition in the life insurance industry and represents an attempt by UniLife to maintain an acceptable spread over their crediting rate of 5% and to more effectively price its products. Total expenses associated with business operations average 2% of assets. UniLife segments its asset base into three main asset classes: short-term/cash-like, long-term fixed-income, and equity instruments. The continued low interest rate environment, as well as improvement in equity markets, has strengthened the quality of UniLife's asset base. The following are statements made during a recent conversation by UniLife's management regarding the portfolio segments:

- "The main purpose of the short-term portfolio is to meet the liquidity requirements of our life insurance and annuity products. Hence, we expect this segment to be invested in assets exceeding or equivalent in safety to 90-day high-grade corporate commercial instruments. The improvement in overall quality of corporate paper has been encouraging."

- "The purpose of our long-term, fixed-income portfolio is to generate sufficient total returns that not only cover the crediting rate, but add to our net interest margin. Investment grade corporates (i.e., rated at least A1) with maturities ranging from 10–20 years are representative assets for this portfolio segment. Again, the improvement of corporate issues is encouraging."

- "The stock portfolio segment exists to provide longer-term growth in company surplus in the hopes of not only improving our financial condition, but also to better meet competitive pricing objectives. The majority of state regulations allow for ample investments in mid- to large-cap domestic equities, but only a small proportion (less than 5%) in international securities. Hence, the equity portfolio should generate returns exceeding the appropriate mid-to-large cap equity indexes such as the S&P MidCap or S&P 500 indexes. The equity market trend has also been positive."

A. **Construct** the risk and return objectives portion of an investment policy statement for UniLife's portfolio segments.

Answer Question 2-A in the template provided.

(12 minutes)

Template for Question Part 2-A

Investment Policy Statement for UniLife Portfolio Segments	
Objectives	**Return Objectives** Short-term portfolio: Long-term bond portfolio: Stock portfolio:
	Risk Tolerance Short-term portfolio: Long-term bond portfolio: Stock portfolio:

B. **Construct** the constraints portion of the investment policy statement for UniLife. Address the time horizon, liquidity, legal/regulatory, tax, and unique circumstances constraints. Address the time horizon and liquidity constraints for each of UniLife's portfolio segments.

Answer Question 2-B in the template provided.

(18 minutes)

©2009 Kaplan, Inc.

Template for Question 2-B

Constraints	**Time Horizon** Short-term portfolio: Long-term portfolio: Stock portfolio:
	Liquidity Short-term portfolio: Long-term portfolio: Stock portfolio:
	Legal/regulatory:
	Taxes:
	Unique considerations:

QUESTION 3 HAS ONE PART FOR A TOTAL OF 9 MINUTES

Bernard Parker, CFA, is a portfolio manager at Net Worth Enhancers. Recently, Parker attended a conference on the outlook for investments over the next decade. During the conference, he heard the following comments:

- "Pension plan participants currently have 90% of their investments in traditional asset classes. Our portfolio management firm has had difficulty getting investors to consider the non-traditional investments that are available through newly introduced exchange traded funds."

- "Despite the recent increase in the CBOE volatility index (VIX) and increasing credit spreads, I have not increased the expected risk premium for stock investments beyond the 4.5% I forecasted earlier this year."

- "The recent bubble in technology stock prices resulted in stock valuations not justifiable by even the most optimistic fundamental analysis. However, it was difficult to exploit the stocks' mispricing because individual investors kept bidding up prices based on their perceptions of the trading of other investors."

Identify the behavioral concept that is best described in each statement. Briefly **describe** each concept.

Answer Question 3 in the template provided.

(9 minutes)

Template for Question 3

Comment	Identify the behavioral concept	Briefly describe the behavioral concept
"Pension plan participants currently have 90% of their investments in traditional asset classes. Our portfolio management firm has had difficulty getting investors to consider the non-traditional investments that are available through newly introduced exchange traded funds."		
"Despite the recent increase in the CBOE volatility index (VIX) and increasing credit spreads, I have not increased the expected risk premium for stock investments beyond the 4.5% I forecasted earlier this year."		
"The recent bubble in technology stock prices resulted in stock valuations not justifiable by even the most optimistic fundamental analysis. However, it was difficult to exploit the stocks' mispricing because individual investors kept bidding up prices as they expected the trend to continue."		

QUESTION 4 HAS ONE PART FOR A TOTAL OF 12 MINUTES

Margaret Knight, CFA, is convinced that reporting portfolio performance according to the Global Investment Performance Standards (GIPS®) will provide her firm a competitive edge in the marketplace. After reading the latest information on the Standards, Knight formulates the following statements as a guide for how she will approach implementation of GIPS at her firm.

- "All composites will have the same beginning and ending annual dates. We will apply accrual accounting to all interest generated by the bonds in our portfolios. Until 2010 we will calculate time-weighted portfolio returns that approximate the effect of daily cash flows. All discretionary, fee-paying portfolios will be included in at least one composite and composites will be defined according to investment strategy and/or objectives."

- "My firm is approximately seven years old. Since GIPS only requires five years of annual investment performance, I can easily meet that requirement. Since my reporting systems are so effective, I also will have no problem maintaining the 5-year reporting requirement into the future."

- "My effective electronic systems will have no trouble capturing and maintaining cost and market values for portfolio valuations. My system automatically generates return information every quarter and, for my international composites, uses the same exchange rate sources for the portfolios and the benchmark."

- "All of my fee-paying portfolios will be included in at least one composite. When clients decide they no longer need my services, my system automatically recalculates previous portfolio performance to reflect the removal of the portfolios from relevant historical performance presentations."

Indicate whether each of Knight's statements is an accurate representation of GIPS. If you find these statements to be inaccurate, **explain** the reason(s) for the inaccuracies.

Answer Question 4 in the template provided.

(12 minutes)

Template for Question 4

Knight's statements	Accurate/inaccurate (circle one)	Reason(s) for inaccuracy
"All composites will have the same beginning and ending annual dates. We will apply accrual accounting to all interest generated by the bonds in our portfolios. Until 2010 we will calculate time-weighted portfolio returns that approximate the effect of daily cash flows. All discretionary, fee-paying portfolios will be included in at least one composite and composites will be defined according to investment strategy and/ or objectives."	Accurate Inaccurate	
"My firm is approximately seven years old. Since GIPS only requires five years of annual investment performance, I can easily meet that requirement. Since my reporting systems are so effective, I also will have no problem maintaining the 5-year reporting requirement into the future."	Accurate Inaccurate	

Knight's statements	Accurate/inaccurate (circle one)	Reason(s) for inaccuracy
"My effective electronic systems will have no trouble capturing and maintaining cost and market values for portfolio valuations. My system automatically generates return information every quarter and, for my international composites, uses the same exchange rate sources for the portfolios and the benchmark."	Accurate Inaccurate	
"All of my fee-paying portfolios will be included in at least one composite. When clients decide they no longer need my services, my system automatically recalculates previous portfolio performance to reflect the removal of the portfolios from relevant historical performance presentations."	Accurate Inaccurate	

QUESTION 5 HAS THREE PARTS FOR A TOTAL OF 27 MINUTES

Julie Carter and Jenny Dumas are senior analysts for Oleander Associates. Oleander provides portfolio management and investment planning for wealthy individuals. Although Oleander has a staff consisting of both analysts and economists, they periodically use outside portfolio managers when appropriate.

Carter and Dumas are currently evaluating the expected performance for a group of portfolio managers they have hired for a subset of their clients' portfolios. For this subset, Carter and Dumas have decided to pursue a core-satellite approach. The data below show the managers' active risk and active returns. Diamond Management uses a value-oriented approach, SRI Advisors uses a socially responsible investing approach, and Wrightsville Managers uses a passive enhanced indexing approach.

	Expected Alpha	Expected Tracking Error	Allocations
Diamond Management	2.80%	5.20%	10%
Hoke Associates	0%	0%	20%
Mosby Investors	2.00%	3.10%	25%
SRI Advisors	3.50%	6.80%	5%
Wrightsville Managers	1.10%	1.62%	40%

A.   **Calculate** the expected active return, expected active risk, and expected information ratio of this subset of managers, given the above allocations.

(9 minutes)

Based on the previous data, Carter and others make the following comments:

- "From your data it appears that your core investment is Hoke associates. Hoke should mitigate the overall risk of your strategy, while the four satellites provide an active return component."
- "The portfolio of Diamond Management is likely weighted towards utility and financial stocks."
- "I expect that investors who pursue an investment approach similar to Hoke Associates will generally have higher information ratios than other investment approaches."
- "We should carefully monitor the style of SRI Advisors because they likely have a bias toward value stocks, given their investment emphasis."

B.   **State** whether or not *each* of these comments is correct or incorrect and **explain** your selection. Rearranging a statement does not constitute an explanation for either a correct or incorrect statement.

Answer Question 5-B in the template provided.

(12 minutes)

Template for Question 5-B

Comment	Correct or incorrect? (circle one)	Explanation, if incorrect
"From your data it appears that your core investment is Hoke associates. Hoke should mitigate the overall risk of your strategy, while the four satellites should provide an active return component."	Correct Incorrect	
"The portfolio of Diamond Management is likely weighted towards utility and financial stocks."	Correct Incorrect	

"I expect that investors who pursue an investment approach similar to Hoke Associates will generally have higher information ratios than other investment approaches."	Correct Incorrect	
"We should carefully monitor the style of SRI Advisors because they likely have a bias toward value stocks, given their investment emphasis."	Correct Incorrect	

Oleander Associates periodically reviews the performance of and fees paid to its outside portfolio managers. Carter and Dumas are in charge of revising the manager questionnaire, reviewing the fee schedules, and preparing a report on the impact of a manager's investment approach on the costs to Oleander.

Under Oleander's current plan, managers are paid 0.40% for the first $20 million under management and 0.35% for asset amounts over $20 million. The primary concern at Oleander is that managers are not provided proper incentive. Under a proposed fee schedule, managers would be paid 0.35% for the first $10 million under management and 0.30% for asset amounts over $10 million plus 10% of all excess returns relative to the manager's benchmark.

During their discussion on these items, Dumas makes the following comments:

- "Our proposed plan should contain high water mark provisions. These provisions state that managers will be paid no less than a certain amount during bear markets. This will prevent us from losing good managers during market downturns and, at the same time, help us avoid paying excess performance fees."
- "Your proposal to cap performance fees is illogical. The cap would discourage your managers from taking the risks necessary to obtain higher returns. Rather than aligning the managers' goals with your own, this could have a very negative effect."

C.   **State** whether *each* of these comments is correct or incorrect and **explain** your selection.

Answer Question 5-C in the template provided.

(6 minutes)

Template for Question 5-C

Comment	Correct or incorrect? (circle one)	Explanation, if incorrect
"Our proposed plan should contain high water mark provisions. These provisions state that managers will be paid no less than a certain amount during bear markets. This will prevent us from losing good managers during market downturns and, at the same time, help us avoid paying excess performance fees."	Correct Incorrect	
"Your proposal to cap performance fees is illogical. The cap would discourage your managers from taking the risks necessary to obtain higher returns. Rather than aligning the managers' goals with your own, this could have a very negative effect."	Correct Incorrect	

QUESTION 6 HAS THREE PARTS FOR A TOTAL OF 18 MINUTES

As part of an attribution analysis, Greg Roberts, CFA, has accumulated the following partial data for his portfolio:

Sectors	Portfolio Sector Weight (%)	Benchmark Sector Weight (%)	Portfolio Sector Return (%)	Benchmark Sector Return (%)
Agricultural	10.55	6.45	−0.82	+1.35
Capital Goods	8.52	8.99	−3.28	−4.34
Consumer Durables	36.22	37.36	1.96	1.98
Energy	5.24	4.65	0.44	0.24
Total Portfolio			1.34	0.56

A.   Using the available data, **calculate** and **explain** the pure sector allocation contribution attributable to the agricultural sector allocation.

(6 minutes)

B.   Using the available data, **calculate** and **explain** the within-sector contribution attributable to the agricultural sector allocation.

(6 minutes)

C.   Using the available data, **calculate** and **explain** the allocation/selection interaction contribution attributable to the agricultural sector allocation.

(6 minutes)

QUESTION 7 HAS THREE PARTS FOR A TOTAL OF 18 MINUTES

Matrix Corporation has decided that since the company has sufficient liquid resources to make any required plan contributions in the future, it will maintain its current asset mix in the defined benefit plan, which is approximately 60% equities and 40% bonds over a wide range of maturities. Matrix officers believe that interest rates are temporarily low, and they do not want to increase the bond allocation for this reason.

Concern remains, however, that if they are wrong, further decreases in interest rates will worsen the underfunded status of the plan and require even greater funding by Matrix over the next several years. Matrix has decided to hedge this risk by taking a position in derivative securities.

Matrix is considering three derivative strategies to provide the hedge described above: exchange-traded interest rate put options, options on Treasury bonds, and futures on Treasury bonds. For each of the alternatives, **describe** the most appropriate strategy, given the goals stated above. For each alternative, **determine** whether the strategy will achieve the stated goal, **support** your conclusion, and **indicate** any potential problems with the strategy.

A.   Exchange-traded interest rate put options.

(6 minutes)

B.   Treasury bond options.

(6 minutes)

C.   Treasury bond futures.

(6 minutes)

QUESTION 8 HAS ONE PART FOR A TOTAL OF 12 MINUTES

Derek May, CFA, recently attended a retirement planning conference on using Monte Carlo techniques in the retirement planning decision. Since it has been a year since May formulated some of his clients' Investment Policy Statements, he decided it might be a good idea to apply some of the concepts discussed at the meeting. May scheduled a meeting with Lacy Dayne, who just returned from her travel abroad and has recently been named executive vice president of marketing for a global provider of wireless portal equipment. In the meeting, May makes the following statements:

- "Since all has gone according to plan since our first meeting a year ago, I think it is time we focus efforts on your retirement. The most important objective is to determine an exact future value goal for your portfolio, integrating an expected rate of return, inflation, and your tax position to produce your retirement profile."

- "Once we have generated the single point estimate for the value of your retirement portfolio, we can apply some Monte Carlo techniques to see various other outcomes. Monte Carlo techniques will generate various portfolio values at retirement but, unfortunately, will not account for the risks inherent in our investment decisions. So, we will just have to pay a little more attention to the various portfolio levels."

- "Think of the various portfolio levels as a range of potential outcomes your portfolio can achieve in ten years. The primary focus when evaluating those outcomes, however, will still be on the risks you wish to avoid in the present, and not necessarily any risks that may occur along the way."

- "Although we can incorporate taxes in our Monte Carlo techniques, the compounding assumptions we made in the single point estimate of portfolio value is just fine. Compounding does not play that much of a role with Monte Carlo, which simplifies the application of the procedure."

State whether you agree or disagree with each of May's statements. **Justify** your answer with a discussion of either a virtue or shortcoming associated with *each* statement.

Answer Question 8 in the template provided.

(12 minutes)

Template for Question 8

Statement	Agree or Disagree (circle one)	Explanation, if incorrect
"Since all has gone according to plan since our first meeting a year ago, I think it is time we focus efforts on your retirement. The most important objective is to determine an exact future value goal for your portfolio, integrating an expected rate of return, inflation, and your tax position to produce your retirement profile."	Agree Disagree	
"Once we have generated the single point estimate for the value of your retirement portfolio, we can apply some Monte Carlo techniques to see various other outcomes. Monte Carlo techniques will generate various portfolio values at retirement but, unfortunately, will not account for the risks inherent in our investment decisions. So, we will just have to pay a little more attention to the various portfolio levels."	Agree Disagree	

"Think of the various portfolio levels as a range of potential outcomes your portfolio can achieve in ten years. The primary focus when evaluating those outcomes, however, will still be on the risks you wish to avoid in the present, and not necessarily any risks that may occur along the way."	Agree Disagree	
"Although we can incorporate taxes in our Monte Carlo techniques, the compounding assumptions we made in the single point estimate of portfolio value is just fine. Compounding does not play that much of a role with Monte Carlo, which simplifies the application of the procedure."	Agree Disagree	

QUESTION 9 HAS THREE PARTS FOR A TOTAL OF 22 MINUTES

Polly Nurnberg and Lilly Hoey are analysts for Greenville Management. Greenville manages the money for individuals and small institutions. Nurnberg and Hoey have been assigned the responsibility of identifying attractive national stock markets. They do so by evaluating the macroeconomic conditions in a country, the strength of its currency, and its future outlook.

Nurnberg and Hoey are currently evaluating the economic data for the European Union, North America, and South America. During a discussion amongst themselves and junior analysts, Nurnberg and Hoey discuss the economic data and prospects of these economies. Hoey has gathered the following data for the Canadian economy:

Neutral rate for Canada	4.0%
Inflation target for Canada	3.5%
GDP long-term trend for Canada	4.5%
Expected Canadian inflation	7.5%
Expected Canadian GDP	6.5%

Based on these figures, Hoey makes the following comments:

• "Using the Taylor rule, I expect the Canadian central bank to target an interest rate of about 6.0%."

• "Based on the information I have gathered, we should be advising clients interested in the Canadian economy to invest in Canadian cash instruments, rather than stocks or bonds."

A. **State** whether *each* of these comments is correct or incorrect. If incorrect, **explain** or **demonstrate** why.

Answer Question 9-A in the template provided.

(4 minutes)

Template for Question 9-A

Comment	Correct or incorrect? (circle one)	Explanation, if incorrect
"Using the Taylor rule, I expect the Canadian central bank to target an interest rate of about 6.0%."	Correct Incorrect	
"Based on the information I have gathered, we should be advising clients interested in the Canadian economy to invest in Canadian cash instruments, rather than stocks or bonds."	Correct Incorrect	

Later in the discussion, Nurnberg makes the following comments regarding the prospects of other economies and currencies:

- "The European Central Bank has been cutting interest rates. One potential impact on the euro is to decrease its value because investors will seek higher returns elsewhere. Unlike most analysts, however, I use a capital flows approach which projects that the euro will actually increase in value."

- "Short-term interest rates on government bonds in Great Britain are 3.2% and 10-year rates are 5.9%. This indicates that, for an investor considering investing in Britain, British corporate bonds would be a better investment than British stocks."

- "Mexico's largest trading partner is the United States. Given that the United States is in the early stages of an economic expansion, Mexican stocks would be attractive investments."

- "Economists project that in the coming months, business confidence in Japan will increase. The Bank of Japan will continue to accommodate growth by keeping interest rates low. Japanese government spending will increase as Japan puts a renewed emphasis on defense spending. Inflation in Japan will fall or remain stable. Given this outlook, I suggest that for an investor with a time horizon of a few years, an allocation to Japanese bonds is warranted."

B. **State** whether *each* of these comments is correct or incorrect. If incorrect, **explain** why.

Answer Question 9-B in the template provided.

(8 minutes)

Template for Question 9-B

Comment	Correct or incorrect? (circle one)	Explanation, if incorrect
"The European Central Bank has been cutting interest rates. One potential impact on the euro is to decrease its value because investors will seek higher returns elsewhere. Unlike most analysts, however, I use a capital flows approach which projects that the euro will actually increase in value."	Correct Incorrect	
"Short-term interest rates on government bonds in Great Britain are 3.2% and 10-year rates are 5.9%. This indicates that, for an investor considering investing in Britain, British corporate bonds would be a better investment than British stocks."	Correct Incorrect	

"Mexico's largest trading partner is the United States. Given that the United States is in the early stages of an economic expansion, Mexican stocks would be attractive investments."	Correct Incorrect	
"Economists project that in the coming months, business confidence in Japan will increase. The Bank of Japan will continue to accommodate growth by keeping interest rates low. Japanese government spending will increase as Japan puts a renewed emphasis on defense spending. Inflation in Japan will fall or remain stable. Given this outlook, I suggest that for an investor with a time horizon of a few years, an allocation to Japanese bonds is warranted."	Correct Incorrect	

Hoey assigns the junior analysts the task of estimating the return on a stock market using the earnings multiplier approach. The following data are for an aggregate stock market:

Current index price	$40.00
Equity risk premium	6.50%
Estimated dividend next period	$1.50
Estimated earnings next period	$5.00
Financial leverage	1.25
Government bond rate	4.00%
Net profit margin	6.00%
Total asset turnover	1.30

C.   **Calculate** the expected rate of return for this stock market using the data above.

(10 minutes)

END OF MORNING SESSION

Exam 1 Afternoon Session
Topic Breakdown

Question	Topic	Minutes
10	Ethical and Professional Standards	18
11	Ethical and Professional Standards	18
12	Portfolio Management—Institutional/GIPS	18
13	Fixed Income/Derivatives	18
14	Fixed Income/Derivatives	18
15	Fixed Income/Derivatives	18
16	Alternative Investments	18
17	Portfolio Management—Individual	18
18	Derivatives	18
19	Monitoring and Rebalancing	18
	Total	180

Exam 1 Selected Response Item Set Answer Sheet

The afternoon session of the Level 3 exam contains 10 Selected Response Item Sets, each with six questions, and you must answer them by filling in a bubble sheet with a number 2 or HB pencil. For realism, we suggest that you use this answer sheet and darken the bubbles corresponding to your answers. This sheet will also facilitate entering your answers into our online Performance Tracker. You have 180 minutes for this session of the exam. That equates to 3 minutes per item set question, so budget your time well.

10.1.	(A) (B) (C)			15.1.	(A) (B) (C)	
10.2.	(A) (B) (C)			15.2.	(A) (B) (C)	
10.3.	(A) (B) (C)			15.3.	(A) (B) (C)	
10.4.	(A) (B) (C)			15.4.	(A) (B) (C)	
10.5.	(A) (B) (C)			15.5.	(A) (B) (C)	
10.6.	(A) (B) (C)			15.6.	(A) (B) (C)	
11.1.	(A) (B) (C)			16.1.	(A) (B) (C)	
11.2.	(A) (B) (C)			16.2.	(A) (B) (C)	
11.3.	(A) (B) (C)			16.3.	(A) (B) (C)	
11.4.	(A) (B) (C)			16.4.	(A) (B) (C)	
11.5.	(A) (B) (C)			16.5.	(A) (B) (C)	
11.6.	(A) (B) (C)			16.6.	(A) (B) (C)	
12.1.	(A) (B) (C)			17.1.	(A) (B) (C)	
12.2.	(A) (B) (C)			17.2.	(A) (B) (C)	
12.3.	(A) (B) (C)			17.3.	(A) (B) (C)	
12.4.	(A) (B) (C)			17.4.	(A) (B) (C)	
12.5.	(A) (B) (C)			17.5.	(A) (B) (C)	
12.6.	(A) (B) (C)			17.6.	(A) (B) (C)	
13.1.	(A) (B) (C)			18.1.	(A) (B) (C)	
13.2.	(A) (B) (C)			18.2.	(A) (B) (C)	
13.3.	(A) (B) (C)			18.3.	(A) (B) (C)	
13.4.	(A) (B) (C)			18.4.	(A) (B) (C)	
13.5.	(A) (B) (C)			18.5.	(A) (B) (C)	
13.6.	(A) (B) (C)			18.6.	(A) (B) (C)	
14.1.	(A) (B) (C)			19.1.	(A) (B) (C)	
14.2.	(A) (B) (C)			19.2.	(A) (B) (C)	
14.3.	(A) (B) (C)			19.3.	(A) (B) (C)	
14.4.	(A) (B) (C)			19.4.	(A) (B) (C)	
14.5.	(A) (B) (C)			19.5.	(A) (B) (C)	
14.6.	(A) (B) (C)			19.6.	(A) (B) (C)	

EXAM 1
AFTERNOON SESSION

QUESTION 10 HAS SIX PARTS FOR A TOTAL OF 18 MINUTES

Theresa Bair, CFA, a portfolio manager for Brinton Investment Company (BIC), has recently been promoted to lead portfolio manager for her firm's new small capitalization closed-end equity fund, the Quaker Fund. BIC is an asset management firm headquartered in Holland with regional offices in several other European countries.

After accepting the position, Bair received a letter from the three principals of BIC. The letter congratulated Bair on her accomplishment and new position with the firm and also provided some guidance as to her new role and the firm's expectations. Among other things, the letter stated the following:

> "Because our firm is based in Holland and you will have clients located in many European countries, it is essential that you determine what laws and regulations are applicable to the management of this new fund. It is your responsibility to obtain this knowledge and comply with appropriate regulations. This is the first time we have offered a fund devoted solely to small capitalization securities, so we will observe your progress carefully. You will likely need to arrange for our sister companies to quietly buy and sell Quaker Fund shares over the first month of operations. This will provide sufficient price support to allow the fund to trade closer to its net asset value than other small-cap closed-end funds. Because these funds generally trade at a discount to net asset value, if our fund trades close to its net asset value, the market may perceive it as more desirable than similar funds managed by our competitors."

Bair heeded the advice from her firm's principals and collected information on the laws and regulations of three countries: Norway, Sweden, and Denmark. So far, all of the investors expressing interest in the Quaker Fund are from these areas. Based on her research, Bair decides the following policies are appropriate for the fund:

Note: Laws mentioned below are assumed for illustrative purposes.

- For clients located in Norway the fund will institute transaction crossing, since, unlike in Holland, the practice is not prohibited by securities laws or regulations. The process will involve internally matching buy and sell orders from Norwegian clients whenever possible. This will reduce brokerage fees and improve the fund's overall performance.

- For clients located in Denmark, account statements that include the value of the clients' holdings, number of trades, and average daily trading volume will be generated on a monthly basis as required by Denmark's securities regulators, even though the laws in Holland only require such reports to be generated on a quarterly basis.
- For clients located in Sweden, the fund will not disclose differing levels of service that are available for investors based upon the size of their investment. This policy is consistent with the laws and regulations in Holland. Sweden's securities regulations do not cover this type of situation.

Three months after the inception of the fund, its market value has grown from $200 million to $300 million and Bair's performance has earned her a quarter-end bonus. Since it is now the end of the quarter, Bair is participating in conference calls with companies in her fund. Bair calls into the conference number for Swift Petroleum. The meeting doesn't start for another five minutes, however, and as Bair waits, she hears the CEO and CFO of Swift discussing the huge earnings restatement that will be necessary for the financial statement from the previous quarter. The restatement will not be announced until the year's end, six months from now. Bair does not remind the officers that she can hear their conversation. Once the call has ended, Bair rushes to BIC's compliance officer to inform him of what she has learned during the conference call. Bair ignores the fact that two members of the firm's investment banking division are in the office while she is telling the compliance officer what happened on the conference call. The investment bankers then proceed to sell their personal holdings of Swift Petroleum stock. After her meeting, Bair sells the Quaker Fund's holdings of Swift Petroleum stock.

10.1. Do the suggestions in the letter from the principals of BIC violate any CFA Institute Standards of Professional Conduct?
 A. No.
 B. Yes, because the suggestions are intended to manipulate market data in order to attract investors for the fund.
 C. Yes, because the compliance officer should be responsible for knowing applicable laws and regulations, not Bair.

10.2. With regard to the treatment of clients in Norway and Denmark, do the policies that Bair has selected for the Quaker Fund violate any CFA Institute Standards of Professional Conduct?

	Norway	Denmark
A.	No	Yes
B.	Yes	No
C.	No	No

10.3. With regard to the treatment of clients in Sweden, does the policy that Bair has selected for the Quaker Fund violate any CFA Institute Standards of Professional Conduct?
   A. Yes, Bair's policy will violate Standard III(B) Fair Dealing.
   B. No, because disclosure in Sweden would disadvantage clients residing in other countries.
   C. No, because disclosure in any country would break the confidentiality that Bair owes to her clients.

10.4. After her conference call with Swift Petroleum, Bair should have:
   A. included the information in a research report to make it public before selling the holdings from the Quaker Fund.
   B. attempted to have Swift publicly disclose the earnings restatement before informing the compliance officer of the information.
   C. informed the compliance officer and then publicly disclosed the information in a research report before selling the Swift stock.

10.5. By selling their personal holdings of Swift Petroleum, did the employees of BIC's investment banking division violate any CFA Institute Standards of Professional Conduct?
   A. Yes, because they breached their fiduciary duty and were disloyal to the clients of the Quaker Fund.
   B. Yes, because they did not maintain the confidentiality of the information they overheard in the compliance officer's office.
   C. Yes, because they knowingly traded on information that, if it had been publicly known, would have affected the price of Swift stock.

10.6. By selling the Quaker Fund's shares of Swift Petroleum, did Bair violate any CFA Institute Standards of Professional Conduct?
   A. Yes, Bair violated Standard II Integrity of Capital Markets.
   B. No, because she ensured public dissemination of the earnings restatement information before she traded the shares.
   C. Yes, because waiting to trade the stock would severely disadvantage investors in her fund and would have violated her duty of loyalty to her clients.

QUESTION 11 HAS SIX PARTS FOR A TOTAL OF 18 MINUTES

Stephanie Mackley is a portfolio manager for Durango Wealth Management (DWM), a regional money manager catering to wealthy investors in the southwestern portion of the United States. Mackley's clients vary widely in terms of their age, net worth, and investment objectives, but all must have at least $1 million in net assets before she will accept them as clients.

Many of Mackley's clients are referred to her by Kern & Associates, an accounting and consulting firm. DWM does not provide any direct compensation to Kern & Associates for the referrals, but Mackley, who is the president of her local CFA Society, invites Kern & Associates to give an annual presentation to the society on the subject of tax planning and minimization strategies that Kern & Associates provides for its clients. Kern & Associates' competitors have never received an invitation to present their services to the society. When Mackley receives a referral, she informs the prospect of the arrangement between DWM and Kern & Associates.

DWM maintains a full research staff that analyzes and recommends equity and debt investments. All of the in-house research is provided to the firm's portfolio managers and their clients. In addition, DWM provides a subscription service to outside investors and portfolio managers. Aaron Welch, CFA, a private contractor, researches and reports on high-tech firms in the United States and other developed countries for several portfolio management clients. One of his latest reports rated InnerTech, Inc., a small startup that develops microscopic surgical devices, as a strong buy. After reviewing the report carefully, Mackley decides to purchase shares of InnerTech for clients with account values over $6 million. She feels that accounts with less than this amount cannot accept the risk level associated with InnerTech stock.

Two days after purchasing InnerTech for her clients, the stock nearly doubles in value, and the clients are ecstatic about the returns on their portfolios. Several of them give her small bouquets of flowers and boxes of chocolates, which she discloses to her supervisor at DWM. One client even offers her the use of a condo in Vail, Colorado for two weeks during ski season, if she can reproduce the results next quarter. Mackley graciously thanks her clients and asks that they refer any of their friends and relatives who are in need of asset management services. She provides brochures to a few clients who mention that they have friends who would be interested. The brochure contains a description of Mackley's services and her qualifications. At the end of the brochure, Mackley includes her full name followed by "a Chartered Financial Analyst" in bold font of the same size as her name. Following is an excerpt from the brochure:

"DWM can provide many of the investment services you are likely to need. For those services that we do not provide directly, such as estate planning, we have standing relationships with companies that do provide such services. I have a long history with DWM, serving as an investment analyst for six years and then in my current capacity as a portfolio manager for twelve years. My clients have been very satisfied with my past performance and will likely be very satisfied with my future performance, which I attribute to my significant investment experience as well as my participation in the CFA Program. I earned the right to use the CFA designation thirteen years ago. All CFA charterholders must pass a series of three rigorous examinations that cover investment management and research analysis."

Two weeks later, some of Mackley's clients request that she provide supporting documentation for the research report on InnerTech, so they can familiarize themselves with how DWM analyzes investment opportunities. Mackley asks Welch for the documents, but Welch is unable to provide copies of his supporting research since he disposed of them, according to the company's policy, one week after issuing and distributing the report. Mackley informs Welch that obtaining the supporting documents is of the utmost importance, since one of the clients requesting the materials, Craig Adams, is about to inherit $20 million and as a result will be one of the firm's most important clients. Welch agrees to recreate the research documents in order to support the firm's relationship with Adams.

11.1. Does the arrangement between Mackley and Kern & Associates violate any CFA Institute Standards of Professional Conduct?
A. Yes.
B. No, because the referral agreement is fully disclosed to all clients and prospects before they employ Mackley's services.
C. No, because Mackley only accepts clients with net assets above $1 million who are likely to know that the arrangement is common in the industry.

11.2. Were any CFA Institute Standards of Professional Conduct violated in conjunction with Welch's report on InnerTech and Mackley's purchase of InnerTech stock?

	Welch	Mackley
A.	No	Yes
B.	Yes	No
C.	Yes	Yes

11.3. According to the Standards of Professional Conduct, Mackley must do which of the following regarding the gifts offered to her by her clients? She may:

A. accept the flowers and chocolates and the use of the condo without disclosing the gifts to her employer.

B. not accept the flowers and chocolates or the use of the condo without disclosing the gifts to her employer.

C. accept the flowers and chocolates but may not accept the use of the condo without first receiving written approval from her employer.

11.4. Does Mackley's signature at the end of her brochure violate any CFA Institute Standards of Professional Conduct?

A. No.

B. Yes, because "a Chartered Financial Analyst" should not be written in bold.

C. Yes, because "a Chartered Financial Analyst" should not be written in bold and should not include "a."

11.5. In her marketing brochure, did Mackley violate any CFA Institute Standards of Professional Conduct in her reference to her investment performance or her reference to the CFA Program?

	Performance	CFA Program
A.	Yes	Yes
B.	No	Yes
C.	Yes	No

11.6. In her discussions with Welch, where she asks him to recreate the supporting research for the InnerTech report, has Mackley violated any CFA Institute Standards of Professional Conduct?

A. No.

B. Yes, because the request creates a conflict of interest between Mackley and Welch.

C. Yes, because she failed to preserve the confidentiality of her client's information.

QUESTION 12 HAS SIX PARTS FOR A TOTAL OF 18 MINUTES

Jack Rose and Ryan Boatman are analysts with Quincy Consultants. Quincy provides advice on risk management and performance presentation to pension plans, insurance firms, and other institutional portfolio managers throughout the United States and Canada.

Rose and Boatman are preparing an analysis of the defined benefit pension plans for four mature corporations in the United States. In an effort to ascertain the risk to the firm's shareholders from the plans, Rose and Boatman gather the information in Figure 1.

Figure 1: Pension Plan Data

	Firm A	Firm B	Firm C	Firm D
Market value of plan assets ($ million)	$1,300	$980	$1,400	$710
Market value of plan liabilities ($ million)	$1,460	$900	$1,330	$870
Percentage of plan assets in bonds	35%	57%	65%	25%

While discussing how the weighted average cost of capital (WACC) for a corporation can be adjusted to incorporate pension asset risk, Rose and Boatman make the following comments:

- Rose: "From what I understand, in order to calculate a true weighted average cost of capital, management should consider the assets held in their pension plan. Because pension plans hold equity securities as assets, the plan assets usually have a higher weighted average beta than the sponsoring firm's operating assets. This means the typical firm's weighted average asset beta and cost of capital are higher than when calculated using only the operating assets. If management bases their accept/reject decisions on a weighted average cost of capital that considers only operating assets, they might accept projects that really should have been rejected."
- Boatman: "I'm not sure I agree with you. To match the maturity of their liabilities, pension plans like to hold at least half their assets in long maturity bonds. Then, since the bonds have a long weighted average duration, they have considerable interest rate sensitivity. This is really what makes the pension assets riskier than the firm's operating assets. However, since debt securities have zero betas, they have a low weighted average asset beta and the firm has a lower weighted average cost of capital when pension assets are considered than when they are not considered. The result of considering only the operating assets is that the weighted average cost of capital is inflated and management tends to incorrectly reject projects that could have been accepted."

In a visit to the headquarters of Beeman Enterprises, Rose and Boatman explain how in an expanded balance sheet format, a change in a pension plan's asset allocation can result in a change in the firm's financial ratios. To illustrate the concept to the firm's chief financial officer, they provide three different scenarios (shown in Figure 2) indicating necessary changes in the firm's capital structure under the assumption that the firm's pension plan increases its allocation to equity and management wants to keep the sponsoring firm's cost of equity capital constant (i.e., constant equity beta).

Figure 2: Cost of Capital Scenarios

	Debt to Equity Ratio	Total Assets Beta	Equity Beta	Amount of Equity Capital
Scenario A	Increase	Constant	Constant	Increase
Scenario B	Decrease	Increase	Constant	Increase
Scenario C	Increase	Decrease	Constant	Constant

Quincy Consultants has also provided advice to Monroe Portfolio Managers. Among its investments, Monroe has a real estate portfolio that invests in shopping centers and office buildings throughout the southern United States. The firm has provided the following data to calculate and report quarterly returns to current and prospective investors. Additionally, the capital contribution came on day 47 (0.52 into the quarter) and the capital disbursement came on day 67 (0.74 into the quarter).

Total capital as of	1/1/2007	$18,000,000
Capital contribution on	2/16/2007	2,300,000
Capital disbursement on	3/8/2007	850,000
Capital expenditure		1,000,000
Property taxes paid		219,000
Property sales		1,820,000
Total non-recoverable expenses		178,000
Interest paid on borrowed funds		152,000
Accrued investment income		58,000
Market value — beg. of quarter	1/1/2007	19,100,000
Market value — end of quarter	3/31/2007	20,200,000

After calculating the capital return and income return for the portfolio, Rose and Boatman discuss the performance presentation standards for real estate and private equity portfolios. Discussing the differences between the general provisions of the GIPS standards and those for real estate and private equity portfolios, Rose states the following:

1. "The general provisions require that valuations take place monthly until 2010. For real estate, valuations could be done annually until 2008, but starting in 2008 quarterly valuations are required. For private equity, valuations should be performed annually."

2. "The performance standards in the general provisions for real estate and for private equity require that both gross-of-fees and net-of-fees returns are presented."

Also commenting on the differences between the various GIPS requirements, Boatman states the following:

1. "Although the general provisions for GIPS make the verification of GIPS compliance by an outside third-party voluntary, the valuation of real estate and private equity by an outside third party is required by GIPS."

2. "The GIPS general provisions for real estate and for private equity require that both income and capital gains are included in the calculation and presentation of returns."

12.1. From the data provided in Figure 1, determine the firm or firms that *probably* have the greatest risk arising from pension plan assets.
   A. Firm A.
   B. Firms B and C.
   C. Firm D.

12.2. Regarding the comments by Rose and Boatman on the incorporation of pension plan risk into the weighted average cost of capital, determine whether they are correct or incorrect.
   A. Only Rose is correct.
   B. Only Boatman is correct.
   C. Neither is correct.

12.3. Of the three scenarios (see Figure 2) presented to the Beeman Enterprises executives, which would represent the appropriate reaction to increasing the pension plan allocation to equity, if management wishes to maintain its current equity beta?
   A. Scenario A.
   B. Scenario B.
   C. Scenario C.

12.4. The capital return and income return for Monroe are *closest* to:

	Capital return	Income return
A.	5.8%	−2.6%
B.	5.8%	0.3%
C.	10.2%	−2.6%

12.5. Determine whether Rose's two statements on the GIPS standards are correct or incorrect.
   A. Only statement 1 is correct.
   B. Only statement 2 is correct.
   C. Both statements are correct.

12.6. Determine whether Boatman's two statements on the GIPS standards are correct or incorrect.
   A. Only statement 1 is correct.
   B. Only statement 2 is correct.
   C. Both are incorrect.

QUESTION 13 HAS SIX PARTS FOR A TOTAL OF 18 MINUTES

Daniel Castillo and Ramon Diaz are chief investment officers at Advanced Advisors (AA), a boutique fixed-income firm based in the United States. AA employs numerous quantitative models to invest in both domestic and international securities.

During the week, Castillo and Diaz consult with one of their investors, Sally Michaels. Michaels currently holds a $10,000,000 fixed-income position that is selling at par. The maturity is 20 years, and the coupon rate of 7% is paid semiannually. Her coupons can be reinvested at 8%. Castillo is looking at various interest rate change scenarios, and one such scenario is where the interest rate on the bonds immediately changes to 8%.

Diaz is considering using a repurchase agreement to leverage Michaels's portfolio. Michaels is concerned, however, with not understanding the factors that impact the interest rate, or repo rate, used in her strategy. In response, Castillo explains the factors that affect the repo rate and makes the following statements:

1. "The repo rate is directly related to the maturity of the repo, inversely related to the quality of the collateral, and directly related to the maturity of the collateral. U.S. Treasury bills are often purchased by Treasury dealers using repo transactions, and since they have high liquidity, short maturities, and no default risk, the repo rate is usually quite low. "

2. "The greater control the lender has over the collateral, the lower the repo rate. If the availability of the collateral is limited, the repo rate will be higher."

Castillo consults with an institutional investor, the Washington Investment Fund, on the effect of leverage on bond portfolio returns as well as their bond portfolio's sensitivity to changes in interest rates. The portfolio under discussion is well-diversified, with small positions in a large number of bonds. It has a duration of 7.2. Of the $200 million value of the portfolio, $60 million was borrowed. The duration of borrowed funds is 0.8. The expected return on the portfolio is 8% and the cost of borrowed funds is 3%.

The next day, the chief investment officer for the Washington Investment Fund expresses her concern about the risk of their portfolio, given its leverage. She inquires about the various risk measures for bond portfolios. In response, Diaz distinguishes between the standard deviation and downside risk measures, making the following statements:

1. "Portfolio managers complain that using variance to calculate Sharpe ratios is inappropriate. Since it considers all returns over the entire distribution, variance and the resulting standard deviation are artificially

inflated, so the resulting Sharpe ratio is artificially deflated. Since it is easily calculated for bond portfolios, managers feel a more realistic measure of risk is the semi-variance, which measures the distribution of returns below a given return, such as the mean or a hurdle rate."

2. "A shortcoming of VAR is its inability to predict the size of potential losses in the lower tail of the expected return distribution. Although it can assign a probability to some maximum loss, it does not predict the actual loss if the maximum loss is exceeded. If Washington Investment Fund is worried about catastrophic loss, shortfall risk is a more appropriate measure, because it provides the probability of not meeting a target return."

AA has a corporate client, Shaifer Materials with a €20,000,000 bond outstanding that pays an annual fixed coupon rate of 9.5% with a 5-year maturity. Castillo believes that euro interest rates may decrease further within the next year below the coupon rate on the fixed rate bond. Castillo would like Shaifer to issue new debt at a lower euro interest rate in the future. Castillo has, however, looked into the costs of calling the bonds and has found that the call premium is quite high and that the investment banking costs of issuing new floating rate debt would be quite steep. As such, he is considering using a swaption to create a synthetic refinancing of the bond at a lower cost than an actual refinancing of the bond. He states that in order to do so, Shaifer should buy a payer swaption, which would give Shaifer the option to pay a lower floating interest rate if rates drop.

Diaz retrieves current market data for payer and receiver swaptions with a maturity of one year. The terms of each instrument are provided below:

Payer swaption fixed rate	7.90%
Receiver swaption fixed rate	7.60%
Current Euribor	7.20%
Projected Euribor in one year	5.90%

Diaz states that, assuming Castillo is correct, Shaifer can exercise a swaption in one year to effectively call in their old fixed rate euro debt paying 9.5% and refinance at a floating rate, which would be 7.5% in one year.

13.1. Calculated in bond equivalent yield terms, Michaels's return over the next year, if interest rates change as expected, is *closest* to:
A. 2.56%.
B. −2.56%.
C. 3.50%.

13.2. Determine whether each of Castillo's statements about repos is correct or incorrect.
A. Both are correct.
B. Neither is correct.
C. One is correct.

13.3. The return on the Washington Investment Fund portfolio is *closest* to:
A. 7.14%.
B. 10.14%.
C. 11.00%.

13.4. The duration on the Washington Investment Fund portfolio is *closest* to:
A. 6.4.
B. 8.0.
C. 9.9.

13.5. Regarding the statements made by Diaz about downside risk measures, are the statements correct?
A. Only statement 1 is correct.
B. Only statement 2 is correct.
C. Neither statement is correct.

13.6. Regarding their statements concerning the synthetic refinancing of the Shaifer Materials fixed rate euro debt, are the statements correct?
A. Only Castillo is correct.
B. Only Diaz is correct.
C. Both Castillo and Diaz are incorrect.

QUESTION 14 HAS SIX PARTS FOR A TOTAL OF 18 MINUTES

Ellen Truxel is the principal at Truxel Investment Management. Her firm uses bonds for income enhancement as well as capital gains. She occasionally uses sector-quality bets and yield curve positioning to exploit her beliefs on the relative changes in sector credit quality and the direction of interest rates. She has recently hired John Timberlake to assist her in preparing data for the analysis of bond portfolios. Timberlake is a recent graduate of an outstanding undergraduate program in finance.

Truxel is considering investing in international bonds, as this is an arena she has previously ignored. During conversations, Truxel says it is her understanding that changes in international bond markets have made it easier to manage the duration of an international bond portfolio. Timberlake notes that the European Monetary Union has increased the availability of corporate bonds, making it easier to rotate across sectors.

In the domestic arena, Truxel is considering constructing a portfolio that matches the index on quality, call, sector, and cash flow dimensions and tilts the portfolio duration small amounts to take advantage of predictions of yield curve shifts. She states that this would be referred to as enhanced indexing with minor mismatches. Timberlake tells her that the most important determinant of her performance relative to other bond managers will be her ability to perform credit analysis.

Truxel then tells Timberlake that before they venture into new areas, she wants him to prepare an analysis of their current positions. Timberlake obliges and presents the following data on Truxel's current portfolio.

Bond Rating	Percent Weight in Truxel Portfolio	Sector Effective Duration	Percent Weight in Index Portfolio
AAA	12%	5.3	35%
AA	30%	5.4	30%
A	30%	5.5	25%
BBB	28%	5.0	10%

14.1. Regarding the conversation on the attributes of international bond investing, are Truxel and Timberlake correct or incorrect?
A. Both are correct.
B. Neither is correct.
C. One is correct.

14.2. Regarding the conversation on domestic bond portfolio management, are Truxel and Timberlake correct or incorrect?
   A. Both are correct.
   B. Neither is correct.
   C. One is correct.

14.3. Given a parallel shift in the yield curve of 60 basis points for Treasury yields, the approximate percent change in the value of the Truxel portfolio is *closest* to:
   A. 3.2.
   B. 3.4.
   C. 5.3.

14.4. If the OAS for all bond sectors changes by 60 basis points while Treasury yields remain unchanged, the approximate percent change in the Truxel portfolio is *closest* to:
   A. 3.2.
   B. 3.4.
   C. 5.3.

14.5. If the OAS for all bond sectors changes by 100 basis points while Treasury yields remain unchanged, which sector or sectors would contribute the most to tracking error for Truxel's portfolio?
   A. BBB.
   B. AAA.
   C. AA and A, which contribute about the same.

14.6. In evaluating relative valuation methodologies, which of the following rationales for trading in the secondary bond market is *least* appropriate?
   A. Cash flow reinvestment.
   B. New issue swaps.
   C. Seasonality.

QUESTION 15 HAS SIX PARTS FOR A TOTAL OF 18 MINUTES

Mark Rolle, CFA, is the manager of the international bond fund for the Ryder Investment Advisory. He is responsible for bond selection as well as currency hedging decisions. His assistant is Joanne Chen, a candidate for the Level 1 CFA Exam.

Rolle is interested in the relationship between interest rates and exchange rates for Canada and Great Britain. He observes that the spot exchange rate between the Canadian dollar (C$) and the British pound is C$1.75/£. Also, the 1-year interest rate in Canada is 4.0% and the 1-year interest rate in Great Britain is 11.0%. The current 1-year forward rate is C$1.60/£.

Rolle is evaluating the bonds from the Knauff company and the Tatehiki company, for which information is provided in the table below. The Knauff company bond is denominated in euros and the Tatehiki company bond is denominated in yen. The bonds have similar risk and maturities, and Ryder's investors reside in the United States.

Return on Knauff bond in euros	8.00%
Risk-free rate in the European Union	5.00%
Expected change in the euro relative to the U.S. dollar	–1.20%
Return on Tatehiki bond in yen	6.00%
Risk-free rate in Japan	2.00%
Expected change in the yen relative to the U.S. dollar	2.00%
Risk-free rate in United States	4.80%

Provided this information, Rolle must decide which country's bonds are most attractive if a forward hedge of currency exposure is used. Furthermore, assuming that both countries' bonds are bought, Rolle must also decide whether or not to hedge the currency exposure.

Rolle also has a position in a bond issued in Korea and denominated in Korean won. Unfortunately, he is having difficulty obtaining a forward contract for the won on favorable terms. As an alternative hedge, he has entered a forward contract that allows him to sell yen in one year, when he anticipates liquidating his Korean bond. His reason for choosing the yen is that it is positively correlated with the won.

One of Ryder's services is to provide consulting advice to firms that are interested in interest rate hedging strategies. One such firm is Crawfordville Bank. One of the certificates of deposit (CDs) Crawfordville has outstanding is a jumbo CD the issued requiring the payment of LIBOR plus 150 basis points. The chief financial officer at Crawfordville is worried that interest rates may increase and would like to hedge this exposure. Rolle is contemplating either an interest rate cap or an interest rate floor as a hedge.

Additionally, Rolle is analyzing the best hedge for Ryder's portfolio of fixed-rate coupon bonds. Rolle is contemplating using either a covered call or a protective put on a T-bond futures contract.

15.1. Given the current forward rate of C$1.60/£, what is the exact forward premium or discount for the £ against the C$?
A. −9.37%.
B. −8.57%.
C. 8.57%.

15.2. What must the 1-year forward exchange rate be between the C$ and Great Britain pound (£) so that no arbitrage opportunities are available?
A. 0.6364 C$ per £.
B. 1.6396 C$ per £.
C. 1.8510 C$ per £.

15.3. Assuming Rolle uses forward contracts to hedge the currency risk of the bond investment, determine which bond is the better investment.
A. The Knauff bond because its return is 8.0%.
B. The Tatehiki bond because its excess return is 4.0%.
C. The Knauff bond because its excess currency return is 3.2%.

15.4. Calculate the expected return for both bonds if Rolle uses forward contracts to hedge the currency risk of the Knauff company bond and leaves the Tatehiki company bond unhedged.

	Knauff bond	Tatehiki bond
A.	6.8%	8.1%
B.	6.8%	8.8%
C.	7.8%	8.1%

15.5. The hedge that Rolle uses to hedge the currency exposure of the Korean bond is *best* referred to as a:
A. proxy hedge.
B. cross hedge.
C. forward hedge.

15.6. The *best* hedges of the Crawfordville position and the Ryder portfolio are:

	Crawfordville	Ryder
A.	Cap	Covered call
B.	Cap	Protective put
C.	Floor	Covered call

QUESTION 16 HAS SIX PARTS FOR A TOTAL OF 18 MINUTES

Cynthia Farmington, CFA, manages the Lewis family's $600 million securities portfolio. Farmington and the Lewis family have agreed that they should hire a manager of alternative investments to manage a portion of the portfolio containing those assets. As part of the hiring process, they attempted to do the necessary due diligence. They assessed each manager's organization, the relative efficiency of the markets each manager has invested in, the character of each manager, and the service providers, such as lawyers, that each manager has used. In particular, they hoped to find a manager who has run an operation with low employee turnover, has invested in efficient and transparent markets, has sound character, and has utilized reputable providers of external services.

Eventually, Farmington hires the firm owned and managed by Bruce Carnegie, CFA, to diversify the Lewis portfolio into alternative investments. Carnegie will manage the portion of the portfolio containing these assets, and Farmington will continue to manage the remainder of the portfolio in a mix of approximately 50/50 high-grade stocks and bonds. Over the past ten years, the stock portion of the portfolio has closely tracked the S&P 500 and the bond portfolio has closely tracked a broad bond index.

Carnegie and Farmington meet to discuss how Carnegie should proceed. Farmington mentions that she and the Lewis family have agreed that the main goal of the alternative investments that Carnegie will manage should be to enhance the return of the overall portfolio. Diversification is only a secondary goal. In particular, Farmington says the Lewis family has expressed an interest in having the portfolio take positions in private equity. Farmington says that she envisions that Carnegie should take five positions of about $5 million each in distinct private equity investments, and each position should have about a 5-year horizon.

Farmington states that she has grown very dependent on benchmarks for her investing activities, and she has concerns with respect to how she and Carnegie will monitor the success of the portfolio allocation in private equity. She has read that there can be a problem with the valuation of private equity indices in that they depend on price-revealing events like IPOs, mergers, and new financing. Thus, the repricing of the index occurs infrequently. Carnegie concludes that the solution is to follow the commonly accepted practice of creating their own private equity benchmark.

Farmington asks Carnegie to explain the choices that exist in the private equity market. Carnegie explains that there are two basic categories: venture capital funds and buyout funds. Farmington asks that Carnegie explain the pros and cons of one over the other. Carnegie states that buyout funds would probably have higher return potential, fewer losses, earlier cash flows, and less error in the measurement of the returns.

Carnegie comments that before he proceeds he will need to communicate with the clients. Farmington says this communication is not necessary because the Lewis family has largely followed her advice with very few questions. Even when the market has fallen and the portfolio has not done well, the Lewis family has not asked for any changes.

16.1. With respect to the criteria that Farmington used to choose a manager of alternative assets, which of the following is not a due diligence checkpoint? Finding a manager who:
A. has low staff turnover.
B. invests only in efficient and transparent markets.
C. has stable providers of external services.

16.2. Given that Farmington states that high return is more important than diversification, the choice to focus on private equity is:
A. not appropriate because private equity offers good diversification, but the returns are comparatively low.
B. appropriate because private equity offers a high return but relatively low diversification.
C. appropriate because private equity offers both a high return and good diversification.

16.3. Regarding Farmington's recommended private equity allocations and time horizon, which of her guidelines is *least* appropriate?
A. The horizon is too short.
B. Too few positions for proper diversification.
C. Too much invested given the size of the overall portfolio.

16.4. With respect to the issue of benchmarks, Farmington made an observation concerning the potential problem with benchmarks, and Carnegie offered a solution. With respect to their discussion, are Farmington and Carnegie correct or incorrect?
A. Only Farmington is correct.
B. Only Carnegie is correct.
C. Both are correct -OR- both are incorrect.

16.5. With respect to the pros and cons Carnegie listed concerning buyout funds over venture capital funds, Carnegie was correct in all of the points except that buyout funds tend to have:
A. higher return potential.
B. earlier cash flows.
C. less error in the measurement of the returns.

16.6. With respect to the special issues that an alternative investment manager should address with a private wealth client, from the conversation between Farmington and Carnegie, Carnegie will need to discuss all of the following with the possible exception of:

A. tax issues.

B. other closely held investments.

C. decision risk.

QUESTION 17 HAS SIX PARTS FOR A TOTAL OF 18 MINUTES

Bill Ogilvey, CFA, manages money for clients residing in various countries. Some of them reside in countries that do not currently have tax-advantaged accounts. Ogilvey stays abreast of tax laws of the countries to be able to quickly advise his clients when new tax-advantaged accounts become available.

Ogilvey often counsels his clients with regard to how they should manage their investment accounts for tax purposes. One of his newest clients, Tilly Beamer, lives in a country with a tax regime that has a flat rate for ordinary income, dividends, and capital gains, but provides favorable treatment for interest income. Her portfolio is in a taxable account and is equally allocated among interest-paying assets, dividend-paying assets, and non-dividend-paying growth stocks.

Beamer is interested in Ogilvey's advice about her retirement planning and which tax-advantaged account(s) would be most beneficial to her. Beamer is young and her income is modest, but she has a high degree of job security and expects her income to increase dramatically over the upcoming ten years. Her objective is to fund a retirement income approximately equal to her wage income at retirement. She is specifically concerned with managing her risk exposure and wonders how a planned reduction in her portfolio risk will affect her expected returns, investment time horizon, and tax drag.

Ogilvey has another client, Steven Vance, who lives in a country with a heavy capital gains tax regime. The current tax law in Vance's country does not provide for tax-advantaged accounts, but that is expected to change, as tax-exempt accounts may soon become available.

To fund a new tax-exempt account, Vance will need to sell some appreciated stock, and he is concerned with the ramifications of harvesting gains. In specific, Vance has a position in TTT stock, which he accumulated over several years at successively higher prices. If this position is liquidated, taxes will be payable on his investment gains. He asks Ogilvey his advice concerning the best way to handle the sale of the shares and how to measure the tax consequences of realizing the gains.

17.1. The tax regime in Beamer's country can be *best* classified as:
   A. Flat and Heavy.
   B. Flat and Light.
   C. Heavy Capital Gain Tax.

17.2.   Assume that Beamer's interest paying assets are held in a taxable account. The account is currently worth €1,000,000, the pretax interest income is 7%, and the tax rate, assessed annually, is 25%. If there are no deposits or withdrawals from this account and compounding is annual, what will her investment be worth in 15 years?
   A.   €2,097,228.
   B.   €2,154,426.
   C.   €2,759,032.

17.3.   Beamer's plan to reduce her investment risk will *most likely*:
   A.   decrease her investment horizon because the resulting tax drag will be less than the applicable tax rate.
   B.   increase her investment horizon but result in tax drag that is less than the applicable tax rate.
   C.   increase both her investment horizon and result in tax drag that exceeds the applicable tax rate.

17.4.   Assume that Vance sells some of his TTT stock. The pretax return on the TTT stock averaged 12% per year over 10 years, the capital gains tax rate is 35%, and the cost basis is $250,000. What is the after-tax gain on the investment?
   A. $254,200.
   B. $342,200.
   C. $592,200.

17.5   Which of the following is *closest* to the percentage tax drag Vance will experience with sale of the TTT stock?
   A.   25%.
   B.   35%.
   C.   40%.

17.6.   Suppose that Vance's after-tax proceeds on his TTT stock sale were $150,000, his cost basis was $60,000, the pre-tax return was 13%, and the holding period was 9 years. The accrual equivalent after-tax return is *closest* to:
   A.   10.7%.
   B.   17.7%.
   C.   27.8%.

QUESTION 18 HAS SIX PARTS FOR A TOTAL OF 18 MINUTES

Gabrielle Reneau, CFA, and Jack Belanger specialize in options strategies at the brokerage firm of Damon and Damon. They employ fairly sophisticated strategies to construct positions with limited risk, to profit from future volatility estimates, and to exploit arbitrage opportunities. Damon and Damon also provide advice to outside portfolio managers on the appropriate use of options strategies. Damon and Damon prefer to use, and recommend, options written on widely traded indices such as the S&P 500 due to their higher liquidity. However, they also use options written on individual stocks when the investor has a position in the underlying stock or when mispricing and/or trading depth exists.

In order to trade in the one-year maturity puts and calls for the S&P 500 stock index, Reneau and Belanger contact the chief economists at Damon and Damon, Mark Blair and Fran Robinson. Blair recently joined Damon and Damon after a successful stint at a London investment bank. Robinson has been with Damon and Damon for the past ten years and has a considerable record of success in forecasting macroeconomic activity. In his forecasts for the U.S. economy over the next year, Blair is quite bullish, for both the U.S. economy and the S&P 500 stock index. Blair believes that the U.S. economy will grow at 2% more than expected over the next year. He also states that labor productivity will be higher than expected, given increased productivity through the use of technological advances. He expects that these technological advances will result in higher earnings for U.S. firms over the next year and over the long run.

Reneau believes that the best S&P 500 option strategy to exploit Blair's forecast involves two options of the same maturity, one with a low exercise price, and the other with a high exercise price. The beginning stock price is usually below the two option strike prices. She states that the benefit of this strategy is that the maximum loss is limited to the difference between the two option prices.

Belanger is unsure that Blair's forecast is correct. He states that his own reading of the economy is for a continued holding pattern of low growth, with a similar projection for the stock market as a whole. He states that Damon and Damon may want to pursue an options strategy where a put and call of the same maturity and same exercise price are purchased. He asserts that such a strategy would have losses limited to the total cost of the two options.

Reneau and Belanger are also currently examining various positions in the options of Brendan Industries. Brendan Industries is a large-cap manufacturing firm with headquarters in the midwestern United States. The firm has both puts and calls sold on the Chicago Board Options Exchange. Their options have good liquidity for the near money puts and calls and for those puts and calls with maturities less than four months. Reneau believes that Brendan Industries will benefit from the economic expansion forecasted by Mark Blair, the Damon and Damon economist. She decides that the best option strategy to exploit these expectations is for her to pursue the same strategy she has delineated for the market as a whole.

Shares of Brendan Industries are currently trading at $38. The following are the prices for their exchange-traded options.

Option Type	Strike Price	Maturity	Price
Call	$35	30 days	$4.50
Call	$40	30 days	$1.50
Put	$35	30 days	$1.80
Put	$40	30 days	$3.50

As a mature firm in a mature industry, Brendan Industries stock has historically had low volatility. However, Belanger's analysis indicates that with a lawsuit pending against Brendan Industries, the volatility of the stock price over the next 60 days is greater by several orders of magnitude than the implied volatility of the options. He believes that Damon and Damon should attempt to exploit this projected increase in Brendan Industries' volatility by using an options strategy where a put and call of the same maturity and same exercise price are utilized. He advocates using the least expensive strategy possible.

During their discussions, Reneau cites a counter example to Brendan Industries from last year. She recalls that Nano Networks, a technology firm, had a stock price that stayed fairly stable despite expectations to the contrary. In this case, she utilized an options strategy where three different calls were used. Profits were earned on the strategy because Nano Networks' stock price stayed fairly stable. Even if the stock price had become volatile, losses would have been limited.

Later that week, Reneau and Belanger discuss various credit option strategies during a lunch time presentation to Damon and Damon client portfolio managers. During their discussion, Reneau describes a credit option strategy that pays the holder a fixed sum, which is agreed upon when the option is written, and occurs in the event that an issue or issuer goes into default. Reneau declares that this strategy can take the form of either puts or calls. Belanger states that this strategy is known as either a credit spread call option strategy or a credit spread put option strategy.

Reneau and Belanger continue by discussing the benefits of using credit options. Reneau mentions that credit options written on an underlying asset will protect against declines in asset valuation. Belanger says that credit spread options protect against adverse movements of the credit spread over a referenced benchmark.

18.1. Regarding their statements concerning the use of options strategies to exploit changes in the broad stock market, are Reneau and Belanger correct or incorrect?
A. Only Belanger is correct.
B. Only Reneau is correct.
C. Both are correct -OR- both are incorrect.

18.2. If Brendan Industries will experience the same growth as the overall economy (as projected by Blair), the breakeven stock price and maximum loss on Reneau's intended option strategy are *closest* to:

	Breakeven	Maximum loss
A.	$38	Unlimited
B.	$43	$6
C.	$38	$3

18.3. If Belanger is correct regarding Brendan Industries' volatility, and if the stock price at expiration is $45 and he pursues a lower cost strategy, his described strategy has a profit at expiration of:
A. $3.70.
B. $5.00.
C. $0.00.

18.4. Assume Reneau applies the options strategy used earlier for Nano Networks. Assuming there is a 3-month 45 call on Brendan Industries trading at $1.00, calculate the maximum gain and maximum loss on this position.

	Max gain	Max loss
A.	$2.50	−$2.50
B.	$5.00	−$5.00
C.	$3.00	−$2.00

18.5. Regarding their comments concerning the credit option strategy that pays the holder a fixed sum, are Reneau and Belanger correct or incorrect?
A. Only Belanger is correct.
B. Only Reneau is correct.
C. Both are correct -OR- both are incorrect.

18.6. Regarding their comments concerning the benefits of using credit options, are Reneau and Belanger correct or incorrect?
A. Only Belanger is correct.
B. Only Reneau is correct.
C. Both are correct -OR- both are incorrect.

QUESTION 19 HAS SIX PARTS FOR A TOTAL OF 18 MINUTES

Wealth Management's top economist, Frederick Milton, is an economic cycle forecaster. Milton's economic forecasts indicate an economic upswing that will impact all goods and services sectors. Milton presents his economic findings to the rest of Wealth Management's professionals at their monthly meeting. All are excited about Milton's forecast of an improving economic condition that should translate into a steadily rising stock market.

Nathaniel Norton and Timothy Tucker have confidence in Milton's capabilities and decide to meet with their clients. Their first meeting is with Elizabeth Mascarella to whom Norton recommends a dynamic asset allocation strategy to take advantage of Milton's forecast. However, Mascarella is concerned because the somewhat persistent back-and-forth of economic activity has translated into an oscillating stock market. Mascarella questions Norton's recommendation and asks Tucker which strategy should be followed if the market continues as it has, instead of making such "wonderful" strides.

It is one year later and Frederick Milton's economic forecast has been correct, and the market has trended upward as expected. Mascarella's strategic allocation to equity, which was $600,000 of a total portfolio of $1,000,000, has increased 20%. Her overall portfolio, which contains equity, debt, and some cash, is now valued at $1,150,000. Tucker meets with Mascarella and indicates it may be time to rebalance her portfolio.

19.1. Assuming a steadily rising market, the *best* strategy for Mascarella is:
   A. buy and hold.
   B. constant mix.
   C. constant proportion portfolio insurance.

19.2. Determine the preferred dynamic rebalancing strategy if the market is expected to be highly volatile, but more or less flat.
   A. Buy and hold.
   B. Constant mix.
   C. Constant proportion portfolio insurance.

19.3. Which of the following statements about CPPI strategies is probably *least* correct?
   A. CPPI strategies represent the purchase of portfolio insurance because they will buy stocks as they rise and sell them as they fall.
   B. CPPI strategies offer good upside potential because they increase exposure to risky assets as the market rises.
   C. Due to the concave nature of CPPI strategies, they offer good downside protection.

19.4. Mascarella has instructed Tucker to rebalance annually to maintain a corridor of ± 5% for equity. Given the constraint, Tucker should:
   A. reallocate an additional $50,000 to equity.
   B. reallocate the entire $120,000 to debt and cash.
   C. make no adjustments.

19.5. Tucker has tried to make Mascarella understand the benefits of percentage-of-portfolio rebalancing relative to calendar rebalancing. Which of the following statements made by Tucker is probably *least* correct?
   A. Calendar rebalancing provides discipline while requiring less monitoring.
   B. Percentage-of-portfolio rebalancing minimizes the amount by which the allocations stray from their strategic levels.
   C. Percentage of portfolio rebalancing is better than calendar rebalancing because it keeps allocations closer to their strategic levels.

19.6. Which of the following would generally suggest a narrower tolerance band?
   A. Assets in the portfolio tend to be illiquid.
   B. Highly volatile assets.
   C. Correlated portfolio assets.

END OF AFTERNOON SESSION

Exam 2
Score Sheet

MORNING SESSION		
Question	Maximum Points	Your Estimated Score
1	20	
2A	6	
2B	12	
2C	10	
3	10	
4A	12	
4B	16	
5A	4	
5B	10	
5C	9	
6A	9	
6B	7	
6C	6	
7	14	
8	12	
9A	8	
9B	3	
9C	3	
10A	6	
10B	3	
Total	180	

AFTERNOON SESSION		
Question	Maximum Points	Your Score
11	18	
12	18	
13	18	
14	18	
15	18	
16	18	
17	18	
18	18	
19	18	
20	18	
Total	180	

Certain Passing Score: 252 of 360 (70%)
Probable Passing Score: 234 (65%)

Please note that we write these exams to be as challenging and representative as possible. However, due to the relaxed conditions that most candidates apply when they "take" these tests (e.g., "I need a break. I think I'll go to the refrigerator and get a snack"), you should adjust your score downward by 10–15 percentage points to get a more accurate measure of the score you would have actually received on exam day. Also, you must be honest with yourself for your score on this exam to have any meaning. Don't assume, for example, that if your essay answer is close, the graders will be generous with points.

EXAM 2 MORNING SESSION TOPIC BREAKDOWN

Question	Topic	Minutes
1	Portfolio Management—Individual	20
2	Portfolio Management—Institutional	28
3	Benchmarks	10
4	Capital Market Expectations	28
5	Equity Portfolio Management	23
6	Asset Allocation	22
7	Portfolio Management—Institutional	14
8	Global Investment Performance Standards	12
9	Performance Evaluation	14
10	Portfolio Management—Institutional/Equity Portfolio Management	9
	Total	180

Exam 2
Morning Session

QUESTION 1 HAS ONE PART FOR A TOTAL OF 20 MINUTES

Barney Smythe, 40, and his wife Heather, 39, are considering what to do with a recent windfall they received after the untimely death of Heather's mother. The windfall is estimated to be $2,500,000 (after taxes). Barney is currently a supervising mechanic at a local luxury car dealership and has a salary of $48,750 annually. Heather is, and always has been, a stay-at-home mom. The Smythes have two children, Lenny, 12, and Buford, 10. By design, the Smythes owe no debt and pay their expenses on a monthly basis. Family expenses last year amounted to approximately $150,000.

In addition to the inheritance they will receive, the Smthyes have an additional $1,250,000 in savings. Barney and Heather have approached Net Worth Enhancers, PC, for assistance in managing their portfolio. The Smythes made the following statements at a recent client discovery meeting:

- "One of our goals at this stage in our lives is to pay for the college education of our children. We would like both of them to go to Heather's alma mater, which is a prestigious liberal arts institution."
- "We expect our annual expenses to increase at the general rate of inflation of 2%."
- "We want to retire at 65 and be able to live comfortably, but not extravagantly."
- "We are taxed at 25% on both income and capital gains."
- "We believe our portfolio should never suffer an annual loss of more than 5%. In addition, we do not want to invest in any individual investment or security that is too risky."
- "We do not foresee any unusual expenses over the short term. As always, we would like to have enough cash on hand for emergencies."

Determine the Smythes' willingness and ability to tolerate risk, their overall risk tolerance, and their required return for the next year. **Determine** the Smythes' time horizon, liquidity needs, and legal, regulatory and tax considerations.

Answer Question 1 in the template provided.

(20 minutes)

Template for Question 1

Investment Policy Statement for the Smythes	
Objectives	Risk Tolerance
	Return
Constraints	Time Horizon
	Liquidity
	Legal/Regulatory
	Taxes
	Unique Circumstances

QUESTION 2 HAS THREE PARTS FOR A TOTAL OF 28 MINUTES

Matrix Corporation is a multidivisional company with operations in energy, telecommunications, and shipping. Matrix sponsors a traditional defined benefit pension plan. Plan assets are valued at $5.5 billion, while recent declines in interest rates have caused plan liabilities to balloon to $8.3 billion. Average employee age at Matrix is 57.5, which is considerably higher than the industry average, and the ratio of active to retired lives is 1.1. Joe Elliot, Matrix's CFO, has made the following statement about the current state of the pension plan.

> "Recent declines in interest rates have caused our pension liabilities to grow faster than ever experienced in our long history, but I am sure these low rates are temporary. I have looked at the charts and estimated the probability of higher interest rates at more than 90%. Given the expected improvement in interest rate levels, plan liabilities will again come back into line with our historical position. Our investment policy will therefore be to invest plan assets in aggressive equity securities. This investment exposure will bring our plan to an over-funded status, which will allow us to use pension income to bolster our profitability."

A. **Critique** Elliot's statement with respect to investing Matrix's plan assets by addressing the following three points:

    i. Behavioral characteristic exhibited.
    ii. Plan risk and return objectives.
    iii. Using pension plan income to bolster firm profitability.

(6 minutes)

B.   Based on the information provided, **formulate** a return objective and a risk objective for the Matrix Corporation pension plan. (No calculations required.)

Answer Question 2-B in the template provided.

(12 minutes)

Template for Question 2-B

Investment Policy Statement for Matrix Corporation
Risk
Return

C.   Based on the information provided, **formulate** an appropriate constraints section for the investment policy statement for the pension fund.

Answer Question 2-C in the template provided.

(10 minutes)

Template for Question 2-C

Constraints	Time Horizon	
	Liquidity	
	Legal/ Regulatory	
	Taxes	
	Unique	

QUESTION 3 HAS ONE PART FOR A TOTAL OF 10 MINUTES

John Carpenter is considering using fixed income securities, hedge funds, and international stocks as vehicles for his more wealthy clients. Before doing so, he consults with Tom McKnealey, who is president of Benchmark Associates, a firm that specializes in the construction of benchmarks for portfolio managers. During a meeting with Carpenter, McKnealey makes the following statements about the proper construction of benchmarks for fixed income, hedge fund, and international stock portfolio managers:

- "The popularity bias can cause problems for measuring value-weighted hedge fund benchmark performance. The popularity bias argues that out-performing hedge funds as well as hedge fund styles tend to attract additional funding, so as they grow in popularity their performance tends to have a greater and greater impact on the value-weighted index's measured performance. This creates a double impact on the value-weighted hedge fund index return; the individual funds have good returns, and their increasing size means they have a greater weight in the index. The result is that the index's return has an upward bias. This bias, however, can be counteracted by utilizing two indices, one long and one short. Since most hedge fund managers attempt to generate alpha through both long and short positions, they can have a net zero weight or even a net negative weight. A single, long-only benchmark will not capture the performance of both strategies."

- "If an investor is averse to market value risk, the bond benchmark used should have a long maturity so they can lock in a yield to maturity."

- "The recommended solution to the 'free float' problem in international markets is to determine the amount of shares to be floated by an issuer in the upcoming year and use that to recalculate the issuer's weight in market capitalization weighted indices."

- "For bond investors such as foundations who desire a stable stream of income, long-term bond benchmarks should be used."

Determine which of McKnealey's statements are correct or incorrect, and if incorrect, **justify** your response.

Answer Question 3 in the template provided.

(10 minutes)

Template for Question 3

Comment	Is this statement correct or incorrect? (circle one)	Explanation, if incorrect
"The popularity bias can cause problems for measuring value-weighted hedge fund benchmark performance. The popularity bias argues that out-performing hedge funds as well as hedge fund styles tend to attract additional funding, so as they grow in popularity their performance tends to have a greater and greater impact on the value-weighted index's measured performance. This creates a double impact on the value-weighted hedge fund index return; the individual funds have good returns, and their increasing size means they have a greater weight in the index. The result is that the index's return has an upward bias. This bias, however, can be counteracted by utilizing two indices, one long and one short. Since most hedge fund managers attempt to generate alpha through both long and short positions, they can have a net zero weight or even a net negative weight. A single, long-only benchmark will not capture the performance of both strategies."	Correct Incorrect	–

Comment	Is this statement correct or incorrect? (circle one)	Explanation, if incorrect
"If an investor is averse to market value risk, the bond benchmark used should have a long maturity so they can lock in a yield to maturity."	Correct Incorrect	
"The recommended solution to the 'free float' problem in international markets is to determine the amount of shares to be floated by an issuer in the upcoming year and use that to recalculate the issuer's weight in market capitalization weighted indices."	Correct Incorrect	
"For bond investors such as foundations who desire a stable stream of income, long-term bond benchmarks should be used."	Correct Incorrect	

QUESTION 4 HAS TWO PARTS FOR A TOTAL OF 28 MINUTES

William Barkley and David McFalls are economists for Irvington Advisors, a U.S.-based firm. Irvington provides independent economic and investment advice to portfolio managers, research analysts, and others. Barkley and McFalls are discussing the state of developed and emerging market economies and stock markets.

Barkley and McFalls use economic data from a variety of sources to form their forecasts of international economies. At their regular Monday morning staff meeting, the two economists discuss the usefulness of economic data with their junior economists and research analysts. During the meeting, Barkley makes the following comments:

- "The stock returns in emerging markets are quite impressive. The mean returns are quite high and the risk is lower than many investors expect. Consider the example of the country of Yalewian. An index of Yalewian stocks had high returns for the period January 1, 1995 to December 31, 2006. This includes the period of crisis for emerging market stocks in 1997 and 1998. Yalewian stocks escaped from this crisis unscathed as their returns were positive during these years."

- "After extensive research on stock price patterns in 30 developed and emerging markets, I have uncovered a turn of the month effect in the United States. Specifically, the returns for U.S. stocks are higher in the first half of every month compared to the returns during the latter part of the month. The reason why this pattern is found in the United States and not in the other countries is because U.S. investors tend to invest after they have been paid their wages at the end of the month."

- "Using data for U.S. inflation from 1960 to 2006, the average rate was 3.4%. Accordingly, I expect U.S. inflation for the next year to be equal to this historical rate."

- "After evaluating the historical data for the U.S. and European stock markets, I have found that when the central bank is increasing the growth of the money supply, stock returns are higher. When they are restricting the growth, stock returns are lower. In fact, the correlation between the central bank discount rate and stock returns is 0.74 on average, indicating that central bank monetary policy is very influential for stock returns."

A. **State** whether or not *each* of these comments is susceptible to problems associated with using economic data to forecast. If susceptible, **identify** and **describe** the problem.

Answer Question 4-A in the template provided.

(12 minutes)

Template for Question 4-A

Comment	Is the statement susceptible to problems in using economic data to forecast? (circle one)	If yes, identify and describe the problem
"The stock returns in emerging markets are quite impressive. The mean returns are quite high and the risk is lower than many investors expect. Consider the example of the country of Yalewian. An index of Yalewian stocks had high returns for the period January 1, 1995 to December 31, 2006. This includes the period of crisis for emerging market stocks in 1997 and 1998. Yalewian stocks escaped from this crisis unscathed as their returns were positive during these years."	Yes No	
"After extensive research on stock price patterns in 30 developed and emerging markets, I have uncovered a turn of the month effect in the United States. Specifically, the returns for U.S. stocks are higher in the first half of every month compared to the returns during the latter part of the month. The reason why this pattern is found in the United States and not in the other countries is because U.S. investors tend to invest after they have been paid their wages at the end of the month."	Yes No	

"Using data for U.S. inflation from 1960 to 2006, the average rate was 3.4%. Accordingly, I expect U.S. inflation for the next year to be equal to this historical rate."	Yes No	
"After evaluating the historical data for the U.S. and European stock markets, I have found that when the central bank is increasing the growth of the money supply, stock returns are higher. When they are restricting the growth, stock returns are lower. In fact, the correlation between the central bank discount rate and stock returns is 0.74 on average, indicating that central bank monetary policy is very influential for stock returns."	Yes No	

Barkley and McFalls are evaluating the stock returns for two economies, the country of Airedale and the country of Bermiese. Airedale is a developed country with mature capital markets and few restrictions on cross border capital flows. Bermiese is an emerging country that puts restrictions on investment in its stock market by foreign investors. Specifically, foreign investors in total may hold no more than 5% of the outstanding shares of a single stock. McFalls has gathered the following data for the two countries and is deciding whether they would be an attractive addition to a portfolio. He uses the MSCI World Index as the global portfolio and uses a financial equilibrium model approach to evaluate the markets.

Sharpe ratio of the MSCI World Index	0.26
Standard deviation of the MSCI World Index	10.00%
Risk-free rate of return	3.50%
Degree of market integration for Airedale	85.00%
Degree of market integration for Bermiese	65.00%
Standard deviation of Airedale stock returns	11.00%
Standard deviation of Bermiese stock returns	21.00%
Correlation of Airedale with MSCI World Index	0.79
Correlation of Bermiese with MSCI World Index	0.58
Estimated illiquidity premium for Airedale	0.00%
Estimated illiquidity premium for Bermiese	2.60%

B.   **Calculate** the expected returns and betas for the two countries' stock markets. **Calculate** the covariance between the two countries' stock markets.

(16 minutes)

©2009 Kaplan, Inc.

QUESTION 5 HAS THREE PARTS FOR A TOTAL OF 23 MINUTES

Aaron Bell, a portfolio manager, is focusing his attention on investment style, and whether style should be a factor in investment decision making. Bell decides to play it safe and investigate how he can use different instruments related to style indices or indexing strategies to see if he can add value to his customers' portfolios.

A.   **Explain** holdings-based style analysis. **Discuss** *one* disadvantage of holdings-based style analysis and *one* advantage over returns-based style analysis.

(4 minutes)

B.   **Explain** returns-based style analysis. **Reproduce** the general form of the regression equation used for returns-based style analysis, including any constraints, and label *each* component of the equation. **Discuss** *one* disadvantage of returns-based style analysis and *one* advantage over holdings-based style analysis.

(10 minutes)

C.   Bell is considering indexing strategies and a colleague has suggested three alternatives: full replication; stratified sampling; and optimization. **Explain** *each* along with the conditions under which each would be appropriate to use and provide *one* disadvantage for *each*.

(9 minutes)

QUESTION 6 HAS THREE PARTS FOR A TOTAL OF 22 MINUTES

Wyatt Washington is the portfolio manager for Mark Beitia, a recent retiree. He is currently exploring a change in Beitia's strategic asset allocation. He gathers data on the expected returns, standard deviations, and correlations for five assets. Using these market expectations, he derives an efficient frontier. Washington uses the following information in his construction of the asset allocation:

- Beitia's asset base = $5,000,000.
- Annual after-tax spending amount = $150,000.
- Estimate of future inflation = 3.5%.
- Beitia will donate $750,000 to his alma mater in one year in one lump sum.
- Risk-free rate = 4.0%.
- Beitia's income tax rate = 25%.
- Beitia's risk aversion value = 5.0.

Washington forms four corner portfolios from his efficient frontier and calculates the following expected returns and standard deviations:

Corner Portfolio	Expected Before Tax Return	Expected Std. Dev.	Sharpe Ratio	Weights in assets 1 to 5				
				1	2	3	4	5
1	6.50%	4.10%	0.610	0%	20%	80%	0%	0%
2	8.50%	5.80%	0.776	0%	15%	85%	0%	0%
3	9.70%	7.80%	0.731	60%	10%	30%	0%	0%
4	13.50%	10.60%	0.896	100%	0%	0%	0%	0%

A.   **Calculate** the required before-tax return for Beitia's portfolio and Beitia's expected utility from holding each of the corner portfolios.

(9 minutes)

B. Assuming that Washington combines two corner portfolios to meet Beitia's desired return (calculated in Part A), **calculate** the weights of the appropriate corner portfolios that will be used (assume no borrowing or short-selling) and the resulting portfolio standard deviation.

(7 minutes)

C. Assuming that Washington combines a corner portfolio with the risk-free asset to meet Beitia's desired return (calculated in Part A), **calculate** the weights of the appropriate corner portfolio and the risk-free asset that will be used (assume no borrowing) and the resulting portfolio standard deviation.

(6 minutes)

QUESTION 7 HAS ONE PART FOR A TOTAL OF 14 MINUTES

A1 Casualty, Inc. writes property and casualty insurance policies for individuals, homeowners, and small businesses located in the Southeastern portion of the United States. For the last three years, market forces have caused A1 to more competitively price their policies to increase underwriting volume. This competitive pricing environment coincides with a somewhat slowing general business cycle. Two months ago, a massive hurricane hit the panhandle of Florida and southeast Alabama, causing unprecedented damages to property. Approximately 50% of A1's homeowners' policies are written in that geographic region, but as of yet, claims processing has been much less than expected from the area. Stan Carnay, A1's CEO, has been busy preparing the latest investment portfolio report for the Board of Directors' meeting in two weeks and has asked Eileen Carlyle, CFA, A1's most recent addition to the investment group, for assistance in updating a decades-old investment policy statement. In preliminary discussions, Carlyle indicated the following:

- "Underwriting activity, although somewhat improved over the past decade, has not been as profitable as expected during the last three years. The competitive marketplace in which we operate has directly impacted our ability to profitably price our insurance products."

- "We should count our blessings that so few claims from the recent hurricane have been submitted. Actuarial estimates indicate our potential exposure from this weather event is approximately $75 million, which represents 75% of our surplus portfolio. Since claim submission has been almost non-existent, we can transition our investment portfolio into a greater proportion of common stock, taking our stock to surplus ratio from 90% to close to 100%. That action should help strengthen our long-term competitive position."

- "Recent economic conditions have slowed, but numerous other comparable casualty companies are optimistic that economic conditions will improve over the next 9 to 12 months. Although market economists continue forecasting a slightly longer downturn in the national economy, we consider those forecasts overly pessimistic."

Without using calculations, **formulate** an investment policy statement appropriate for A1.

Answer Question 7 in the template provided.

(14 minutes)

Template for Question 7

Investment Policy Statement for A1 Casualty	
Objectives	Return Objectives
	Risk Tolerance
Constraints	Time Horizon
	Liquidity
	Legal/Regulatory
	Taxes
	Unique Circumstances

QUESTION 8 HAS ONE PART FOR A TOTAL OF 12 MINUTES

Bailey Investments is a U.S.-based investment management firm. They began operations on January 1, 2004. Their client base has grown considerably over the last few years and in order to ensure accurate and consistent performance data they have decided to pursue GIPS® compliance. The following includes composite data and notes relating to the first presentation for one of their composites in which they claim GIPS compliance.

Year	Total Return (%)	Benchmark Return (%)	Number of Portfolios	Composite Dispersion (%)	Total Firm Asset ($ millions)
2005	6.54	7.25	15	2.5	86
2006	8.74	9.25	19	3.2	135
2007	9.45	8.67	28	4.1	276
2008	7.53	7.45	35	4.5	332

Bailey Investments has prepared and presented this report in compliance with the Global Investment Performance Standards (GIPS®).

Notes:

1. Valuations are obtained by Reuters and computed using the U.S. dollar.

2. Bailey Investments is a dedicated equity portfolio manager that invests entirely in U.S. securities and has no affiliates.

3. The benchmark composition is 100% S&P 500. The annualized compound benchmark return is 8.15%. The annualized compound composite return is 8.06%.

4. Composite dispersion is the annualized monthly standard deviation of composite returns.

5. No modifications to the composites as presented here have occurred as a result of changes in personnel or for any other reason at any time.

6. Performance results are presented before management and custodial fees but after all trading commissions.

7. The composite includes discretionary and non-discretionary fee-paying portfolios.

List *four* non-compliant items in the presentation. For *each*, **state** the necessary corrective action.

Answer Question 8 in the template provided.

(12 minutes)

Template for Question 8

Errors in presentation and corrective action.
1.
2.
3.
4.

QUESTION 9 HAS THREE PARTS FOR A TOTAL OF 14 MINUTES

One year has passed since HNW Advisors first started operations. Their overall equity portfolio has returned 28.2% versus a return of 22.4% for the S&P 500. The standard deviation of the S&P 500 is 20%, and Maggie Day, CFA, has estimated the standard deviation of HNW Advisor's equity portfolio at 45%. HNW Advisor's equity portfolio has a beta of 1.35, and the risk-free rate is 4.4%.

A major HNW client is attempting to evaluate the relative performance of HNW's equity fund. The client is unsure whether the Sharpe measure or the Treynor measure is appropriate for the HNW portfolio.

A.   Using the Sharpe and Treynor measures for the HNW portfolio and the S&P 500, **determine** how HNW has performed relative to the S&P 500.

(8 minutes)

B.   Assume that, using the Sharpe ratio to measure performance, the S&P 500 outperformed the HNW portfolio, but using the Treynor measure, the HNW portfolio outperformed the S&P 500. **Explain**, in terms of systematic and unsystematic risk, how this change in ranking could have occurred.

(3 minutes)

C. **Compute** M^2 for the HNW portfolio, assuming management uses the market as a benchmark. **Explain**, in terms of relative returns and volatility, the circumstances under which M^2 for HNW would equal M^2 for the market.

(3 minutes)

QUESTION 10 HAS TWO PARTS FOR A TOTAL OF 9 MINUTES

Tom Groh is the President of Opportunity Banks. Opportunity has historically operated in the northeastern United States, with most of its business in Maryland, Delaware, and New Jersey. Opportunity has been in business since 1987 and has built its business on making mortgages and construction loans to residential developers. Opportunity has been very profitable, because developers value the services the bank provides. This allows Opportunity to price their construction loans with higher interest rates. Opportunity services and retains ownership of the its loans. It historically has had a near-zero leverage-adjusted duration gap.

In the most recent fiscal year, Opportunity has experienced important changes in their business as follows:

1. Due to pressure from local activists, Opportunity has stepped up lending in low-income areas. Groh expects the default rate on these loans to be higher than the loans currently in their portfolio.

2. Opportunity has bought a regional bank with operations in North Carolina, South Carolina, and Georgia. The acquired bank's loan portfolio consists mostly of commercial loans to small, local businesses.

3. A recent downturn in interest rates has caused many of Opportunity's variable rate mortgages to be refinanced to 15 and 30-year fixed-rate mortgages. Opportunity has retained the business of most of its customers who have refinanced.

A.   In each of the scenarios provided, **determine** *one* effect on the investment objectives, constraints, or investment policies of the bank's security portfolio. **Evaluate** *each* scenario in isolation from the others.

   Answer Question 10-A in the template provided.

   (6 minutes)

Template for Question 10-A

Scenario	Effect on Bank's Policies
1. Due to pressure from local activists, Opportunity has stepped up lending to low-income areas. Groh expects the default rate on these loans to be higher than the loans currently in their portfolio.	
2. Opportunity has bought a regional bank with operations in North Carolina, South Carolina, and Georgia. The acquired bank's loan portfolio consists mostly of commercial loans to small, local businesses.	
3. A recent downturn in interest rates has caused many of Opportunity's variable rate mortgages to be refinanced to 15- and 30-year fixed rate mortgages. Opportunity has retained the business of most of its customers who have refinanced.	

B.   Groh is advising one of the bank's clients on the management of the client's family trust. Previously the family trust hired a portfolio manager whose fee was a fixed 1% of assets. The family is now considering another portfolio manager who is paid a lower fixed 0.30% of assets but also charges 20% of any excess return above their benchmark. **Discuss** *one* advantage and *two* disadvantages of the new manager's fee structure.

(3 minutes)

END OF MORNING SESSION

Exam 2 Afternoon Session Topic Breakdown

Question	Topic	Minutes
11	Ethics and Professional Standards	18
12	Ethics and Professional Standards	18
13	Fixed Income/Swaps	18
14	Fixed Income/Risk Management	18
15	Fixed Income	18
16	Alternative Investments	18
17	Fixed Income/Equity/Derivatives	18
18	Fixed Income/Derivatives	18
19	Execution of Portfolio Decisions	18
20	Risk Management/Performance Evaluation	18
	Total	180

EXAM 2 SELECTED RESPONSE ITEM SET ANSWER SHEET

The afternoon session of the Level 3 exam contains 10 Selected Response Item Sets, each with six questions, and you must answer them by filling in a bubble sheet with a number 2 or HB pencil. For realism, we suggest that you use this answer sheet and darken the bubbles corresponding to your answers. This sheet will also facilitate entering your answers into our online Performance Tracker. You have 180 minutes for this session of the exam. That equates to 3 minutes per item set question, so budget your time well.

11.1. Ⓐ	Ⓑ	Ⓒ		16.1. Ⓐ	Ⓑ	Ⓒ
11.2. Ⓐ	Ⓑ	Ⓒ		162. Ⓐ	Ⓑ	Ⓒ
11.3. Ⓐ	Ⓑ	Ⓒ		16.3. Ⓐ	Ⓑ	Ⓒ
11.4. Ⓐ	Ⓑ	Ⓒ		16.4. Ⓐ	Ⓑ	Ⓒ
11.5. Ⓐ	Ⓑ	Ⓒ		16.5. Ⓐ	Ⓑ	Ⓒ
11.6. Ⓐ	Ⓑ	Ⓒ		16.6. Ⓐ	Ⓑ	Ⓒ
12.1. Ⓐ	Ⓑ	Ⓒ		17.1. Ⓐ	Ⓑ	Ⓒ
12.2. Ⓐ	Ⓑ	Ⓒ		17.2. Ⓐ	Ⓑ	Ⓒ
12.3. Ⓐ	Ⓑ	Ⓒ		17.3. Ⓐ	Ⓑ	Ⓒ
12.4. Ⓐ	Ⓑ	Ⓒ		17.4. Ⓐ	Ⓑ	Ⓒ
12.5. Ⓐ	Ⓑ	Ⓒ		17.5. Ⓐ	Ⓑ	Ⓒ
12.6. Ⓐ	Ⓑ	Ⓒ		17.6. Ⓐ	Ⓑ	Ⓒ
13.1. Ⓐ	Ⓑ	Ⓒ		18.1. Ⓐ	Ⓑ	Ⓒ
13.2. Ⓐ	Ⓑ	Ⓒ		18.2. Ⓐ	Ⓑ	Ⓒ
13.3. Ⓐ	Ⓑ	Ⓒ		18.3. Ⓐ	Ⓑ	Ⓒ
13.4. Ⓐ	Ⓑ	Ⓒ		18.4. Ⓐ	Ⓑ	Ⓒ
13.5. Ⓐ	Ⓑ	Ⓒ		18.5. Ⓐ	Ⓑ	Ⓒ
13.6. Ⓐ	Ⓑ	Ⓒ		18.6. Ⓐ	Ⓑ	Ⓒ
14.1. Ⓐ	Ⓑ	Ⓒ		19.1. Ⓐ	Ⓑ	Ⓒ
14.2. Ⓐ	Ⓑ	Ⓒ		19.2. Ⓐ	Ⓑ	Ⓒ
14.3. Ⓐ	Ⓑ	Ⓒ		19.3. Ⓐ	Ⓑ	Ⓒ
14.4. Ⓐ	Ⓑ	Ⓒ		19.4. Ⓐ	Ⓑ	Ⓒ
14.5. Ⓐ	Ⓑ	Ⓒ		19.5. Ⓐ	Ⓑ	Ⓒ
14.6. Ⓐ	Ⓑ	Ⓒ		19.6. Ⓐ	Ⓑ	Ⓒ
15.1. Ⓐ	Ⓑ	Ⓒ		20.1. Ⓐ	Ⓑ	Ⓒ
15.2. Ⓐ	Ⓑ	Ⓒ		20.2. Ⓐ	Ⓑ	Ⓒ
15.3. Ⓐ	Ⓑ	Ⓒ		20.3. Ⓐ	Ⓑ	Ⓒ
15.4. Ⓐ	Ⓑ	Ⓒ		20.4. Ⓐ	Ⓑ	Ⓒ
15.5. Ⓐ	Ⓑ	Ⓒ		20.5. Ⓐ	Ⓑ	Ⓒ
15.6. Ⓐ	Ⓑ	Ⓒ		20.6. Ⓐ	Ⓑ	Ⓒ

Exam 2
Afternoon Session

QUESTION 11 HAS SIX PARTS FOR A TOTAL OF 18 MINUTES

Rowan Brothers is a full service investment firm offering portfolio management and investment banking services. For the last ten years, Aaron King, CFA, has managed individual client portfolios for Rowan Brothers, most of which are trust accounts over which King has full discretion. One of King's clients, Shelby Pavlica, is a widow in her late 50s whose husband died and left assets of over $7 million in a trust, for which she is the only beneficiary.

Pavlica's three children are appalled at their mother's spending habits and have called a meeting with King to discuss their concerns. They inform King that their mother is living too lavishly to leave much for them or Pavlica's grandchildren upon her death. King acknowledges their concerns and informs them that, on top of her ever-increasing spending, Pavlica has recently been diagnosed with a chronic illness. Since the diagnosis could indicate a considerable increase in medical spending, he will need to increase the risk of the portfolio to generate sufficient return to cover the medical bills and spending and still maintain the principal. King restructures the portfolio accordingly and then meets with Pavlica a week later to discuss how he has altered the investment strategy, which was previously revised only three months earlier in their annual meeting.

During the meeting with Pavlica, King explains his reasoning for altering the portfolio allocation but does not mention the meeting with Pavlica's children. Pavlica agrees that it is probably the wisest decision and accepts the new portfolio allocation adding that she will need to tell her children about her illness, so they will understand why her medical spending requirements will increase in the near future. She admits to King that her children have been concerned about her spending. King assures her that the new investments will definitely allow her to maintain her lifestyle and meet her higher medical spending needs.

One of the investments selected by King is a small allocation in a private placement offered to him by a brokerage firm that often makes trades for King's portfolios. The private placement is an equity investment in ShaleCo, a small oil exploration company. In order to make the investment, King sold shares of a publicly traded biotech firm, VNC Technologies. King also held shares of VNC, a fact that he has always disclosed to clients before purchasing VNC for their accounts. An hour before submitting the sell order for the VNC shares in Pavlica's trust account, King placed an order to sell a portion of his position in VNC stock. By the time Pavlica's order was sent to the trading floor, the price of VNC had risen, allowing Pavlica to sell her shares at a better price than received by King.

Although King elected not to take any shares in the private placement, he purchased positions for several of his clients, for whom the investment was deemed appropriate in terms of the clients' objectives and constraints as well as the existing composition of the portfolios. In response to the investment support, ShaleCo appointed King to their board of directors. Seeing an opportunity to advance his career while also protecting the value of his clients' investments in the company, King gladly accepted the offer. King decided that since serving on the board of ShaleCo is in his clients' best interest, it is not necessary to disclose the directorship to his clients or his employer.

For his portfolio management services, King charges a fixed percentage fee based on the value of assets under management. All fees charged and other terms of service are disclosed to clients as well as prospects. In the past month, however, Rowan Brothers has instituted an incentive program for its portfolio managers. Under the program, the firm will award an all-expense-paid vacation to the Cayman islands for any portfolio manager who generates two consecutive quarterly returns for his clients in excess of 10%. King updates his marketing literature to ensure that his prospective clients are fully aware of his compensation arrangements, but he does not contact current clients to make them aware of the newly created performance incentive.

11.1. In discussing Pavlica's spending and medical condition with Pavlica's children, did King violate any CFA Institute Standards of Professional Conduct?
A. No.
B. Yes, because he violated his client's confidentiality.
C. Yes, because he created a conflict of interest between himself and his employer.

11.2. In reallocating the portfolio after the meeting with Pavlica's children, did King violate any CFA Institute Standards of Professional Conduct?
A. Yes, he violated Standard III(A) Loyalty, Prudence, and Care.
B. No, because he had a reasonable basis for making adjustments to the portfolio.
C. No, because Pavlica agreed with the investment choices and King has discretion over the portfolio.

11.3. In his statements to Pavlica after the reallocation, did King violate any CFA Institute Standards of Professional Conduct?
A. No.
B. Yes, because he misrepresented the expected performance of the strategy.
C. Yes, because he met with her before their annual meeting which is unfair to clients who only meet with King annually.

11.4. Did King's actions with regard to allocating the private placement and the sale of VNC stock violate any CFA Institute Standards of Professional Conduct?

	Private placement	VNC sale
A.	Yes	Yes
B.	No	No
C.	No	Yes

11.5. According to the CFA Institute Standards of Professional Conduct, which of the following statements is correct concerning King's directorship with ShaleCo?
   A. King may not accept the directorship since it creates a conflict of interest.
   B. King may accept the directorship as long as it is disclosed to clients and prospects.
   C. King may accept the directorship as long as it is disclosed to his employer, clients, and prospects.

11.6. Does the fee structure at Rowan Brothers and King's disclosure of the compensation structure violate any CFA Institute Standards of Professional Conduct?

	Fee structure	Disclosure
A.	No	Yes
B.	Yes	No
C.	No	No

QUESTION 12 HAS SIX PARTS FOR A TOTAL OF 18 MINUTES

Johnny Bracco, CFA, is a portfolio manager in the trust department of Canada National (CNL) in Toronto. CNL is a financial conglomerate with many divisions. In addition to the trust department, the firm sells financial products and has a research department, a trading desk, and an investment banking division.

Part of the company's operating procedures manual contains detailed information on how the firm allocates shares in oversubscribed stock offerings. Allocation is effected on a pro rata basis based upon factors such as the size of a client's portfolio, suitability, and previous notification to participate in IPOs. Additionally, company policy discloses to clients that any trade needs to meet a minimum transaction size in an effort to control trading costs and to comply with best execution procedures.

One of Bracco's trust accounts is the Carobilo family trust, which contains a portion of nondiscretionary funds managed by Stephen Carobilo. Carobilo has a friend who runs a brokerage firm called First Trades, to which Carobilo tells Bracco to direct trades from the nondiscretionary accounts. Bracco has learned that First Trades charges a slightly higher trading fee than other brokers providing comparable services, and he discloses this to Carobilo.

Due to high prices and limited supplies of oil, Bracco has been following companies in the energy sector. He believes this area of the economy is in turmoil and should present some mispricing opportunities. One company he has been researching is Stiles Corporation, which is working on a new type of hydrogen fuel cell that uses fusion technology to create energy. To date, no one has been able to successfully sustain a fusion reaction for an extended period of time. Bracco has been in close contact with Stiles' pubic relations department, has toured their laboratories, and has thoroughly researched fusion technology and Stiles' competitors. Bracco is convinced from his research, based upon various public sources, that Stiles is on the verge of perfecting this technology and will be the first firm to bring it to the marketplace. Jerry McNulty, CFA and vice president of the investment banking division of CNL, has been working with Stiles to raise new capital via a secondary offering of Stiles common shares. One day Bracco happened to be in a stall in the bathroom when McNulty and a colleague came in and discussed the fact that Stiles had perfected the fuel-cell technology, which will greatly increase the price of Stiles' stock.

Stiles Corporation's board of directors includes Dr. Elaine James, who is a physics professor at the University of Toronto. She also works part-time for Stiles Corporation as a consultant in their fusion technology laboratory. Her husband is a materials engineer who recently started performing consulting work for Stiles.

A routine audit by the quality control department at CNL discovered trading errors in several of Bracco's accounts involving an oversubscribed IPO. Some accounts received shares they should not have and others did not receive shares they should have. Bracco and his supervisor Jaime Gun, CFA, are taking responsibility to reverse the incorrect trades. Bracco told Gun, "I'll correct the trades based on our clients' investment policy statements, previous notification of intent, and according to the company's formula for allocating shares on a pro rata basis. In so doing, we will fairly allocate shares so even small accounts that did not meet minimum size requirements will receive some shares of the IPO." Gun replied to Bracco by saying, "I'll credit short-term interest back to the accounts that should not have received the shares and subtract interest from the accounts that should have received the shares."

That evening, Bracco and his wife attended the company holiday party for CNL employees and their spouses. Jerry McNulty, whose wife was ill and could not come to the party, arrived drunk from a meeting with Stiles' upper management. During the party McNulty made inappropriate advances toward many of the female employees and joked about the inadequacies of Stiles' managers.

While cleaning up after the party, a janitor found McNulty's pocket notebook that he apparently dropped accidentally during the party. In the notebook, McNulty wrote the recommended amount and date of the secondary offering as well as several details on the nature of the new product. Not knowing exactly what to do with the notebook, the janitor gave it to Burt Sampson, CFA, a trader at CNL. Later that night, Sampson called many of his relatives and friends and told them about the upcoming offering. First thing the following Monday morning, McNulty submitted an order to buy the stock for his personal portfolio.

12.1. Has Bracco violated any soft dollar standards regarding the Carobilo family trust? Bracco has:
   A. violated soft dollar standards because he did not satisfy the requirement of best execution.
   B. violated the soft dollar standards because client brokerage is to be used only for research purposes to benefit the client.
   C. not violated any soft dollar standards since Carobilo requested that the trades be sent to a specific broker.

12.2. If after overhearing McNulty's conversation in the bathroom Bracco placed trades to purchase shares of the Stiles Corporation for some of his clients, would Bracco have violated any of the Standards of Professional conduct?
   A. No, because the information regarding the Stiles Corporation was not acquired in a breach of confidence.
   B. No, since he performed his own research and is allowed to trade based on the mosaic theory.
   C. Yes, since he possesses insider information, he is not allowed to trade based on this information.

12.3. Which of the following statements regarding Elaine James's participation on the board of directors of Stiles Corporation is *most* accurate? James's participation:
   A. does not violate effective corporate governance policies because she provides relevant expertise to the board.
   B. does not violate effective corporate governance policies since boards are allowed to hire outside consultants when making decisions.
   C. violates effective corporate governance policies because she is paid by the company as a consultant and is therefore not independent.

12.4. Regarding the statements made by Bracco and Gun on how to correct the trading errors:
   A. only Gun's statement is correct.
   B. only Bracco's statement is correct.
   C. both are correct or both are incorrect.

12.5. Did McNulty's behavior at the holiday party violate the:

	Code of Ethics?	Standards of Professional Conduct?
A.	Yes	Yes
B.	No	Yes
C.	Yes	No

12.6. Based solely on the information provided in the last paragraph, determine whether McNulty and/or Sampson violated the Code and Standards.

	McNulty	Sampson
A.	No	No
B.	Yes	Yes
C.	No	Yes

QUESTION 13 HAS SIX PARTS FOR A TOTAL OF 18 MINUTES

Tiffany Morrison, CFA, a manager for Sierra Fund, is investigating the use of relative value methodologies for global corporate bond portfolio management. As a recent college graduate, Bernard Tabler has been assisting Morrison in data gathering and analysis.

Morrison is a firm believer that corporate yield spreads have a tendency to revert to their historical mean values. Accordingly, Tabler has compiled relevant information for three corporate issues. Morrison and Tabler use the information below to conduct mean reversion analysis.

Bond Issue	Current Spread	Mean Spread for Past 12 Months	Standard Deviation of Spread
VV	125	98	28
XX	100	75	15
YY	85	100	10

Note: All spreads are expressed in basis points.

Morrison's research has also included a study of the implications of secular and cyclical changes in the primary corporate bond market. As a result of her research, she states that the implication of both cyclical and secular changes in the primary corporate bond market for fixed-income portfolio management is that effective duration and aggregate interest rate risk will increase. Tabler adds that it also appears that credit-based derivatives will increasingly be used to achieve desired exposure to credit sectors, issuers, and structures.

During the presentation to a client, Morrison discusses corporate curve analysis. She states that corporate spread curves tend to change with the economic cycle, so in order to properly conduct this analysis the analyst must examine credit and yield curves carefully. Tabler adds that corporate spreads usually narrow during upturns and widen during downturns.

Morrison is also considering using repurchase agreements to fund some overnight investment activities. Watching the financial news, she observes that the Federal Reserve has increased the federal funds rate to combat potential inflation. She notes that this will increase the borrowing costs of investment strategies using repurchase agreements. Tabler chimes in that the strategy's interest cost could be reduced by using hot collateral such as on-the-run U.S. Treasuries.

Morrison is also providing advice to a client on the best way to hedge a floating rate loan using a swap. The client is paying 120 basis points over LIBOR. Morrison suggests that the client enter a 5-year LIBOR-based swap. The swap fixed rate is 100 basis points over the U.S. Treasury rate. The floating rate is LIBOR flat. LIBOR is 5.60% and the Treasury rate is 5.20% when this swap is being considered.

13.1. Based on the mean-reversion analysis only, which of the three bonds is the most attractive candidate for Morrison to purchase for the Sierra Fund?
A. VV.
B. XX.
C. YY.

13.2. Regarding their statements on the implications of secular and cyclical changes in the primary corporate bond market, determine if Morrison and Tabler are correct or incorrect.
A. Only Morrison is correct.
B. Only Tabler is correct.
C. Both are incorrect.

13.3. Over lunch, Morrison and Tabler get into a heated debate over the relative performance of callable and non-callable bonds in a dynamic interest rate environment. In terms of relative performance, determine which of the following relationships is *least* correct.
A. If rates are significantly greater than coupon rates, embedded call options are practically worthless, so callable bonds perform as if they are non-callable.
B. As interest rates increase, the option to call a callable bond decreases. If required returns are below coupon rates and expected to increase, non-callable bonds are probably better investments than callable bonds.
C. The value of a callable bond is significantly affected by the value of the embedded call option. For example, as its required return falls below (increases above) its coupon rate, the value of the embedded option consumes an increasing (a decreasing) proportion of the total value of the bond.

13.4. Regarding their statements on corporate curve analysis, are Morrison and Tabler correct or incorrect?
A. Both are correct.
B. Neither is correct.
C. One is correct.

13.5. Regarding their statements on investment strategies using repurchase agreements, are Morrison and Tabler correct or incorrect?
A. Only Morrison is correct.
B. Only Tabler is correct.
C. Both are correct.

13.6. In the swap hedge of the floating rate loan, the net fixed rate that the client will pay is *closest* to:
A. 5.8%.
B. 7.4%.
C. 7.8%.

QUESTION 14 HAS SIX PARTS FOR A TOTAL OF 18 MINUTES

Carl Cramer is a recent hire at Derivatives Specialists Inc. (DSI), a small consulting firm that advises a variety of institutions on the management of credit risk. Some of DSI's clients are very familiar with risk management techniques whereas others are not. Cramer has been assigned the task of creating a handbook on credit risk, its possible impact, and its management. His immediate supervisor, Christine McNally, will assist Cramer in the creation of the handbook and will review it. Before she took a position at DSI, McNally advised banks and other institutions on the use of value-at-risk (VAR) as well as credit-at-risk (CAR).

Cramer's first task is to address the basic dimensions of credit risk. He states that the first dimension of credit risk is the probability of an event that will cause a loss. The second dimension of credit risk is the amount lost, which is a function of the dollar amount recovered when a loss event occurs. Cramer recalls the considerable difficulty he faced when transacting with Johnson Associates, a firm which defaulted on a contract with the Grich Company. Grich forced Johnson Associates into bankruptcy, and Johnson Associates was declared in default of all its agreements. Unfortunately, DSI then had to wait until the bankruptcy court decided on all claims before it could settle the agreement with Johnson Associates.

McNally mentions that Cramer should include a statement about the time dimension of credit risk. She states that the two primary time dimensions of credit risk are current and future. Current credit risk relates to the possibility of default on current obligations, while future credit risk relates to potential default on future obligations. If a borrower defaults and claims bankruptcy, a creditor can file claims representing the face value of current obligations and the present value of future obligations. Cramer adds that combining current and potential credit risk analysis provides the firm's total credit risk exposure and that current credit risk is usually a reliable predictor of a borrower's potential credit risk.

As DSI has clients with a variety of forward contracts, Cramer then addresses the credit risks associated with forward agreements. Cramer states that long forward contracts gain in value when the market price of the underlying increases above the contract price. McNally encourages Cramer to include an example of credit risk and forward contracts in the handbook. She offers the following:

> *A forward contract sold by Palmer Securities has six months until the delivery date and a contract price of 50. The underlying asset has no cash flows or storage costs and is currently priced at 50. In the contract, no funds were exchanged upfront.*

Cramer also describes how a client firm of DSI can control the credit risks in their derivatives transactions. He writes that firms can make use of netting arrangements, create a special purpose vehicle, require collateral from counterparties, and require a mark-to-market provision. McNally adds that Cramer should include a discussion of some newer forms of credit protection in his handbook. McNally thinks credit derivatives represent an opportunity for DSI. She believes that one type of credit derivative that should figure prominently in their handbook is total return swaps. She asserts that to purchase protection through a total return swap, the holder of a credit asset will agree to pass the total return on the asset to the protection seller (e.g., a swap dealer) in exchange for a single, fixed payment representing the discounted present value of expected cash flows from the asset.

A DSI client, Weaver Trading, has a bond that they are concerned will increase in credit risk. Weaver would like protection against this event in the form of a payment if the bond's yield spread increases beyond LIBOR plus 3%. Weaver Trading prefers a cash settlement.

Later that week, Cramer and McNally visit a client's headquarters and discuss the potential hedge of a bond issued by Cuellar Motors. Cuellar manufactures and markets specialty luxury motorcycles. The client is considering hedging the bond using a credit spread forward because he is concerned that a downturn in the economy could result in a default on the Cuellar bond. The client holds $2,000,000 in par of the Cuellar bond, and the bond's coupons are paid annually. The bond's current spread over the U.S. Treasury rate is 2.5%. The characteristics of the forward contract are shown below.

Information on the Credit Spread Forward

Contract spread	3%
Risk factor	10
Spread at maturity	4.5%
Notional principal of credit spread forward	$2 million

14.1. Determine which of the following is *most likely* responsible for the difficulty Cramer faced when transacting with the firm Johnson Associates.
     A. A cross-default provision.
     B. A jump-to-default provision.
     C. A credit protection provision.

14.2. Regarding their statements concerning current and future credit risk, determine whether Cramer and McNally are correct or incorrect.
A. Only Cramer is correct.
B. Only McNally is correct.
C. Both are correct -OR- both are incorrect.

14.3. Determine whether the forward contracts sold by Palmer Securities have current and/or potential credit risk.
A. The contract has current credit risk only.
B. The contract has potential credit risk only.
C. The contract has neither potential credit risk nor current credit risk.

14.4. Regarding their statements concerning controlling credit risk, determine whether Cramer and McNally are correct or incorrect.
A. Only Cramer is correct.
B. Only McNally is correct.
C. Both are incorrect.

14.5. Of the following, determine which would *most likely* provide the *best* hedge desired by Weaver Trading.
A. Credit default swap.
B. Credit spread call option.
C. Credit spread put option.

14.6. Assuming the $2,000,000 in par of the Cuellar bond is hedged using the given credit spread forward, the payoff to the buyer or seller from the credit spread forward contract is *closest* to:
A. $300,000 to the seller.
B. $300,000 to the buyer.
C. $100,000 to the buyer.

QUESTION 15 HAS SIX PARTS FOR A TOTAL OF 18 MINUTES

Jack Thomas and Tim Bentley are analysts for Bond Analytics (BA). BA provides bond analysis for mutual fund managers, hedge fund managers, and institutional money managers in the United States. BA specializes in the valuation of international bonds and callable bonds, using intrasector analysis to find undervalued bonds. In addition to valuing the bonds, they also advise clients on whether to hedge currency risk for international bonds. Thomas has been a particularly strong advocate of hedging the currency risk of international bonds, especially in emerging markets, using forward contracts when they are available.

At a morning meeting, Thomas and Bentley are trying to decide whether to hedge the currency risk of a large issue of bonds from a Thai manufacturer of pressed steel, Nakhon Metals. The client considering purchasing the bonds is a large U.S. mutual fund, Epsilon Funds. Epsilon has started to explore the possibility of earning higher returns through currency management using forward contracts. Thomas and Bentley discuss the various hedges of currency risk for the Nakhon Metals bond. One possibility is using a forward hedge position on the Thai baht. A second possibility is using forward contracts where the baht is delivered for Korean won. Thomas states that the second hedge would be pursued if the won was expected to appreciate more against the U.S. dollar than the baht. In the second hedge, the manager would sell won for dollars at the future spot rate.

Thomas and Bentley gather the following information on the expected changes in the various currencies, the 1-year cash rates in the respective countries, and the expected return on the Nakhon bond.

Yield on Nakhon Metals bond in Thai baht terms	5.20%
Cash rate in Thailand	2.50%
Expected change in the baht relative to the U.S. dollar	2.80%
Cash rate in Korea	3.20%
Expected change in the won relative to the U.S. dollar	6.40%
Cash rate in Japan	4.20%
Expected change in the yen relative to the U.S. dollar	3.50%
Cash rate in United States	6.50%

Additionally, the Nakhon Metals bond has a duration of 7.30 and is being compared against a bond denominated in U.S. dollars, issued by Powhatan Industries. The Powhatan bond has a duration of 4.2 and a yield of 4.50%. Whichever bond is purchased will be held for the next year. Thomas projects that the yield for the Nakhon Metals bond is expected to increase by 15 basis points, while the yield on the Powhatan Industries bond is expected to stay constant.

©2009 Kaplan, Inc.

The following day, Thomas and Bentley discuss the market for and valuation of callable and long duration bonds. They believe that interest rates are temporarily low and for this reason want to be careful about their bond investments. Although they could hedge interest rate risk, they prefer not to because they believe it reduces the ultimate long-term return.

Thomas says that due to secular changes in the bond market, bonds with structures are expected to become more scarce. He says that the problem with callable bonds has been that they typically trade at a premium due to their scarcity. Bentley states that bonds with long durations also trade at a premium because they are scarce as well.

Thomas states that the performance of callables and non-callables may differ when interest rates change due to the inherent call risk. He discusses the relative performance under two scenarios:

- Scenario A: Interest rates are near coupon rates and fall for both callables and non-callables by the same amount.
- Scenario B: Interest rates are historically very low and rise for both callables and non-callables by the same amount.

15.1. The second hedge that Thomas recommends for the Nakhon Metals bond is *most likely* an example of which of the following currency hedging strategies?
   A. Cross hedge.
   B. Proxy hedge.
   C. Forward hedge.

15.2. Based on their cash rates determine which of the currencies (Thai baht, Korean won, and Japanese yen) should trade at forward discount to the dollar.
   A. Only the yen should trade at a forward discount.
   B. The baht and the won should trade at a forward discount.
   C. None of the currencies should trade at a forward discount.

15.3. Based on interest rate expectations and ignoring currency effects, determine whether the Nakhon Metals bond or Powhatan Industries bond should be more attractive over the one-year time horizon.
   A. The Nakhon Metals bond should be more attractive.
   B. The Powhatan Industries bond should be more attractive.
   C. Neither bond should be more attractive.

15.4.   After Thomas and Bentley review the cash rates and expectations data they have gathered on the won, baht, yen, and dollar, Thomas says, "I'm going to recommend to my U.S. managers that they remain unhedged in Japanese bond investments because they'll pick up an additional currency return not predicted by the market when they translate back into dollars."

Overhearing Thomas, a friend of Bentley's replies, "You're off your bean, old boy. The difference in the cash rates in the dollar and the yen is already reflected in their spot and forward rates. Since you have to exchange dollars for yen now and yen for dollars later, you won't gain anything that isn't already incorporated into the currencies."

Based on cash rates and expectations data provided above, determine whether Thomas and Bentley's friend are correct or incorrect.
A. Only Bentley's friend is correct.
B. Only Thomas is correct.
C. Both are incorrect.

15.5.   Determine whether Thomas and Bentley are correct or incorrect regarding their statements about the scarcity and pricing of callable and long duration bonds.
A. Only Thomas is correct.
B. Only Bentley is correct.
C. Both are correct.

15.6.   Which of the following *best* describes the relative performance of callables and non-callables under the two scenarios?
A. Callables will outperform non-callables under both scenarios.
B. Callables will outperform non-callables under scenario A only.
C. Callables will outperform non-callables under scenario B only.

QUESTION 16 HAS SIX PARTS FOR A TOTAL OF 18 MINUTES

William Bliss, CFA, runs a hedge fund that uses both managed futures strategies and positions in physical commodities. He is reviewing his operations and strategies to increase the return of the fund. Bliss has just hired Joseph Kanter, CFA, to help him manage the fund because he realizes that he needs to increase his trading activity in futures and to engage in futures strategies other than fully hedged, passively managed positions. Bliss also hired Kanter because of Kanter's experience with swaps, which Bliss hopes to add to his choice of investment tools.

Bliss explains to Kanter that his clients pay 2% on assets under management and a 20% incentive fee. The incentive fee is based on profits after having subtracted the risk-free rate, which is the fund's basic hurdle rate, and there is a high water mark provision. Bliss is hoping that Kanter can help his business because his firm did not earn an incentive fee this past year. This was the case despite the fact that, after two years of losses, the value of the fund increased 14% during the previous year. That increase occurred without any new capital contributed from clients. Bliss is optimistic about the near future because the term structure of futures prices is particularly favorable for earning higher returns from long futures positions.

Kanter says he has seen research that indicates inflation may increase in the next few years. He states this should increase the opportunity to earn a higher return in commodities and suggests taking a large, margined position in a broad commodity index. This would offer an enhanced return that would attract investors holding only stocks and bonds. Bliss mentions that not all commodity prices are positively correlated with inflation, so it may be better to choose particular types of commodities in which to invest. Furthermore, Bliss adds that commodities traditionally have not outperformed stocks and bonds either on a risk-adjusted or absolute basis. Kanter says he will research companies who do business in commodities because buying the stock of those companies to gain commodity exposure is an efficient and effective method for gaining indirect exposure to commodities.

Bliss agrees that his fund should increase its exposure to commodities and wants Kanter's help in using swaps to gain such exposure. Bliss asks Kanter to enter into a swap with a relatively short horizon to demonstrate how a commodity swap works. Bliss notes that the futures prices of oil for six months, one year, eighteen months, and two years are $55, $54, $52, and $51 per barrel, respectively, and the risk-free rate is less than 2%.

Bliss asks how a seasonal component could be added to such a swap. Specifically, he asks if either the notional principal or the swap price can be higher during the reset closest to the winter season and lower for the reset period closest to the summer season. This would allow the swap to more effectively hedge a commodity like oil, which would have a higher demand in the winter than the summer. Kanter says that a swap can only have seasonal swap prices, and the notional principal must stay constant. Thus, the solution in such a case would be to enter into two swaps: one that has an annual reset in the winter and one that has an annual reset in the summer.

16.1. Given the information, the *most likely* reason that Bliss's firm did not earn an incentive fee in the past year was because:
   A. the normal return was subtracted.
   B. the 2% asset-under-management fee is greater than the risk-free rate.
   C. of a high water mark provision, which states the value of the fund must exceed its previous high point before managers are paid an incentive fee.

16.2. Bliss has probably *not* earned a very high return on the futures portion of his business because:
   A. of high normal backwardation.
   B. he has used fully hedged, passively managed positions.
   C. of high collateral return.

16.3. Bliss is optimistic about the near future because the term structure of futures prices is particularly favorable for earning higher returns from long positions. This would be the case if the term structure is:
   A. negative but upward sloping.
   B. negative and relatively flat.
   C. negative and steep.

16.4. The points made by Kanter and Bliss during their discussion of commodity returns given high inflation expectations were correct with the exception of:
   A. Kanter's assertions concerning the indirect method of investing in stocks to gain commodity exposure.
   B. Bliss's assertion that not all commodities are positively correlated with inflation.
   C. Kanter's assertion that a broad index would benefit from inflation.

16.5. Based on the given information, the fixed price for the 2-year swap with semi-annual reset is probably:
   A. undefined since the futures price decreases with the time horizon.
   B. closest to $55.
   C. closest to $53.

16.6. Kanter's comment concerning seasonal swaps is:
   A. not correct because neither swap price nor notional principal can be seasonal.
   B. not correct because both a seasonal notional principal and swap price are possible.
   C. not correct because it is the notional principal that can be seasonal and not the swap price.

QUESTION 17 HAS SIX PARTS FOR A TOTAL OF 18 MINUTES

Jerry Edwards is an analyst with DeLeon Analytics. He is currently advising the CFO of Anderson Corp., a multinational manufacturing corporation based in Newark, New Jersey, USA. Jackie Palmer is Edwards's assistant. Palmer is well versed in risk management, having worked at a large multinational bank for the last ten years prior to coming to Anderson.

Anderson has received a $2 million note with a duration of 4.0 from Weaver Tools for a shipment delivered last week. Weaver markets tools and machinery from manufacturers of Anderson's size. Edwards states that in order to effectively hedge the price risk of this instrument, Anderson should sell a series of interest rate calls. Palmer states that an alternative hedge for the note would be to enter an interest rate swap as the fixed-rate payer.

As well as selling products from a Swiss plant in Europe, Anderson sells products in Switzerland itself. As a result, Anderson has quarterly cash flows of 12,000,000 Swiss franc (CHF). In order to convert these cash flows into dollars, Edwards suggests that Anderson enter into a currency swap without an exchange of notional principal. Palmer contacts a currency swap dealer with whom they have dealt in the past and finds the following exchange rate and annual swap interest rates:

Exchange Rate (CHF per dollar)	1.24
Swap interest rate in U.S. dollars	2.80%
Swap interest rate in Swiss franc	6.60%

Discussing foreign exchange rate risk in general, Edwards states that it is transaction exposure that is most often hedged because the amount to be hedged is contractual and certain. Economic exposure, he states, is less certain and thus harder to hedge.

To finance their U.S. operations, Anderson issued a $10 million fixed-rate bond in the United States five years ago. The bond had an original maturity of ten years and now has a modified duration of 4.0. Edwards states that Anderson should enter a 5-year semiannual pay floating swap with a notional principal of about $11.4 million to take advantage of falling interest rates. The duration of the fixed-rate side of the swap is equal to 75% of its maturity or 3.75 ($= 0.75 \times 5$). The duration of the floating side of the swap is 0.25. Palmer states that Anderson's position in the swap will have a negative duration.

For another client of DeLeon, Edwards has assigned Palmer the task of estimating the interest rate sensitivity of the client's portfolios. The client's portfolio consists of positions in both U.S. and British bonds. The relevant information for estimating the duration contribution of the British bond and the portfolio's total duration is provided below.

U.S. dollar bond	$275,000
British bond	$155,000
British yield beta	1.40
Duration of U.S. bond	4.0
Duration of British bond	8.5

When discussing portfolio management with clients, Edwards recommends the use of emerging market bonds to add value to a core-plus strategy. He explains the characteristics of emerging market debt to Palmer by stating:

1. "The performance of emerging market debt has been quite resilient over time. After crises in the debt markets, emerging market bonds quickly recover, so long-term returns can be poor."

2. "Emerging market debt is quite volatile due in part to the nature of political risk in these markets. It is therefore important that the analyst monitor the risk of these markets. I prefer to measure the risk of emerging market bonds with the standard deviation because it provides the best representation of risk in these markets."

17.1. Regarding their statements concerning the hedge of the Weaver Tools note, determine if Edwards and Palmer are correct or incorrect.
   A. Both are correct.
   B. Neither is correct.
   C. One is correct.

17.2. If Anderson enters a properly structured currency swap to convert the CHF 12,000,000 to dollars, the amount they will receive is *closest* to:
   A. $4,105,572.
   B. $7,071,429.
   C. $9,677,419.

17.3. Regarding Edward's statements concerning the transaction exposure of currency risk, which of the following *best* describes his statement?
   A. It is inaccurate because transaction exposure is very uncertain.
   B. It accurately describes firms' currency exposures and hedging practices.
   C. It is inaccurate because firms more frequently hedge translation exposure.

17.4. Regarding their statements concerning the hedge of the U.S. dollar-denominated bond Anderson issued, determine whether Edwards and Palmer are correct or incorrect.
   A. Only Edwards is correct.
   B. Only Palmer is correct.
   C. Both are correct.

17.5. Which of the following is *closest* to the duration contribution of the British bond and the portfolio's total duration from a U.S. perspective?

British bond	Portfolio duration
A. 2.19	4.75
B. 3.06	5.62
C. 4.29	6.85

17.6. Regarding his two statements about the characteristics of emerging market debt, is Edwards correct?
   A. Only statement 1 is correct.
   B. Only statement 2 is correct.
   C. Both statements are incorrect.

QUESTION 18 HAS SIX PARTS FOR A TOTAL OF 18 MINUTES

Mary Thomas works for Kershaw-Ross, a large investment bank located in London. Kershaw-Ross provides advice to portfolio managers, securities dealers, and hedge funds. Jack Bentley is Thomas' assistant.

Washington Capital Management, one of Thomas' clients, has a $5 million position in fixed-rate U.S. Treasury bonds. The firm would like to hedge this position using calls on Treasury bonds. The calls each cover $100,000 par value of bonds, have a delta of 0.4, and are out-of-the-money. To hedge this position, Thomas recommends that Washington Capital Management calculate the delta for the call options written on these Treasury bonds.

Later that week, Thomas discusses the particulars of option hedges with Francis Steele, Vice President at Washington Capital Management. Thomas describes how using gamma, the change in delta relative to the change in the underlying asset price, can increase the precision of the hedge. She states that this would be particularly true if the bond portfolio used calls that were at-the-money. Bentley adds that, given the uncertainty surrounding U.S. Federal Reserve monetary policy, Kershaw-Ross has been advising clients to carefully monitor their bond positions for price changes. Bentley states that, in Washington Capital Management's case, if the price of the underlying bond increases by 1% due to a yield curve shift, the call hedge should be decreased because delta would have increased.

Thomas is analyzing the portfolio for one of his investors, Canopy Managers. Last year the portfolio had a market value of $4,881,000 and a dollar duration of $157,200. The current figures for the portfolio are provided below:

	Market Value	Duration	Dollar Duration
Bond 1	$780,000	4.5	$35,100
Bond 2	$2,500,000	3.4	$85,000
Bond 3	$524,000	2.7	$14,148
Bond 4	$413,000	1.9	$7,847
Portfolio	$4,217,000		$142,095

Canopy would like to alter the current dollar duration of the portfolio to last year's duration, and they would like to do so with the least amount of cash possible and a controlling position in one of the bonds.

Canopy Managers has also contracted to take out a 9-month loan for $5 million in three months at LIBOR. Canopy's chief financial officer has become concerned that interest rates might increase and has asked Thomas to investigate the possibility of hedging the position with a forward rate agreement. Thomas finds a forward rate agreement is available with the same maturity as Canopy's loan at a rate of 4.40%. The risk free rate is 3.8%, and LIBOR is projected to be 4.60% at the inception of the loan.

The next week, Thomas and Bentley visit the headquarters of Capital Pension Management, one of Kershaw-Ross's largest clients. Capital is using contingent immunization to immunize a liability, but management is concerned about a possible rise in interest rates. Thomas states that if she were to recommend the most effective strategy to Capital, she would recommend that they use bonds with high yields because immunization will be cheaper. Bentley interjects that the risk from nonparallel shifts in the yield curve can be minimized by concentrating the cash flows around the horizon date.

Due to their tremendous success, Kershaw-Ross has outgrown their current headquarters and is going to expand their current building. Thomas's team has been charged with securing financing for the renovations. They currently are considering a remodeling and addition that would cost approximately £5,000,000.

Thomas has secured the financing necessary for the renovations at a floating interest rate of LIBOR plus 150 basis points, with payments made quarterly over three years. Thomas believes that Kershaw-Ross should be able to complete the renovation of the building and close on the loan in one year. She is concerned, however, that interest rates will increase in the interim and has obtained a swaption to hedge the loan. She states that Kershaw-Ross should use a payer swaption to hedge the loan. Bentley evaluates the forecasts for future swap fixed rates as well as the current terms of various swaptions, which are provided below:

Fixed rate for a 1-year payer swaption	= 8.50%
Fixed rate for a 1-year receiver swaption	= 8.60%
Projected swap fixed rate in one year	= 9.30%
Fixed rate for a 4-year payer swaption	= 9.40%
Fixed rate for a 4-year receiver swaption	= 9.70%
Projected swap fixed rate in four years	= 9.80%

18.1. Determine the most appropriate action to delta hedge the Washington Capital Management's Treasury bond position.
   A. Sell 20 Treasury bond calls.
   B. Buy 20 Treasury bond calls.
   C. Sell 125 Treasury bond calls.

18.2. Regarding their statements to Steele concerning the hedge of Washington Capital Management's Treasury bond position, determine whether Thomas and Bentley are correct or incorrect.
   A. Only Thomas is correct.
   B. Only Bentley is correct.
   C. Both are correct.

18.3. To adjust the dollar duration of the Canopy portfolio to last year's level, the smallest amount Canopy will need to purchase of the bond that acts as a controlling position is *closest* to:
   A. $335,667.
   B. $862,916.
   C. $1,115,667.

18.4. The current credit risk to Canopy from the FRA agreement is *closest* to:
   A. $7,183.
   B. $7,250.
   C. $7,292.

18.5. Regarding their statements concerning the strategy of Capital Asset Management, determine whether Thomas and Bentley are correct or incorrect.
   A. Only Thomas is correct.
   B. Only Bentley is correct.
   C. Both are correct.

18.6. Assuming that their interest rate forecast is correct and they use the appropriate hedge, calculate Kershaw-Ross's first quarterly payment on the building expansion loan.
   A. £125,000.
   B. £126,250.
   C. £136,250.

QUESTION 19 HAS SIX PARTS FOR A TOTAL OF 18 MINUTES

Somerset Investment Limited is a Singapore-based money management firm that is conducting an appraisal of its investment performance. Cameron Li, CFA, has been charged with conducting the appraisal and is to report back to upper management with his findings.

Li is convinced that trade executions play a substantial role in overall portfolio performance, particularly for funds that have a relatively high level of turnover during the year. As a result, he is seeking methods that will allow him to evaluate the quality of trade executions.

He knows that the firm's traders use both market and limit orders, and he is wondering if a framework can be developed to ensure that the best order type is used under the specific circumstances for each trade. When he consults with the firm's head trader, Rick Gleeson, Gleeson tells him that market orders have price uncertainty but no execution uncertainty, while limit orders eliminate price uncertainty but have execution uncertainty. According to Gleeson, rebalancing and liquidity-motivated trades should use limit orders while value-motivated and information-motivated trades should use market orders.

Li knows that bid-ask spreads are a major component of trading costs and asks Gleeson for some recent trade data that he can use for analysis and presentation to management. He receives the following data relating to a series of buy trades for Sumatra Natural Resources (SNR), with all currency values in Singapore dollars:

Trades of Sumatra Natural Resources

Time	Bid Price	Ask Price	Execution Price	Shares Bought
10:30	$22.18	$22.36	$22.33	900
11:15	$22.23	$22.43	$22.43	600
13:45	$22.29	$22.48	$22.47	700
15:00	$22.37	$22.63	$22.65	800

Gleeson also tells Li that the portfolio manager had originally made the decision to purchase 5,000 SNR at 10:00 a.m. when the price was $22.36. The closing price for the day was Leeson's last trade at $22.65, at which point the order for the remaining 2,000 shares was cancelled.

19.1. Which of the following *correctly* summarizes Gleeson's comments concerning the differences between market and limit orders?
   A. He is correct concerning the nature of uncertainty; he is correct concerning when the order types should be used.
   B. He is correct concerning the nature of uncertainty; he is incorrect concerning when the order types should be used.
   C. He is incorrect concerning the nature of uncertainty; he is correct concerning when the order types should be used.

19.2. Concerning the Sumatra Natural Resources price and execution data, the average effective spread and weighted average effective spread are *closest* to:

	Average effective spread	Weighted average effective spread
A.	0.1957	0.1975
B.	0.0971	0.0908
C.	0.1975	0.1957

19.3. Assume that the four trades in Sumatra Natural Resources are the only trades in the security for the day. Determine which of the following statements concerning the volume weighted average price (VWAP) is *most* correct.
   A. The VWAP for the day is 22.470, and the trader's goal would be to have an average cost that is less than the VWAP.
   B. The VWAP for the day is 22.468, and the trader's goal would be to have an average cost that is greater than the VWAP.
   C. The VWAP for the day is 22.468, and the trader's goal would be to have an average cost that is less than the VWAP.

19.4. Calculate the implementation shortfall assuming total commissions paid by Gleeson when he purchased the 3,000 SNR were $210.
   A. 0.303%.
   B. 0.996%.
   C. 2.027%.

19.5. Which of the following statements concerning implementation shortfall and VWAP is incorrect?
   A. Implementation shortfall is greater than zero if any portion of the original order goes unfilled and is cancelled.
   B. VWAP is more appropriate for small trades in non-trending markets.
   C. Implementation shortfall must be adjusted to accurately account for movements in the general market.

19.6. Determine which of the following statements concerning an algorithmic trading strategy is *most* incorrect. An algorithmic trading strategy:

A. ensures that the portfolio does not become over-concentrated (in specific assets or sectors) because it is based on quantitative rules.

B. involves the use of automated processes based on quantitative measures, such as the ratio of the trade size to average daily volume, to guide trading decisions.

C. known as simple logical participation, breaks trades into small pieces to avoid detection and to minimize market impact costs.

QUESTION 20 HAS SIX PARTS FOR A TOTAL OF 18 MINUTES

Jack Mercer and June Seagram are investment advisors for Northern Advisors. Mercer graduated from a prestigious university in London eight years ago, whereas Seagram is newly graduated from a mid-western university in the United States. Northern provides investment advice for pension funds, foundations, endowments, and trusts. As part of their services, they evaluate the performance of outside portfolio managers. They are currently scrutinizing the performance of several portfolio managers who work for the Thompson University endowment.

Over the most recent month, the record of the largest manager, Bison Management, is as follows. On March 1, the endowment account with Bison stood at $11,200,000. On March 16, the university contributed $4,000,000 that they received from a wealthy alumnus. After receiving that contribution, the account was valued at $17,800,000. On March 31, the account was valued at $16,100,000. Using this information, Mercer and Seagram calculated the time-weighted and money-weighted returns for Bison during March. Mercer states that the advantage of the time-weighted return is that it is easy to calculate and administer. Seagram states that the money-weighted return is, however, a better measure of the manager's performance.

Mercer and Seagram are also evaluating the performance of Lunar Management. Risk and return data for the most recent fiscal year are shown below for both Bison and Lunar. The minimum acceptable return (MAR) for Thompson is the 4.5% spending rate on the endowment, which the endowment has determined using a geometric spending rule. The T-bill return over the same fiscal year was 3.5%. The return on the MSCI World Index was used as the market index. The World index had a return of 9% in dollar terms with a standard deviation of 23% and a beta of 1.0.

	Bison	Lunar
Return	14.1%	15.8%
Standard Deviation	31.5%	34.7%
Beta	0.9	1.3
Standard Deviation of returns below the MAR	15.1%	15.9%

The next day at lunch, Mercer and Seagram discuss alternatives for benchmarks in assessing the performance of managers. The alternatives discussed that day are manager universes, broad market indices, style indices, factor models, and custom benchmarks. Mercer states that manager universes have the advantage of being measurable, but they are subject to survivor bias. Seagram states that manager universes possess only one quality of a valid benchmark.

Mercer and Seagram also provide investment advice for a hedge fund, Jaguar Investors. Jaguar specializes in exploiting mispricing in equities and over-the-counter derivatives in emerging markets. They periodically engage in providing foreign currency hedges to small firms in emerging markets when deemed profitable. This most commonly occurs when no other provider of these contracts is available to these firms. Jaguar is selling a large position in Mexican pesos in the spot market. Furthermore, they have just provided a forward contract to a firm in Russia that allows that firm to sell Swiss francs for Russian rubles in 90 days. Jaguar has also entered into a currency swap that allows a firm to receive Japanese yen in exchange for paying the Russian ruble.

20.1. The time-weighted and money-weighted returns for Bison during March (assuming compounding every half-month) are *closest* to:

Time-weighted	Money-weighted
A. 5.9%	6.8%
B. 5.9%	3.4%
C. 11.4%	6.8%

20.2 Regarding their statements about time-weighted and money-weighted returns, determine whether Mercer and Seagram are correct or incorrect.
A. Only Mercer is correct.
B. Both are correct.
C. Neither is correct.

20.3. The M-squared measure for the Bison fund is *closest* to:
A. 2.2%.
B. 6.4%.
C. 11.2%.

20.4. Determine which of the following best describes the relative diversification and performance of the Bison portfolio and Lunar portfolio:
A. The Lunar portfolio is better diversified and, from a downside risk perspective, has superior performance.
B. The Bison portfolio is better diversified, but from a downside risk perspective, the Lunar portfolio has superior performance.
C. The Lunar portfolio is better diversified, but from a downside risk perspective, the Bison portfolio has superior performance.

20.5. Regarding their statements about manager universes, determine whether Mercer and Seagram are correct or incorrect.
A. Only Mercer is correct.
B. Only Seagram is correct.
C. Both are correct.

20.6. Of the following risks, determine which was *most likely not* considered in the series of foreign currency derivative transactions by Jaguar.
A. Credit risk.
B. Herstatt risk.
C. Operations risk.

END OF AFTERNOON SESSION

Exam 3
Score Sheet

MORNING SESSION		
Question	Maximum Points	Your Estimated Score
1	17	
2A	24	
2B	8	
3A	8	
3B	9	
3C	6	
3D	6	
4A	4	
4B	4	
4C	12	
5A	4	
5B	9	
6A	7	
6B	8	
7A	3	
7B	5	
7C	4	
7D	2	
7E	4	
8A	4	
8B	12	
9A	6	
9B	5	
9C	5	
9D	4	
Total	180	

AFTERNOON SESSION		
Question	Maximum Points	Your Score
10	18	
11	18	
12	18	
13	18	
14	18	
15	18	
16	18	
17	18	
18	18	
19	18	
Total	180	

Certain Passing Score: 252 of 360 (70%)
Probable Passing Score: 234 (65%)

Please note that we write these exams to be as challenging and representative as possible. However, due to the relaxed conditions that most candidates apply when they "take" these tests (e.g., "I need a break; I think I'll go to the refrigerator and get a snack"), you should adjust your score downward by 10–15 percentage points to get a more accurate measure of the score you would have actually received on exam day. Also, you must be honest with yourself for your score on this exam to have any meaning. Don't assume, for example, that if your essay answer is close, the graders will be generous with points.

Exam 3 Morning Session
Topic Breakdown

Question	Topic	Minutes
1	Portfolio Management—Individual	17
2	Portfolio Management—Individual	32
3	Equity Portfolio Management	29
4	Fixed Income/Risk Management	20
5	Portfolio Management—Institutional/Equity Portfolio Management	13
6	Global Investment Performance Standards	15
7	Portfolio Management—Institutional/Asset Allocation	18
8	Portfolio Management—Individual	16
9	Global Bonds/Derivatives	20
	Total	180

EXAM 3
MORNING SESSION

QUESTION 1 HAS ONE PART FOR A TOTAL OF 17 MINUTES

Mary Middendorf, 52, is the current marketing director for MCTECH, a multinational supplier of computer and telecommunications equipment. Due to the recent acquisition of her firm by a larger organization, Middendorf has been informed that her position will be terminated in six months. Middendorf is visiting with Michelle Mightman, CFA, to discuss her financial situation. The following information is disclosed in her meeting.

- "My investment portfolio is currently valued close to $3,000,000. MCTECH had a fantastic profit sharing and incentive program. My current holding of MCTECH stock is close to $2,250,000. The rest of my portfolio is in a broad market stock index fund. I also have a money market checking account that carries a relatively constant balance of $10,000."

- "When my position is terminated with MCTECH in six months, I will receive a lump-sum after-tax cash payment of $750,000, which is approximately equal to three years salary. Additionally, the acquisition is an all-stock transaction, so my MCTECH position will be replaced by the stock of the acquiring firm."

- "The all-stock transaction will mean my portfolio will contain a much more stable security. The previous two years were substantially rocky for my investments, so I am happy the MCTECH stock will be replaced. My investment portfolio exhibited a substantial improvement with the news of the acquisition, and I look forward to the continued appreciation of my portfolio, due to the favorable performance of the acquiring company's stock. The new stock will also lower the volatility of my investments, which I will need over the next year or so."

- "Although various firms have given me employment offers commencing in six months, I would like to travel during the six months following my separation from MCTECH. I have worked diligently over the past 20 years, and I need a break before I begin working at another firm. Most employment offers I received are for amounts slightly higher than what I am currently making at MCTECH. I am confident I will be able to get other equivalent offers in a year's time."

- "I am not married, and I have no children. Although I like to travel, my living expenses are otherwise minimal, hence I do not require much in the way of current income."

Without calculations, **prepare** the objectives and constraints portion of an investment policy statement for Middendorf.

Answer Question 1 in the template provided.

(20 minutes)

Template for Question 1

Investment Policy Statement for Middendorf		
Objectives	Risk Tolerance	
	Return Objectives	
Constraints	Time Horizon	
	Liquidity	
	Legal/Regulatory	
	Taxes	
	Unique Circumstances	

QUESTION 2 HAS TWO PARTS FOR A TOTAL OF 32 MINUTES

John and Susan Tran are 81 and 74 years old, respectively, and they have one son, Jared, who is 45. Their current annual spending is $150,000, and they would like to maintain that level over their five-year planning horizon. Their current portfolio contains $200,000 of cash equivalents, a $500,000 position in a diversified bond fund, and a $300,000 position in a diversified equity fund.

The Trans have contacted a local financial planner, Mark Palmer, CFA, to assist them in their planning. Palmer has constructed the mortality table below for the Trans.

| Years | Husband | | Wife | |
	Age	Prob.	Age	Prob.
1	82	0.9248	75	0.9736
2	83	0.8418	76	0.9446
3	84	0.7501	77	0.9125
4	85	0.6489	78	0.8771
5	86	0.5371	79	0.8381

Additionally, Palmer has estimated the inflation rate at 3% and the real risk-free interest rate at 2%.

A.   Fill in all *non-shaded* areas of the following template. Show your calculations.

(24 minutes)

Template for Question 2-A

Year	Combined Probability	Real Annual Spending	Expected Real Spending	Present Value
1		150,000		
2		150,000		
3		150,000		
4		150,000		
5		150,000		
Core Capital				
Excess Capital				

The Trans are contemplating gifting their equity fund to Jared, and they would like to gift the remainder to a local charity. Palmer estimates that the equity fund will earn 7% per year. The Trans tax rate for investment returns is 25%, while their son's tax rate for investment returns is 35%. The inheritance tax rate on the Trans is estimated at 20%. If the Trans gift the equity fund to their son immediately, they can take advantage of a one-time tax-free gift provision in their tax code.

B.   **Determine** whether it is more beneficial for the Trans to transfer the equity fund to their son immediately through a gifting arrangement or later as a bequest in five years by **calculating** the relative after-tax value of the two alternatives. (Show your calculations in the template provided.)

(8 minutes)

Template for Question Part 2-B

Is it more beneficial to gift or bequest the fund? (circle one)	Gift Bequest
Value as Tax-Free Gift	
Value as Bequest	
Relative Value	

QUESTION 3 HAS FOUR PARTS FOR A TOTAL OF 29 MINUTES

Royal Performance Verification provides independent analysis of portfolio manager performance and corporate governance effectiveness for investors worldwide. Carolyn Jensen and Vicki Miller are the senior analysts for Royal. Jensen and Miller are currently evaluating the performance for two portfolio managers, Sycamore Management and Malta Advisors. Both managers use active management. The figures for their most recent year's performance are provided below.

	Sycamore Management	*Malta Advisors*
Investor's benchmark	11.0%	18.0%
Manager return	12.0%	16.0%
Misfit active risk	2.8%	3.5%
Normal portfolio return	15.0%	14.0%
Total active risk	4.0%	4.1%

A.   Using the information provided, **assess** the performance of the two managers individually and **discuss** their relative performance.

(8 minutes)

Jensen and Miller also have responsibility for evaluating the investment style of portfolio managers. They are currently evaluating the style of two funds, one from the Rockford group and one from the Kishwaukee group. The Rockford fund trades as an exchange-traded fund (ETF) and the Kishwaukee fund trades as a mutual fund. Miller characterizes the style of portfolio managers by using a constrained regression where the manager's returns are regressed against various security indices. Jensen evaluates the manager's style by examining the characteristics of the securities in the manager's portfolio. The results of her examination of the broad market and the funds are provided below.

	Rockford Fund	Kishwaukee Fund	Broad Market
Dividend yield	1.2%	3.7%	2.8%
EPS growth for one year	17.3%	2.7%	5.9%
EPS growth for five years	19.7%	5.2%	12.1%
Median market cap (in billions)	$0.80	$47.90	$28.50
P/B ratio	3.27	2.11	2.97
P/E ratio	24.84	15.33	19.47

Industry weight			
Basic industries	7%	12%	14%
Business services	9%	6%	6%
Consumer goods	6%	4%	7%
Consumer services	14%	8%	9%
Energy	3%	4%	11%
Financials	10%	40%	20%
Information technology	27%	6%	16%
Health	18%	1%	12%
Media	5%	1%	1%
Utilities	1%	18%	4%
Total	100%	100%	100%

B.   Based on the information provided, **discuss** the following issues.

    i.   The relative earnings volatility for the two funds.

    ii.   The relative abilities of Jensen's and Miller's style classifications to detect style drift.

    iii.   The tax efficiency of the two funds.

(9 minutes)

The following week, Jensen and Miller evaluate the corporate governance structure of the PharmaScreen Corporation. PharmaScreen provides testing of drugs for pharmaceutical firms so that government approvals for the marketing of the drugs can be expedited. PharmaScreen began nine years ago, assisted with some seed capital from Cape Fear Capital, a large hedge fund located in the United States. PharmaScreen went public three years ago and Cape Fear has sold most of their original holdings. They are still PharmaScreen's single largest investor, however, holding 2.1% of PharmaScreen's outstanding stock.

Due to a series of management mistakes, PharmaScreen's stock has fallen to where it is now considered a small-cap value stock. Despite this, Jensen feels that PharmaScreen's niche within their industry provides the stock with tremendous upside potential. The firm's current market capitalization totals $53 million and its P/E ratio is 7.4.

As part of their investigation, Jensen and Miller examine PharmaScreen's ownership and compensation structures. During their discussion, Jensen makes the following comments:

- "I am encouraged that PharmaScreen has institutions that hold their stock. The institutions will help monitor management and will use their influence to effect the change needed in PharmaScreen's management."

- "PharmaScreen's management needs a compensation structure that more closely aligns the interests of management and shareholders. One possible solution would be to weight management's compensation more heavily towards out-of-the-money stock options so that they have a strong incentive to increase the stock price. The drawback of this form of compensation would be that management would have an incentive to undertake too much risk."

C.   **State** whether or not *each* of these comments is correct or incorrect and **explain** your selection.

Answer Question 3-C in the template provided.

(6 minutes)

Template for Question 3-C

Comment	Correct or incorrect? (circle one)	Explanation
"I am encouraged that PharmaScreen has institutions that hold their stock. The institutions will help monitor management and will use their influence to effect the change needed with PharmaScreen's management."	Correct Incorrect	
"PharmaScreen's management needs a compensation structure that more closely aligns the interests of management and shareholders. One possible solution would be to weight management's compensation more heavily toward out-of-the-money stock options so that they have a strong incentive to increase the stock price. The drawback of this form of compensation is that management would have an incentive to undertake too much risk."	Correct Incorrect	

D. Regarding the role of debt as a corporate governance mechanism, **state** and **discuss**: *two* reasons why it is an effective mechanism and *one* limitation.

(6 minutes)

QUESTION 4 HAS THREE PARTS FOR A TOTAL OF 20 MINUTES

Tom Nicholson is the newly hired risk manager for Antelope Advisors. Antelope has approximately $1.7 billion under management for wealthy individuals. Antelope has teams of managers assigned to their specific asset classes. Antelope recommends investments in U.S. and developed country stocks and bonds, as well as nontraditional assets such as hedge funds, commodities, and emerging market stocks. Antelope also uses futures and options to hedge various positions when deemed appropriate.

During his review of Antelope's risk management policies, Nicholson makes the following comments:

- "Antelope must evaluate the risk of its bond positions and equity index option positions carefully, because of recent volatility in interest rates and in the stock markets. For bonds and options, standard deviation is not the preferred risk management tool. Necessary and sufficient risk measures for bonds and options are the duration of bonds and delta of options."

- "One risk management tool Antelope should consider is maximum loss optimization. This tool involves recognizing those factors with the greatest potential to damage the value of Antelope's portfolio. Antelope could then take steps to limit the damage from these factors."

A.   **State** whether or not *each* of these comments is correct or incorrect and **support** your decison.

Answer Question 4-A in the template provided.

(4 minutes)

©2009 Kaplan, Inc.

Template for Question 4-A

Comment	Correct or incorrect? (circle one)	Explanation
"Antelope must evaluate the risk of its bond positions and equity index option positions carefully because of recent volatility in interest rates and in the stock markets. For bonds and options, standard deviation is not the preferred risk management tool. Necessary and sufficient risk measures for bonds and options are the duration of bonds and delta of options."	Correct Incorrect	
"One risk management tool Antelope should consider is maximum loss optimization. This tool involves recognizing those factors with the greatest potential to damage the value of Antelope's portfolio. Antelope could then take steps to limit the damage from these factors."	Correct Incorrect	

B.   Based on the information provided, **discuss** the following issues.

    i.   Whether Antelope should use a centralized or decentralized enterprise risk management system.

    ii. Which of the three general VAR approaches is *least* appropriate for Antelope.

(4 minutes)

John Sims is the chief investment officer for Antelope. Antelope is considering using outside managers for a portion of their invested assets. The first manager is Andy Davis. Davis has had tremendous success during the past five years by investing in the sovereign debt of emerging market countries. He has consistently beaten his benchmark every year. The other manager under consideration is Bobby Brooks. Brooks invests in the equity of formerly government-owned companies in Eastern Europe.

Antelope specifies a minimum acceptable return of 5.3%, and the appropriate risk-free rate is 4.5%. The performance for both managers is provided in the following table. The returns and standard deviations are annualized using monthly returns.

Figure 1: Available Data for Davis and Brooks

	Davis	*Brooks*
Portfolio return	20.60%	21.30%
Maximum drawdown	15.20%	13.70%
Portfolio standard deviation	33.20%	31.20%
Portfolio downside deviation	15.05%	16.50%

C. Using only the information provided in Figure 1, **evaluate** both managers using *three different* risk-adjusted return measures (i.e., ratios). **Show** your calculations. **Determine** which is the *most appropriate* for evaluation of the managers. **Justify** your choice.

(12 minutes)

QUESTION 5 HAS TWO PARTS FOR A TOTAL OF 13 MINUTES

Jeff Stovall is a consultant to the chief executive officer of a large bank, Capital City Bank. Stovall makes the following statements at a presentation to bank officers and regional money managers:

- "The trust officers at the bank may want to suggest an alpha-beta separation approach. This approach is particularly useful in less efficient markets such as small-cap markets."

- "Portfolio managers should be aware, however, that some institutions may not be able to use an alpha-beta separation approach because of institutional constraints."

A.   **State** whether each of these comments is correct or incorrect and **explain** your decision.

Answer Question 5-A in the template provided.

(4 minutes)

Template for Question 5-A

Comment	Correct or incorrect? (circle one)	Explanation
"The trust officers at the bank may want to suggest an alpha-beta separation approach. This approach is particularly useful in less efficient markets such as small-cap markets."	Correct Incorrect	
"Portfolio managers should be aware, however, that some institutions may not be able to use an alpha-beta separation approach because of institutional constraints."	Correct Incorrect	

B.   Regarding banks, **discuss** the following issues.
i.   The maturity of assets in the bank's security portfolio.
ii.   The liquidity of assets in the bank's security portfolio.
iii. The legal and regulatory constraints for banks.

(9 minutes)

QUESTION 6 HAS TWO PARTS FOR A TOTAL OF 17 MINUTES

Tim Brewer, CFA, is vice president for Wealth Managers, Inc. (WMI). WMI has been asked by a pension board to make a presentation on the ability of the firm to manage assets and consistently generate successful results.

During the presentation, Brewer makes the following statements:

- "Since most of our investments are made in fixed income securities, our performance reflects accrual accounting for bond interest, but not for the interest income of non-fixed income securities."
- "As you can see from all the various countries in which we invest, we have to pay close attention to exchange rate effects. Since some of our investments are in countries where exchange rate information is difficult to retrieve, we use a multitude of sources to calculate the exchange rate effects for our composites and benchmarks. These differential sources of information allow us to find the most accurate exchange rate data and are disclosed in performance presentations."
- "Return performance is presented gross of all fees, expenses, and loads."

A. **State** whether or not *each* of these comments is consistent with the Global Investment Performance Standards® (GIPS). If not consistent, **explain** why.

   Answer Question 6-A in the template provided.

   (7 minutes)

Template for Question 6-A

Comment	Does statement comply with GIPS requirements? (circle one)	Explanation
"Since most of our investments are made in fixed income securities, our performance reflects accrual accounting for bond interest, but not for the interest income of non-fixed income securities."	Yes No	
"As you can see from all the various countries in which we invest, we have to pay close attention to exchange rate effects. Since some of our investments are in countries where exchange rate information is difficult to retrieve, we use a multitude of sources to calculate the exchange rate effects for our composites and benchmarks. These differential sources of information allow us to find the most accurate exchange rate data and are disclosed in performance presentations."	Yes No	
"Return performance is presented gross of all fees, expenses, and loads."	Yes No	

B.   Brewer produces a performance presentation as representative of his firm's work (reproduced below). In the template provided, **list** and **discuss** a combination of four items in the presentation (other than omissions) that are not compliant with GIPS® and would prevent the presentation from being in compliance.

Answer Question 6-B in the template provided.

(8 minutes)

Investment Opportunity Investors
Equity Composite
January 1, 2003 through March 31, 2009

Year	Total Return (%)	Benchmark Return (%)	Number of Portfolios	Composite Dispersion (%)	Total Assets at End of Period (€ millions)	% of Total Firm Assets
2003*	18.71	14.34	28	4.1	189	66
2004	19.54	18.23	29	4.8	183	65
2005	12.81	11.75	34	5.9	329	75
2006	17.30	18.56	37	8.5	346	72
2007	11.86	11.20	36	1.7	333	68
2008	7.59	8.50	42	3.5	284	63
1st Quarter 2009 (annualized)	14.25	9.14	38	6.1	279	60

* 2003 results are not in compliance with GIPS® and accordingly have not been certified.

Investment Opportunity Investors has prepared and presented this report in compliance with the Global Investment Performance Standards (GIPS®).

Notes:

1. The benchmark composition is 100% DAX 100.
2. All values are based on market valuations.
3. Performance results are presented before management and custodial fees but after estimated trading expenses. The management fee schedule is contained in the appendix to this report.
4. This composite was created in January 2003. No modifications to the composites as presented here have occurred as a result of changes in personnel or for any other reason at any time. A complete list and description of firm composites and performance results is available upon request.

5. The dispersion of annual returns is measured by the standard deviation among asset-weighted portfolio returns for portfolios that were in the composite over the entire year.
6. Several non-fee paying accounts are included.
7. All accounts of at least €5,000,000 are included in the composite as of the first quarter under management.
8. All return calculations are geometrically linked and performed as prescribed by the Global Investment Performance Standards (GIPS®).
9. Percentage of total firm assets is calculated using discretionary accounts.

Template for Question 6-B

Four non-compliant items
1.
2.
3.
4.

©2009 Kaplan, Inc.

QUESTION 7 HAS FIVE PARTS FOR A TOTAL OF 18 MINUTES

Within the past year, Ural Industries (UI) of Russia has acquired an American competitor, Peak Metals (PM). As a part of the acquisition, UI was required to assume the pension liabilities and assets accumulated by PM. Coming from a country where the concept of privately funded pensions is relatively new, UI has sought the advice of First Chicago Pension Advisors to help formulate a strategy for dealing with the plan.

Meagan Skalmoski, CFA, and Germaine Wilson, CFA, have been assigned to lead the project for First Chicago. Viktor Yushkinsky has assembled a team from the UI finance department to meet with Skalmoski and Wilson to discuss a variety of issues that will need to be addressed going forward. Yushkinsky's first two questions concern the evaluation of risk tolerance and how pension funds differ from other types of institutional investors.

A.   **List** *three* of the five principal characteristics that should be considered when evaluating pension fund risk tolerance.

(3 minutes)

B.   **List** *three* of the five constraints that require consideration for all institutional investors, and **identify** the key difference between the return requirements of a defined-benefit pension plan compared with an endowment.

(5 minutes)

In his next question, Yushkinsky asked for clarification on the role of the strategic allocation. One member of his team asked why it was necessary to specify such an allocation at all, given that the portfolio manager might need to be able to make adjustments to take advantage of market conditions. Another member asked how the key issues involved in setting an institutional asset allocation differ from those for individual investors.

C.   **Summarize** the role of the strategic asset allocation in terms of specifying the client's risk objectives, and its importance to the determination of long-term returns.

(4 minutes)

D.   **Contrast** and **discuss** the principal difference regarding asset allocation for institutions as compared with individual investors.

(2 minutes)

The final questions from UI's team concerned the responsibilities of the portfolio's investment advisor: What are the advisor's key responsibilities, and what underlying factors are likely to dictate that the pension plan's fundamental investment objectives need to be reviewed and/or altered?

E.   **Describe** the institutional portfolio manager's two principal responsibilities. **Identify** the *two* primary factors that change through time and **indicate** the potential need to rebalance a client's portfolio.

(4 minutes)

QUESTION 8 HAS TWO PARTS FOR A TOTAL OF 16 MINUTES

Jack Easterling is a portfolio manager for Reed Management. Two of Easterling's clients are Mary Fisher and Tom Pollard. He is working with them on determining an asset allocation and the appropriate level of life insurance.

Fisher lives in Washington, D.C. and has been working for the federal government for over 15 years. She has good health care benefits and receives steady raises each year, thanks to the strong employee's union that represents her. She has never been married and lives alone with her two cats and two dogs.

Pollard lives in Northern Virginia and is married with two children. His wife stays at home to care for and home school the two children. Pollard works as a sales representative for a firm that provides pharmaceuticals and medical supplies to hospitals on a competitive bid basis. Although he is quite happy in his job and usually has substantial compensation, he is concerned about his future sales commissions due to declining reimbursements and increasing competition in the health care industry.

During separate meetings in Easterling's office, Fisher and Pollard make the following statements:

- Fisher: "I grew up in a family of four. My parents are deceased and I am estranged from my brother. Thus I will not have any heirs, except for my pets. If possible, I would like to leave a modest amount of funds to the local animal shelter upon my death and make sure my pets are cared for. I am in good health and, given my family's medical history, I expect to live another 30 years."

- Pollard: "I want to be sure my family is financially secure. My wife has never worked and has few professional job prospects. My parents died destitute and I had to pay for both their funerals. My father died at an early age due to a heart attack and my mother died of lung cancer. Although I am very conscious of my health, I do fear that I may be susceptible to the same health issues as my parents."

A.   **Characterize** the *likely* asset allocation as to whether it should be weighted towards stocks or bonds for *each* investor. **Justify** your response with *one* reason for *each* investor. Use only the information previously provided.

(4 minutes)

B.   **Characterize** the *likely* term life insurance requirement as high or low demand for *each* investor using the following factors:
i.   Probability of death.

ii. Human capital.

iii. Bequest preferences.

Justify your responses with *one* reason for *each* investor. Consider each factor *independently* of the others. Use only the information previously provided.

(12 minutes)

QUESTION 9 HAS FOUR PARTS FOR A TOTAL OF 20 MINUTES

Consolidated Trust Company, headquartered in Sydney, Australia, is evaluating some international bond investments. Colin Greystone, CFA, is the portfolio manager. He has identified and is evaluating two bonds in countries X and Y for purchase. Greystone believes that international bonds must be evaluated in terms of their potential for excess returns. He wants to identify the sources of excess returns, and the risks associated with these investments, and has gathered the data in Figure 1:

Figure 1: Data on Bond X, Bond Y, and the Domestic Economy

Bond X	Bond Y	Domestic Economy
$r_x = 4.55\%$	$r_y = 7.05\%$	
$c_x = 3.05\%$	$c_y = 5.65\%$	$c_d = 4.55\%$
Duration = 7	Duration = 6	

Notes: r = return on the bond in its currency
c_i = the cash return in country i

A.   **List** *six* sources of excess return from international bond investing.

(6 minutes)

B.   Suppose that the country beta for Bond X is 1.3, and that Australian domestic interest rates are expected to increase by 80 basis points. **Analyze** the effect on the yield change and value of Bond X.

(5 minutes)

C. The investment horizon is one year. Greystone expects Currency Y
to depreciate 0.95% against the domestic currency during this time.
Recommend and **justify** whether or not the currency risk of the
position should be hedged if he purchases Bond Y.

(5 minutes)

D. Greystone feels that the yield on Bond X will increase about 15 bps
over the coming year while the yield on Bond Y will remain more or
less the same. **Determine**, based only on the data provided for Bonds
X and Y in Figure 1 and Greystone's yield predictions, whether
Bond X or Bond Y should produce the higher return for the coming six
months.

(4 minutes)

END OF MORNING SESSION

Exam 3 Afternoon Session
Topic Breakdown

Question	Topic	Minutes
10	Performance Evaluation and Attribution	18
11	Ethics and Professional Standards	18
12	Capital Market Expectations/Equity Portfolio Management	18
13	Fixed Income	18
14	Fixed Income	18
15	Fixed Income Derivatives	18
16	Economics/Derivatives	18
17	Risk Management	18
18	Derivatives	18
19	Ethics and Professional Standards	18
	Total	180

Exam 3 Selected Response Item Set Answer Sheet

The afternoon session of the Level 3 exam contains 10 Selected Response Item Sets, each with six questions, and you must answer them by filling in a bubble sheet with a number 2 or HB pencil. For realism, we suggest that you use this answer sheet and darken the bubbles corresponding to your answers. This sheet will also facilitate entering your answers into our online Performance Tracker. You have 180 minutes for this session of the exam. That equates to 3 minutes per item set question, so budget your time well.

10.1.	Ⓐ	Ⓑ	Ⓒ	15.1.	Ⓐ	Ⓑ	Ⓒ
10.2.	Ⓐ	Ⓑ	Ⓒ	15.2.	Ⓐ	Ⓑ	Ⓒ
10.3.	Ⓐ	Ⓑ	Ⓒ	15.3.	Ⓐ	Ⓑ	Ⓒ
10.4.	Ⓐ	Ⓑ	Ⓒ	15.4.	Ⓐ	Ⓑ	Ⓒ
10.5.	Ⓐ	Ⓑ	Ⓒ	15.5.	Ⓐ	Ⓑ	Ⓒ
10.6.	Ⓐ	Ⓑ	Ⓒ	15.6.	Ⓐ	Ⓑ	Ⓒ
11.1.	Ⓐ	Ⓑ	Ⓒ	16.1.	Ⓐ	Ⓑ	Ⓒ
11.2.	Ⓐ	Ⓑ	Ⓒ	16.2.	Ⓐ	Ⓑ	Ⓒ
11.3.	Ⓐ	Ⓑ	Ⓒ	16.3.	Ⓐ	Ⓑ	Ⓒ
11.4.	Ⓐ	Ⓑ	Ⓒ	16.4.	Ⓐ	Ⓑ	Ⓒ
11.5.	Ⓐ	Ⓑ	Ⓒ	16.5.	Ⓐ	Ⓑ	Ⓒ
11.6.	Ⓐ	Ⓑ	Ⓒ	16.6.	Ⓐ	Ⓑ	Ⓒ
12.1.	Ⓐ	Ⓑ	Ⓒ	17.1.	Ⓐ	Ⓑ	Ⓒ
12.2.	Ⓐ	Ⓑ	Ⓒ	17.2.	Ⓐ	Ⓑ	Ⓒ
12.3.	Ⓐ	Ⓑ	Ⓒ	17.3.	Ⓐ	Ⓑ	Ⓒ
12.4.	Ⓐ	Ⓑ	Ⓒ	17.4.	Ⓐ	Ⓑ	Ⓒ
12.5.	Ⓐ	Ⓑ	Ⓒ	17.5.	Ⓐ	Ⓑ	Ⓒ
12.6.	Ⓐ	Ⓑ	Ⓒ	17.6.	Ⓐ	Ⓑ	Ⓒ
13.1.	Ⓐ	Ⓑ	Ⓒ	18.1.	Ⓐ	Ⓑ	Ⓒ
13.2.	Ⓐ	Ⓑ	Ⓒ	18.2.	Ⓐ	Ⓑ	Ⓒ
13.3.	Ⓐ	Ⓑ	Ⓒ	18.3.	Ⓐ	Ⓑ	Ⓒ
13.4.	Ⓐ	Ⓑ	Ⓒ	18.4.	Ⓐ	Ⓑ	Ⓒ
13.5.	Ⓐ	Ⓑ	Ⓒ	18.5.	Ⓐ	Ⓑ	Ⓒ
13.6.	Ⓐ	Ⓑ	Ⓒ	18.6.	Ⓐ	Ⓑ	Ⓒ
14.1.	Ⓐ	Ⓑ	Ⓒ	19.1.	Ⓐ	Ⓑ	Ⓒ
14.2.	Ⓐ	Ⓑ	Ⓒ	19.2.	Ⓐ	Ⓑ	Ⓒ
14.3.	Ⓐ	Ⓑ	Ⓒ	19.3.	Ⓐ	Ⓑ	Ⓒ
14.4.	Ⓐ	Ⓑ	Ⓒ	19.4.	Ⓐ	Ⓑ	Ⓒ
14.5.	Ⓐ	Ⓑ	Ⓒ	19.5.	Ⓐ	Ⓑ	Ⓒ
14.6.	Ⓐ	Ⓑ	Ⓒ	19.6.	Ⓐ	Ⓑ	Ⓒ

EXAM 3
AFTERNOON SESSION

QUESTION 10 HAS SIX PARTS FOR A TOTAL OF 18 MINUTES

Powerful Performance Presenters (PPP) is a performance attribution and evaluation firm for pension consulting firms and has recently been hired by Stober and Robertson to conduct a performance attribution analysis for TopTech. Tom Harrison and Wendy Powell are the principals for PPP. Although performance attribution has come under fire lately because of its shortcomings, Stober believes PPP provides a needed service to its clients. Robertson shares Stober's view of performance attribution analysis.

Stober and Robertson request that Harrison and Powell provide a discussion of performance measures. During a conversation on complements to attribution analysis, Harrison notes the uses of the Treynor ratio. He states that the Treynor ratio is appropriate only when the investor's portfolio is well diversified. Powell states that the Sharpe ratio and the Treynor ratio will typically yield the same performance rankings for a set of portfolios.

Stober requests that PPP do some performance attribution calculations on TopTech's managers. In order to facilitate the analysis, Stober provides the information in the following table:

Composite	Weighting		Return	
	TopTech	Benchmark	TopTech	Benchmark
Small-cap value	50%	60%	18.7%	28.6%
Large-cap value	30%	25%	15.8%	12.4%
Financials	20%	15%	12.5%	8.85%

Harrison states one of PPP's services is that it will determine if TopTech has chosen a valid benchmark. Stober volunteers that indeed his firm's benchmark possesses the properties of a valid benchmark and describes its composition. The benchmark has the following characteristics:

- It uses the top 10% of U.S. portfolio managers each year in each asset class as the benchmark for TopTech managers;
- TopTech is very careful to make sure that its managers are familiar with the securities in each benchmark asset class;
- The identities and weights of various securities in the TopTech benchmark are clearly defined.

During a presentation to Stober, Robertson, and other TopTech executives, Harrison and Powell describe how macro attribution analysis can decompose an entire fund's excess returns into various levels. In his introduction, Robertson delineates the six levels as net contributions, risk-free return, asset categories, benchmarks, investment managers, and allocations effects.

Robertson states that TopTech has performed impressively at the investment managers level for three years in a row. Harrison and Powell then describe the levels in greater detail. Harrison describes the benchmark level as the difference between active managers' returns and their benchmark returns. Powell states that the investment managers' level reflects the returns to active management on the part of the fund's managers, weighted by the amount actually allocated to each manager.

At the request of Stober, Harrison and Powell explore alternatives to the benchmark TopTech is currently using for its small-cap value manager. After some investigation of the small-cap value manager's emphasis, Harrison and Powell derive four potential custom benchmarks and calculate two measures to evaluate the benchmarks: (1) the return to the manager's active management, or A = portfolio return – benchmark return; and (2) the return to the manager's style, or S = benchmark return – broad market return.

The following characteristics are presented below for each benchmark: (1) the beta between the benchmark and the small-cap value portfolio; (2) the tracking error (i.e., the standard deviation of A); (3) the turnover of the benchmark; and (4) the correlation between A and S.

	Benchmark A	Benchmark B	Benchmark C
Beta	1.23	1.08	1.53
Tracking error	12%	10%	11%
Benchmark turnover	8%	7%	8%
Correlation between A and S	0.52	0.09	0.33

Harrison and Powell evaluate the benchmarks based on the four measures.

10.1. Regarding their statements concerning the Sharpe and the Treynor ratios, are Harrison and Powell correct or incorrect?
A. Only Harrison is correct.
B. Only Powell is correct.
C. Both are incorrect.

10.2. Based on an overall attribution analysis, does TopTech demonstrate superior ability to select sectors?
A. No the pure allocation effect is –1.8%.
B. Yes the pure allocation effect is 1.8%.
C. Yes the pure allocation effect is 3.2%.

10.3. Based on an overall attribution analysis, does TopTech demonstrate superior ability to select stocks?
A. No, the within-sector selection effect is –4.5%.
B. No, the within-sector selection effect is –3.2%.
C. Yes, the within-sector selection effect is 1.3%.

10.4. The TopTech benchmark contains all the following properties of a valid benchmark *except*:
A. it is investable.
B. it is unambiguous.
C. it is reflective of current investment opinion.

10.5. Regarding their statements concerning macro attribution analysis, determine whether Harrison and Powell are correct or incorrect.
A. Only Harrison is correct.
B. Only Powell is correct.
C. Both Harrison and Powell are incorrect.

10.6. Of the three benchmarks, determine which would be *most* appropriate for the small cap value manager.
A. Benchmark A.
B. Benchmark B.
C. Benchmark C.

QUESTION 11 HAS SIX PARTS FOR A TOTAL OF 18 MINUTES

Jacques Lepage, CFA, is a portfolio manager for MontBlanc Securities and holds 4 million shares of AirCon in client portfolios. Lepage issues periodic research reports on AirCon to both discretionary and nondiscretionary accounts. In his October investment report, Lepage stated, "In my opinion, AirCon is entering a phase which could put it "in play" as a takeover target. Nonetheless, this possibility appears to be fully reflected in the market value of the stock."

One month has passed since Lepage's October report and AirCon has just announced the firm's executive compensation packages, which include stock options (50% of which expire in one year), personal use of corporate aircraft (which can be used in conjunction with paid vacation days), and a modest base salary that constitutes a small proportion of the overall package. While he has not asked, he believes that the directors of MontBlanc will find the compensation excessive and sells the entire position immediately after the news. Unbeknownst to Lepage, three days earlier an announcement was made via Reuters and other financial news services that AirCon had produced record results that were far beyond expectations. Moreover, the firm has established a dominant position in a promising new market that is expected to generate above-average firm growth for the next five years.

A few weeks after selling the AirCon holdings, Lepage bought 2.5 million shares of Spectra Vision over a period of four days. The typical trading volume of this security is about 1.3 million shares per day, and his purchases drove the price up 9% over the 4-day period. These trades were designated as appropriate for 13 accounts of differing sizes, including performance-based accounts, charitable trusts, and private accounts. The shares were allocated to the accounts on a pro rata basis at the end of each day at the average price for the day.

One of the investment criteria used in evaluating equity holdings is the corporate governance structure of the issuing company. Because Lepage has dealt with this topic extensively, he has been asked to present a talk of corporate governance issues to the firm's portfolio managers and analysts at the next monthly meeting. At the meeting, Lepage makes the following comments:

"When evaluating the corporate governance policies of a company, you should begin by assessing the responsibilities of the company's board of directors. In general, the board should have the responsibility to set long-term objectives that are consistent with shareholders' interests. In addition, the board must be responsible for hiring the CEO and setting his or her compensation package such that the CEO's interests are aligned with those of the shareholders. In that way the board can spend its time on matters other than monitoring the CEO. A firm with good corporate governance policies should also have an audit committee made up of independent board members that are experienced in auditing and related legal matters. The audit committee should have full access to the firm's financial statements and the ability to question auditors hired by the committee."

11.1. According to the CFA Institute Standards, Lepage's statement that AirCon could be put "in play" is:
A. permissible.
B. not permissible because it blurs the distinction between opinion and fact.
C. permissible if he is aware that a client of MontBlanc's M&A division is secretly preparing a tender offer for AirCon.

11.2. Which of the following is a correct assessment of Lepage's decision to sell the shares of AirCon? Lepage's decision to sell the shares was:
A. an appropriate discharge of his duties as portfolio manager if the details of the compensation structure had not previously been made public.
B. an appropriate discharge of his duties as portfolio manager if the details of the compensation structure had previously been made public.
C. not an appropriate discharge of his duties as portfolio manager.

11.3. According to the CFA Institute Code and Standards, Lepage's ignorance of AirCon's press release to Reuters three days before he sold shares of the company:
A. constitutes a violation.
B. is not a violation because he does not have access to Reuters at MontBlanc Securities.
C. constitutes a violation because, by trading on the information, Lepage would have traded on information that was already incorporated into the stock price and, thus, would have constituted an unwarranted trade.

11.4. Which of the following statements *correctly* characterizes Lepage's method of distributing the shares of Spectra Vision to the 13 relevant accounts? Lepage's allocation method:
A. does not violate CFA Institute Standards on fair dealing.
B. violates CFA Institute Standards because he obtained the shares through trades that altered the market price of the stock.
C. violates CFA Institute Standards because he has a fiduciary responsibility to see that the charitable trusts receive full allocations prior to the performance-based fee accounts.

11.5. Which of the following statements regarding the compensation packages given to executives at AirCon is *most* correct?
   A. The base salary should make up a larger portion of the compensation package.
   B. The use of the corporate aircraft does not pose any problems for shareholder interests.
   C. The stock options cause a potential misalignment between management and shareholder interests.

11.6. Determine whether Lepage's statements in his presentation to MontBlanc's portfolio managers and analysts regarding the responsibilities of the board of directors and the audit committee are correct or incorrect.
   A. Only the statement regarding the board is correct.
   B. Only the statement regarding the audit committee is correct.
   C. Both statements are correct -OR- both statements are incorrect.

QUESTION 12 HAS SIX PARTS FOR A TOTAL OF 18 MINUTES

Security analysts Andrew Tian, CFA, and Cameron Wong, CFA, are attending an investment symposium at the Singapore Investment Analyst Society. The focus of the symposium is capital market expectations and relative asset valuations across markets. Many highly-respected practitioners and academics from across the Asia-Pacific region are on hand to make presentations and participate in panel discussions.

The first presenter, Lillian So, President of the Society, speaks on market expectations and tools for estimating intrinsic valuations. She notes that analysts attempting to gauge expectations are often subject to various pitfalls that subjectively skew their estimates. She also points out that there are potential problems relating to a choice of models, not all of which describe risk the same way. She then provides the following data to illustrate how analysts might go about estimating expectations and intrinsic values.

Index	Value	D_0	$\hat{g}$	Risk-Free	Expected Risk Premium
Singapore	3,750	90	6.0%	2.4%	?
Taiwan	?	450	4.5%	2.7%	1.10 × Singapore's E(Risk premium)

The next speaker, Clive Smyth, is a member of the exchange rate committee at the Bank of New Zealand. His presentation concerns the links between spot currency rates and forecasted exchange rates. He states that foreign exchange rates are linked by several forces including purchasing power parity (PPP) and interest rate parity (IRP). He tells his audience that the relationship between exchange rates and PPP is strongest in the short run, while the relationship between exchange rates and IRP is strongest in the long run. Smyth goes on to say that when a country's economy becomes more integrated with the larger world economy, this can have a profound impact on the cost of capital and asset valuations in that country.

The final speaker in the session directed his discussion toward emerging market investments. This discussion, by Hector Ruiz, head of emerging market investment for the Chilean Investment Board, was primarily concerned with how emerging market risk differs from that in developed markets and how to evaluate the potential of emerging market investments. He noted that sometimes an economic crisis in one country can spread to other countries in the area, and that asset returns often exhibit a greater degree of non-normality than in developed markets.

Ruiz concluded his presentation with the data in the tables below to illustrate factors that should be considered during the decision-making process for portfolio managers who are evaluating investments in emerging markets.

Characteristics for Russia and Brazil

Characteristic	Brazil	Russia
Foreign exchange to short-term debt	93%	182%
Debt as a percentage of GDP	86%	38%

Characteristics for China and India

Characteristic	China	India
Population growth	0.8%	1.3%
Labor force participation growth	1.8%	0.5%
Growth on spending on new capital inputs	1.3%	1.4%
Growth in total factor productivity	0.9%	0.4%
Expected savings relative to investment	Surplus	Deficit

12.1.   When the first presenter refers to skewed estimates and problems with a choice of models, she is referring to:
A. psychological traps and risk specification error.
B. selective bias syndrome and risk specification error.
C. psychological traps and model and input uncertainty.

12.2.   Based upon the information provided by So, the equity risk premium in Singapore and the intrinsic value of the Taiwan index are *closest* to:

	Singapore E(risk premium)	Taiwan Index Value
A.	6.0%	9,800
B.	6.1%	9,500
C.	8.4%	7,125

12.3.   Regarding Smyth's statements concerning exchange rate links:
A. only the statement regarding PPP is correct.
B. only the statement regarding IRSP is correct.
C. both statements are correct -OR- both statements are incorrect.

12.4. Determine which of the following characteristics of emerging market debt investing presents the global fixed income portfolio manager with the best potential to generate enhanced returns.

    A. Increasing quality of emerging market sovereign debt coupled with the ability of emerging market governments to access global capital.

    B. The Emerging Markets Bond Index Plus (EMBI+) index is dominated by Latin American debt securities.

    C. Emerging market debt can be highly volatile with negatively skewed returns distributions.

12.5. With regard to Ruiz's statements concerning emerging market risk, when an economic crisis spreads from one country to other countries in the area, this is known as:

    A. contagion, and non-normality of returns precludes the use of non-parametric models to estimate risk.

    B. contagion, and non-normality of returns makes it more difficult to estimate risk using parametric models.

    C. macro transmission, and non-normality of returns makes it more difficult to estimate risk using parametric models.

12.6. Based upon the data provided, which of the following statements is *most* correct?

    A. Brazil would be favored for equity investment.

    B. China would be favored for either equity or bond investment.

    C. Russia would be favored for bond investment.

QUESTION 13 HAS SIX PARTS FOR A TOTAL OF 18 MINUTES

Eugene Price, CFA, a portfolio manager for the American Universal Fund (AUF), has been directed to pursue a contingent immunization strategy for a portfolio with a current market value of $100 million. AUF's trustees are not willing to accept a rate of return less than 6% over the next five years. The trustees have also stated that they believe an immunization rate of 8% is attainable in today's market. Price has decided to implement this strategy by initially purchasing $100 million in 10-year bonds with an annual coupon rate of 8.0%, paid semiannually.

Price forecasts that the prevailing immunization rate and market rate for the bonds will both rise from 8% to 9% in one year.

While Price is conducting his immunization strategy he is approached by April Banks, a newly hired junior analyst at AUF. Banks is wondering what steps need to be taken to immunize a portfolio with multiple liabilities. Price states that the concept of single liability immunization can fortunately be extended to address the issue of immunizing a portfolio with multiple liabilities. He further states that there are two methods for managing multiple liabilities. The first method is cash flow matching which involves finding a bond with a maturity date equal to the liability payment date, buying enough in par value of that bond so that the principal and final coupon fully fund the last liability, and continuing this process until all liabilities are matched. The second method is horizon matching which ensures that the assets and liabilities have the same present values and durations.

Price warns Banks about the dangers of immunization risk. He states that it is impossible to have a portfolio with zero immunization risk, because reinvestment risk will always be present. Price tells Banks, "Be cognizant of the dispersion of cash flows when conducting an immunization strategy. When there is a high dispersion of cash flows about the horizon date, immunization risk is high. It is better to have cash flows concentrated around the investment horizon, since immunization risk is reduced."

13.1.   The initial cushion spread for Price's strategy is *closest* to:
    A.   100 bps.
    B.   200 bps.
    C.   300 bps.

13.2.   The initial dollar safety margin is *closest* to:
    A. $9.21 million.
    B. $34.39 million.
    C. $42.74 million.

13.3. Given Price's forecast for interest rates in one year, the dollar safety margin, assuming coupons are reinvested at 8% semiannually, will be *closest* to:
A. $3.10 million.
B. $7.58 million.
C. $31.29 million.

13.4. Assuming an immediate (today) increase in the immunized rate to 11%, the portfolio required return that would most likely make Price turn to an immunization strategy is *closest* to:
A. 11.0%.
B. 11.7%.
C. 12.5%.

13.5. Regarding Price's statements on the two methods for managing multiple liabilities, determine whether his descriptions of cash flow matching and horizon matching are correct.
A. Only his statement about cash flow matching is correct.
B. Only his statement about horizon matching is correct.
C. Both statements are correct -OR- both statements are incorrect.

13.6. Price has stated that, because of the need to reinvest coupons, it is impossible to totally eliminate immunization risk. He has also stated that an increased dispersion of asset maturities around the horizon date increases immunization risk. Determine which of these statements is (are) correct.
A. Only the statement about totally eliminating immunization risk is correct.
B. Only the statement about the dispersion of cash flows is correct.
C. Both statements are correct -OR- both statements are incorrect.

QUESTION 14 HAS SIX PARTS FOR A TOTAL OF 18 MINUTES

Mary Rolle and Betty Sims are portfolio managers for RS Global Investments, located in Toronto, Canada. RS specializes in seeking undervalued stocks and bonds throughout the North American, Asian, and European markets. RS has clients throughout North America, however, the majority are Canadian institutional investors. RS has traditionally managed currency risk in their portfolios by assigning it to their portfolio managers. The manager is allowed discretion for hedging currency risk within the confines of the investor's investment policy statement.

Rolle and Sims are currently deciding whether to hedge the currency risk of a portfolio of Japanese stocks. Rolle explores the possibility of using three different currency hedges. Each is an option contract on the yen-Canadian dollar exchange rate.

Hedge A	Buy Yen Puts
Hedge B	Sell Dollar Puts
Hedge C	Sell Yen Calls

RS has a portfolio of European stocks and would like to change its equity risk. They can enter into futures contracts on the Eurostoxx index of large European stocks. The information below provides the characteristics of the futures contract and the portfolio.

Portfolio value in euros	2,000,000
Desired beta value	1.80
Current portfolio beta	0.60
Beta of futures contract	1.02
Value of one futures contract in euros	110,000

RS is also invested in British and Argentine stocks. RS has taken a position in two main sectors of the British economy. The first sector consists of manufacturers who derive a great deal of their business from exporting to the United States and Canada. The other sector consists of British service firms who are largely immune from international competition, because most of their business is localized and cannot be provided by foreign firms. The main investment in the Argentine stocks consists of firms who provide cellular phone service to Argentine consumers. Rolle and Sims discuss which currency positions RS should hedge.

RS occasionally invests in mortgage-backed securities sold in the United States. The growth in these securities has increased tremendously over the past three decades as firms have used securitization to remove the risk of these securities from their balance sheet. RS holds a mortgage security issued by CWC International. This mortgage security has a coupon rate higher than newly issued mortgage securities. Sims discusses the return for this security when hedged with a short position in Treasury bond futures.

Rolle and Sims further discuss how to hedge the risk of mortgage securities. Rolle states that two Treasury bond futures contracts are typically used instead of just one. Sims states that a hedge becomes more important if the volatility of interest rates increases.

14.1.   Which of following *best* describes the approach used by RS to manage currency risk?
A. Currency overlay.
B. Balanced Mandate.
C. Currency as a separate asset allocation.

14.2.   Regarding hedging the currency risk of the Japanese stock portfolio, which hedge would be *most* appropriate?
A. Hedge A.
B. Hedge B.
C. Hedge C.

14.3.   For RS to change the equity risk of their European stocks, the *most* appropriate strategy is to:
A. buy 4 equity futures contracts.
B. sell 4 equity futures contracts.
C. buy 21 equity futures contracts.

14.4.   Regarding the currency hedge of the British and Argentine stocks, which of the following would RS *least likely* hedge?
A. The British service firms.
B. The British manufacturers.
C. The Argentine cellular phone firms.

14.5.   Assuming interest rates fall, what is the *most likely* performance for the CWC International mortgage when hedged with a short position in Treasury bond futures?
A. The return will be weak due to the hedge.
B. The return will be high due to the high coupon.
C. The return will be the risk-free rate due to the hedge.

14.6.   Regarding their statements about hedging mortgage-backed securities, are Rolle and Sims correct or incorrect?
A. Only Rolle is correct.
B. Only Sims is correct.
C. Both Rolle and Sims are correct.

QUESTION 15 HAS SIX PARTS FOR A TOTAL OF 18 MINUTES

John Rawlins is a bond portfolio manager for Waimea Management, a U.S.-based portfolio management firm. Waimea specializes in the management of equity and fixed income portfolios for large institutional investors such as pension funds, insurance companies, and endowments. Rawlins uses bond futures contracts for both hedging and speculative positions. He frequently uses futures contracts for tactical asset allocation because, relative to cash instruments, futures have lower transactions costs and margin requirements. They also allow for short positions and longer duration positions not available with cash market instruments. Rawlins has a total of approximately $750 million of assets under management.

In one of his client portfolios, Rawlins currently holds the following positions:

Bond	Face Amount	Price	Duration Today	Duration in 1 Year
Q	$10m	104.98	10.32	9.46
R	$25m	98.36	8.67	7.83
S	$15m	101.21	7.38	6.51

The dollar duration of the cheapest to deliver bond (CTD) for a 100 basis point change in interest rates is $13,245.46 and the conversion factor is 1.3698.

In a discussion of this bond hedge, Rawlins confers with John Tejada, his assistant. Tejada states that he has regressed the corporate bond's yield against the yield for the CTD and has found that the slope coefficient for this regression is 1.0. He states his results confirm the assumptions made by Rawlins for his hedging calculations. Rawlins states that had Tejada found a slope coefficient greater than one, the number of futures contracts needed to hedge a position would decrease (relative to the regression coefficient being equal to one).

In addition to hedging specific bond positions, Rawlins tends to be quite active in individual bond management by moving in and out of specific issues to take advantage of temporary mispricing. Although the turnover in his portfolio is sometimes quite high, he believes that by using his gut instincts he can outperform a buy-and-hold strategy. Tejada on the other hand prefers using statistical software and simulation to help him find undervalued bond issues. Although Tejada has recently graduated from a prestigious university with a master's degree in finance, Rawlins has not given Tejada full rein in decision-making because he believes that Tejada's approach needs further evaluation over a period of both falling and rising interest rates, as well as in different credit environments.

Rawlins and Tejada are evaluating two individual bonds for purchase. The first bond was issued by Dynacom, a U.S. telecommunications firm. This bond is denominated in dollars. The second bond was issued by Bergamo Metals, an Italian based mining and metal fabrication firm. The Bergamo bond is denominated in euros. The holding period for either bond is three months.

The characteristics of the bonds are as follows:

	Yield on Annual Basis	Modified Duration	Maturity	Current Price	Semiannual Coupon Payment
Dynacom Bond	5.00%	5.13	6.0	100	$2.50
Bergamo Bond	9.00%	2.62	3.0	100	$4.50

3-month cash interest rates are 1% in the United States and 2.5% in the European Union. Rawlins and Tejada will hedge the receipt of euro interest and principal from the Bergamo bond using a forward contract on euros.

Rawlins evaluates these two bonds and decides that over the next three months, he will invest in the Dynacom bond. He notes that although the Bergamo bond has a yield advantage of 1% over the next quarter, the euro is at a three month forward discount of approximately 1.5%. Therefore, he favors the Dynacom bond because the net return advantage for the Dynacom bond is 0.5% over the next three months.

Tejada does his own analysis and states that, although he agrees with Rawlins that the Dynacom bond has a yield advantage, he is concerned about the credit quality of the Dynacom bond. Specifically, he has heard rumors that the chief executive and the chairman of the board at Dynacom are both being investigated by the U.S. Securities and Exchange Commission for possible manipulation of Dynacom's stock price, just prior to the exercise of their options in the firm's stock. He believes that the resulting fallout from this alleged incident could be damaging to Dynacom's bond price.

Tejada analyzes the potential impact on Dynacom's bond price using breakeven analysis. He believes that news of the incident could increase the yield on Dynacom's bond by 0.75%. Under this scenario, he states that he would favor the Bergamo bond over the next three months, assuming that the yield on the Bergamo bond stays constant. Rawlins reviews Tejada's breakeven analysis and states that though he is appreciative of Tejada's efforts, the analysis relies on an approximation.

15.1 The manager wants to completely hedge Bond Q for an expected 80 basis point change in interest rates. The number of futures contracts required is *closest* to:
A. 82.
B. 99.
C. 112.

15.2 The portfolio's dollar duration today, assuming a 100 basis point change in interest rates, is *closest* to:
A. $2,964,708.
B. $4,335,741.
C. $5,235,741.

15.3 Suppose that the original dollar duration for a 100 basis point change in interest rates was $4,901,106 and that the bond prices remain constant during the year. Based upon the durations one year from today, and assuming a proportionate investment in each of the three bonds, the amount of cash that will need to be invested to restore the average dollar duration to the original level is *closest* to:
A. $5,885,167.
B. $10,888,662.
C. $12,793,588.

15.4. Regarding their statements concerning Tejada's regression results, determine if Rawlins and Tejada are correct or incorrect.
A. Only Rawlins is correct.
B. Only Tejada is correct.
C. Both are correct -OR- both are incorrect.

15.5. In their analysis of the Dynacom and Bergamo bonds, the *most likely* basis for the trading of Rawlins and Tejada are:

	Rawlins	Tejada
A.	Yield pickup	Total return approach
B.	Sector rotation	Sector rotation
C.	Total return approach	Yield pickup

15.6. Regarding Tejada's choice of the Bergamo bond and Rawlins' statement concerning breakeven analysis, determine which statement(s) is (are) correct.
A. Only Rawlins is correct.
B. Only Tejada is correct.
C. Both are correct -OR- both are incorrect.

QUESTION 16 HAS SIX PARTS FOR A TOTAL OF 18 MINUTES

International Opportunity Investors (IOI) manages substantial euro-priced equity portfolios for two U.S.-based investors, Mark Taylor and Cindy Amsler. Taylor and Amsler have invested in European stocks because of recent media reports suggesting that, due to continued interest rate increases in the United States, European stocks will outperform U.S. stocks over the next few years. Their portfolios are well diversified and similar to the local index portfolio in capitalization weightings.

Ted Tavinsky, IOI's portfolio manager asks his assistant, Tim Treblehorn, to review the relationship between international asset returns and the level of currency risk assumed when investing in foreign securities. The findings, Tavinsky believes, will prove useful in marketing the fund to North American investors. Treblehorn relays two fundamental conclusions to Taylor. First, correlations between international markets have been increasing, and the result has been reduced diversification benefits for international investors. Second, currency risk is typically less than half that of foreign stock risk, but the actual risk assumed is much lower because currency returns and stock returns are not perfectly positively correlated.

Taylor however is very concerned that the U.S. downturn may spread to the global economy. He states that he would like to explore the possibility of investing in the BRIC countries (Brazil, Russia, India, and China). Tavinsky replies that the prospects for the BRIC countries are quite good. Relative to the current G6 countries (U.S., Japan, U.K., Germany, France, and Italy), the stronger economic growth for emerging markets should result in higher stock returns. Furthermore, the increased growth in these markets will increase the demand for capital, which should strengthen their currency values.

Amsler is a novice investor and has hesitantly invested in the overseas markets. In order to calm her fears, Tavinsky and Treblehorn investigate the possibility of hedging using futures contracts on an equity index as well as a euro forward contract. They have chosen futures contracts written on the Eurostoxx equity index for her portfolio because the price changes of the contract have a high correlation with the returns on Amsler's equity portfolio. Amsler's equity portfolio has a market value of €15,000,000 and a beta of 1.15 relative to the local underlying index.

Tavinsky and Treblehorn collect data for spot exchange rates, futures contract prices and betas, as well as U.S. and European interest rates. Tavinsky and Treblehorn are bearish on the European stock market over the next year as noted by their forecasted return for it.

Relevant values are shown in the table below:

Spot U.S. dollar / euro exchange rate	$1.05
One year risk-free rate in Europe	2%
One year risk-free rate in the United States	4%
Price of futures contract written on the Eurostoxx equity index	€120,000
Beta of futures contract written on the Eurostoxx equity index, relative to the local underlying index	0.975
Forecasted return of the local underlying index over one year	−12%
Forecasted spot U.S. dollar/ exchange rate in one year	$1.12

Tavinsky has told Amsler that he and Treblehorn will calculate the value of her portfolio in hedged and unhedged scenarios. Tavinsky states that if, at the beginning of the year, he were to fully hedge the systematic risk of Amsler's equity portfolio using the index futures, the appropriate futures position to accomplish this would be 125 contracts. Treblehorn states that if they decide to hedge the currency risk of the portfolio as well, the principal for the forward contract that will hedge the currency risk of the hedged equity position will be €15,000,000, using a "hedging the principal" strategy.

Lastly, Tavinsky and Treblehorn calculate the forecasted return on the portfolio assuming that currency risk is hedged. Assuming that both equity and currency risk are hedged, Tavinsky calculates that the dollar return would be 8.8%. Treblehorn states that the forecasted spot U.S. dollar / euro exchange rate in one year of $1.12 should be used for the forward contract rate.

16.1. Which of the following is *least* accurate regarding the BRIC countries?
    A. An increase in investment capital will result in a relatively high level of output.
    B. Per capita income in most BRIC countries is expected to surpass that of G6 countries.
    C. The BRIC countries will experience a decline in their working age population later than that in the G6 countries.

16.2. If IOI wants to hedge the portfolios of Amsler as indicated, Tavinsky should go:
    A. short the equity index futures contract to hedge equity risk and go long a euro forward contract.
    B. long the equity index futures contract to hedge equity risk and go short a euro forward contract.
    C. short the equity index futures contract to hedge equity risk and go short a euro forward contract.

16.3. Regarding their statements on the amounts needed to hedge the equity and currency risk of Amsler's portfolio, determine whether Tavinsky and Treblehorn are correct or not.
A. Only Tavinski is correct.
B. Only Treblehorn is correct.
C. Both are correct.

16.4 Determine which of the following is *closest* to the dollar return on the unhedged Amsler equity portfolio (if equity futures and currency forwards are not used).
A. An 8% loss.
B. A 12% loss.
C. A 7% gain.

16.5 Assuming a futures position based on the expected exchange rate in one year turns out to be a perfect hedge and the currency risk is not hedged, the dollar return on the Amsler equity portfolio is *closest* to:
A. a 9% gain.
B. an 11% gain.
C. a 7% loss.

16.6. Regarding Tavinsky's forecasted dollar returns on Amsler's portfolio (assuming equity and currency risk are both hedged) and Treblehorn's statement about the appropriate forward rate:
A. only Tavinski is correct.
B. only Treblehorn is correct.
C. neither is correct.

QUESTION 17 HAS SIX PARTS FOR A TOTAL OF 18 MINUTES

Maurice Taylor, CFA, FRM, is responsible for managing risk in his firm's commodity portfolios. Taylor has extensive experience in the risk management field and as a result has been appointed the task of mentoring entry-level employees. Steven Jacobs is a newly hired Financial Analyst who has been assigned to research the company's risk management process. To verify the accuracy of his findings he consults Taylor. Taylor agrees to thoroughly review Jacobs' findings and volunteers to contribute his knowledge to enhance any part of the report that mentions Taylor's department.

A week later Jacobs, submits his report to his supervisor without reading Taylor's suggestions. Some excerpts from the report are as follows:

- "Many portfolio managers use a ratio that compares the average alpha to the standard deviation of alpha to measure risk-adjusted performance. This ratio can be used to rank their ability to generate excess returns on a consistent basis."

- "The main difference between risk governance and risk budgeting is that risk governance is concerned with policies and standards, whereas risk budgeting is concerned with allocating risk."

- "In an ERM system individual portfolio managers are charged with measuring, managing, and monitoring their portfolio risk as well as determining their optimal amount of capital at risk. With this information upper management gains a better overall picture of the firm's risk."

- "The two general categories of risk are financial and non-financial risks. Financial risks include market risk and credit risk. Non-financial risks include settlement risk, regulatory risk, model risk, liquidity risk, operations risk, and political risk."

Jacobs' supervisor thanks him for the report and assigns him the next task of researching the firm's VAR calculation methodologies. His supervisor is wondering if the firm should switch to the Monte Carlo Method from the Historical Method. Jacobs again decides to consult Taylor for his expertise. Taylor agrees that using the Monte Carlo Method would be useful since it incorporates returns distributions rather than single point estimates of risk and return. This may be appropriate for Taylor's portfolios since commodity returns can exhibit skewed distributions. Taylor, however, informs Jacobs that there are also advantages to using historical VAR including that it is based on modern portfolio theory (MPT).

Jacobs uses the firm's small cap value portfolio to illustrate the calculation of VAR. The value of the portfolio is $140 million and it has an annual expected return of 12.10%. The annual standard deviation of returns is 18.20%. Assuming a standard normal distribution, 5% of the potential portfolio values are more than 1.65 standard deviations below the expected return.

Jacobs completes his research report on VAR by adding an appendix section on extensions of VAR. He states that one extension that can be particularly valuable in risk management measures the impact of a single asset on the portfolio VAR. This measure captures the effects of the correlations of the individual assets on the overall portfolio VAR.

17.1. In the first statement in his research report, Jacobs is *most likely* describing the:
   A. Sortino ratio.
   B. RoMAD ratio.
   C. information ratio.

17.2. Are Taylor's second and third statements on the differences between risk governance and risk budgeting and ERM systems correct?
   A. Only Taylor's third statement is correct.
   B. Taylor is correct regarding both statements.
   C. Only Taylor's second statement is correct.

17.3. In Jacobs' list of non-financial risks in his fourth statement, all are non-financial *except*:
   A. settlement risk.
   B. operations risk.
   C. liquidity risk.

17.4. Are Taylor's statements on the advantages of the Monte Carlo Method and the Historical VAR correct?
   A. Only the statement about the Monte Carlo method is correct.
   B. Only the statement about Historical VAR is correct.
   C. Both are correct.

17.5. Assuming its returns are normally distributed and there are 250 trading days in the year, the daily VAR Jacobs will calculate for the small cap value portfolio is *closest* to:
   A. $2.59 million.
   B. $25.10 million.
   C. $27.88 million.

17.6. In the Appendix to his research report, the extension to VAR that Jacobs describes is *most likely*:
   A. portfolio VAR.
   B. incremental VAR.
   C. correlation VAR.

QUESTION 18 HAS SIX PARTS FOR A TOTAL OF 18 MINUTES

Smiler Industries is a U.S. manufacturer of machine tools and other capital goods. Dat Ng, the CFO of Smiler, feels strongly that Smiler has a competitive advantage in its risk management practices. With this in mind, Ng hedges many of the risks associated with Smiler's financial transactions, which include those of a financial subsidiary. Ng's knowledge of derivatives is extensive, and he often uses them for hedging and in managing Smiler's considerable investment portfolio.

Smiler has recently completed a sale to Frexa in Italy, and the receivable is denominated in euros. The receivable is €10 million to be received in 90 days. Smiler's bank provides the following information:

	Spot	30 days	60 days	90 days	120 days
$/€	1.42	1.43	1.44	1.45	1.46

Smiler borrows short-term funds to meet expenses on a temporary basis and typically makes semiannual interest payments based on 180-day LIBOR plus a spread of 150 bp. Smiler will need to borrow $25 million in 90 days to invest in new equipment. To hedge the interest rate risk on the loan, Ng is considering the purchase of a call option on 180-day LIBOR with a term to expiration of 90 days, an exercise rate of 4.8%, and a premium of 0.000943443 of the loan amount. Current 90-day LIBOR is 4.8%.

Smiler also has a diversified portfolio of large cap stocks with a current value of $52,750,000, and Ng wants to lower the beta of the portfolio from its current level of 1.25 to 0.9 using S&P 500 futures which have a multiplier of 250. The S&P 500 is currently 1,050, and the futures contract exhibits a beta of 0.98 to the underlying.

Because Ng intends to replace the short-term LIBOR-based loan with long-term financing, he wants to hedge the risk of a 50 bp change in the market rate of the 20-year bond Smiler will issue in 270 days. The current spread to Treasuries for Smiler's corporate debt is 2.4%. He will use a 270-day, 20-year Treasury bond futures contract ($100,000 face value) currently priced at 108.5 for the hedge. The CTD bond for the contract has a conversion factor of 1.259 and a dollar duration of $6,932.53. The corporate bond, if issued today, would have an effective duration of 9.94 and has an expected effective duration at issuance of 9.90 based on a constant spread assumption. A regression of the YTM of 20-year corporate bonds with a rating the same as Smiler's on the YTM of the CTD bond yields a beta of 1.05.

18.1   The type of exchange rate exposure generated by the sale to Frexa is:
    A. economic, and the proceeds from a forward contract would be
        $6.9 million.
    B. economic, and the proceeds from a forward contract would be
        $14.5 million.
    C. transaction, and the proceeds from a forward contract would be
        $14.5 million.

18.2.   If Ng purchases the interest rate call, and 180-day LIBOR at option
    expiration is 5.73%, the annualized effective rate for the 180-day loan is
    closest to:
    A. 6.6982%.
    B. 6.5346%.
    C. 6.3785%.

18.3.   What position should Smiler take to alter the beta of the equity portfolio?
    A. Long 72 futures contracts.
    B. Short 72 futures contracts.
    C. Long 70 futures contracts.

18.4.   Determine the strategy in Treasury bond futures contracts that Ng should
    take to hedge the interest rate risk of the bond Smiler will issue.
    A. Short 244 contracts.
    B. Short 236 contracts.
    C. Short 225 contracts.

18.5.   When hedging the interest rate risk of the bond Smiler will issue, which of
    the following is *not* a likely source of hedging error?
    A. The dollar duration for the corporate bond was incorrect.
    B. Interest rates changed more than expected.
    C. The projected basis of the futures contract at the date the hedge is to be
        removed.

18.6.   Ng is thinking about hedging several foreign exchange positions. Which of
    the following positions would be the *most* difficult to hedge?
    A. Smiler has a loan due in two years that is denominated in yen.
    B. Smiler has an order for German machine parts due in three months,
        payable in euros.
    C. Ng has an investment in British stocks, which he will be converting to
        U.S. dollars in one year.

QUESTION 19 HAS SIX PARTS FOR A TOTAL OF 18 MINUTES

Hilda Olson covers the chemical industry for Bern Securities. Based on conversations with two executives of InterChem, a major producer of synthetic fabrics, she issues a generalized sector report claiming that "according to a survey of industry executives, rayon feedstocks will be in short supply for at least the next 12 months." In addition, Olson recommends Han Chemical, a major producer of rayon, which has routinely reported higher profits than its competitors and should be well positioned to gain further from reduced supply.

In her efforts to learn more about Han Chemical and support her recommendation, Olson scrambles to compile a research report on the firm. She reproduces financial data provided in a research report by Standard & Poor's (S&P) and the Bank of Korea (BOK), the Korean government's central bank. She also obtains two research reports from brokerage firms with operations in Korea, and incorporates portions of the text and charts from these reports into her research report.

Olson describes Han Chemical in her research report as "low risk," even though she knows that the operating risk of the chemical industry is above average and that Han has a higher debt-to-equity ratio than its average competitor. She justifies this to her supervisor by saying that since the market for rayon feedstocks is tight, an investment in Han has a very low risk of suffering a loss in the near term. Olson's supervisor accepts her explanation as valid and the report is issued to the firm's clients.

Shortly after issuing her research report, Olson visited Han Chemical's operations in New Jersey. During her conversation with the firm's vice president of operations, who is also one of Bern's personal trust clients, she was told in confidence that Han Chemical's profit margins are higher than its competitors, partly because they routinely discharge untreated chemical waste into the Delaware River in order to reduce production costs. Such action is a direct violation of U.S. environmental laws.

When Olson returns from her trip to New Jersey, Wolfgang Hundt, director of research at Bern Securities, requests a meeting. Hundt has developed a compliance procedure and has provided relevant written information to employees. Every quarter, he issues written reminders regarding the program to Olson and her peers, so when Olson tells Hundt of Han's chemical dumping, he immediately begins an investigation into the violation.

19.1. With regard to the statement concerning rayon feedstocks, Olson has:
A. not violated CFA Institute Standards.
B. violated CFA Institute Standards since she has failed to use reasonable judgment in gathering her information.
C. violated CFA Institute Standards since she is not permitted to project supply and demand conditions in the industry.

19.2. In her report on Han Chemical, Olson has utilized data from S&P and the BOK. With regard to this data, Olson is allowed to use:
A. both sources of data, but must acknowledge the sources of the data.
B. both sources of data, and need not acknowledge the sources of the data.
C. the S&P data, but not the BOK data, and she must acknowledge the source.

19.3. In her report on Han Chemical, Olson has also utilized two brokerage firms' reports. With regard to these sources, Olson is:
A. allowed to use the text and charts, but must acknowledge the sources.
B. allowed to use the text and charts, and need not acknowledge the sources.
C. not allowed to use the text and charts from other reports.

19.4. Olson's characterization of the risks associated with an investment in Han Chemical is:
A. acceptable since it is clearly an opinion.
B. acceptable since it is supported with facts regarding industry supply and demand.
C. unacceptable since she has not provided enough information for investors to assess Han's risk.

19.5. With regard to the information Olson received from Han Chemical's Vice President of Operations, the *most* appropriate course of action for Olson to take would be to:
A. not divulge such information in her client research since she now lacks independence and objectivity.
B. divulge the information to her employer because, even though received in confidence, it involves an illegal act.
C. divulge the information in her client's research department in order to demonstrate due diligence in performing her research.

19.6. Olson is concerned that Hundt's compliance actions as director of the firm's research department are inconsistent with CFA Institute Standards. Which of the following properly characterize Hundt's compliance activities? Hundt's actions are:
A. consistent with CFA Institute Standards.
B. improper with respect to both the investigation procedures and the periodic reminders.
C. improper regarding the periodic reminders, as these do not constitute regular training.

END OF AFTERNOON SESSION

EXAM 1
MORNING SESSION ANSWERS

QUESTION 1

Reference: Book 1, Study Session 4, LOS 14.j,k, 19.c,d
Book 2, Study Session 8, LOS 26.g
Book 5, Study Session 17, LOS 46.p

Cross-reference to CFA Institute® assigned readings: Readings 14, 26, and 46

Answer for Question 1-A

<table>
<tr><td colspan="3">Investment Policy Statement for the Marks</td></tr>
<tr>
<td>Objectives</td>
<td>Risk Objective</td>
<td>

For the Exam:
Willingness: Below average.
Ability: Average.
Overall: Below average.

Discussion:

Willingness is below average because Marks states he does not want to lose more than 2% in any year. This statement indicates that Marks's focus is on risk and a desire for stability.

Ability is average. Marks' fairly substantial portfolio and fairly low required return indicate above-average ability to tolerate risk. The portfolio must meet all living expenses for the Marks family, however, and that indicates below-average risk tolerance. Considering the two indicators together, we can say Marks has average ability to tolerate risk.

Overall risk tolerance is below average, because willingness to tolerate risk is less than ability to tolerate risk and we honor the lesser (i.e., more risk-averse) of the two.

Note: On the exam you could see a client with above-average ability to tolerate risk due to a very large portfolio (> $10 million or so) and very small required return (< 2% to 3%), but the client has below-average willingness to tolerate risk. In that case, you would be safe averaging the two and saying the client has average overall risk tolerance. As justification, state that significant wealth and low required return mean the portfolio has the ability to sustain considerable reduction in value before the client's goals are placed in jeopardy.

</td>
</tr>
</table>

Objectives	Risk Objective	Here are a few rules of thumb for determining risk tolerance for an individual:
		Willingness: 1. Remember, willingness to tolerate risk is psychological. 2. Always start out at average and then look for statements or actions that might indicate the need to move up or down a notch (i.e., to above average or below average). 3. If the client makes specific statements about risk, this usually indicates that the client is concerned with risk and you should drop willingness a notch. 4. Look at the client's past investments and strategies for indications of risk tolerance. The client might make a statement like, "I have average risk tolerance." When you look at the client's past investments, however, you see emerging market equities, commodities, derivatives, etc. In this case actions speak far louder than words. "Average" to this client is above average for anyone else, so move up a notch. The bottom line is that you can usually ignore client statements about risk aversion. The client's actions are usually more relevant. **Ability:** 1. The client's ability to tolerate risk depends on the portfolio's ability to tolerate risk without putting the client's liquidity needs in jeopardy. This will be determined jointly by the size of the portfolio relative to liquidity needs and the time horizon. (Remember, *liquidity needs* refers to expenditures that must be met by the portfolio; expenditures that are not covered by the client's salary or other income sources.) Holding **portfolio size** constant: • As time horizon increases → ability to tolerate risk increases. • As liquidity needs increase → ability to tolerate risk decreases. Holding **liquidity needs** constant: • As wealth (portfolio size) increases → ability to tolerate risk increases. 2. Starting at average ability to tolerate risk, look for reasons to move up or down a notch: • If the client's salary covers all living and other required expenditures, the client's ability to tolerate risk is usually average or above average, depending on the size of the portfolio and the time horizon. • Having to take living or other expenses out of the portfolio decreases the typical client's ability to tolerate risk. If the client is quite wealthy, however, the expenditures might have no affect. The key is the size of the required expenditure(s) relative to the client's portfolio. Even if the portfolio must meet all living expenses (e.g., retired client), if they amount to less than 1% or 2% of the portfolio, the client's ability to tolerate risk is probably unaffected.

Examples: These examples include discussions of ability to tolerate risk as well as demand for life insurance, based solely on the data provided. In determining life insurance demand on the exam you should also look for indications of the individual's willingness to tolerate risk as well as statements about dependents. You will probably be asked to determine whether or not the individual will demand life insurance, not the dollar amount of life insurance. Since life insurance is a hedge against dying and the accompanying loss of human capital, however, the typical amount of life insurance would be the present value of human capital.

1. Retired individual; 15-year time horizon; $50 million portfolio; $500,000 annual expenses are met by portfolio; little or no desire for bequest → *above-average ability*.
    *   Not concerned with value of portfolio at death, and expenditures amount to only 1% of the portfolio per year. Overall risk tolerance will depend on the client's willingness to tolerate risk.
        *   If willingness is below average, go with average overall and recommend counseling to reconcile the difference.
        *   If willingness is average, go with average overall and recommend counseling to reconcile the difference.
        *   If willingness is above average, go with above average overall.

    Life insurance. Probably no demand for life insurance because of high wealth and low utility derived from leaving an estate.

2. Retired individual; 15-year time horizon; $50 million portfolio; $500,000 annual expenses are met by portfolio; desire for maximum bequest → *average ability*.
    *   This one is somewhat vague, but seems to imply the client wants to leave at least $50 million. An important consideration is the inability of the client to make further contributions to the portfolio. Since the portfolio must meet all expenses and the client wants to maintain or grow the value of the portfolio, we would probably conclude that the client has average ability to tolerate risk. If the client had a time horizon of five years or so, we would no doubt conclude that ability is below average. In this case the client's willingness to tolerate risk will have a somewhat smaller impact on overall risk tolerance.
        *   If willingness is below average, go with average overall and recommend counseling to reconcile the difference.
        *   If willingness is average, go with average overall.
        *   If willingness is above average, go with average overall and recommend counseling to reconcile the difference.

    Life insurance: Based on wealth, little or no demand for life insurance. Since strong desire to maximize bequest, however, this investor probably wants life insurance.

3. Working individual; 30 years until retirement; $1 million portfolio; $150,000 annual expenses are approximately equal to after-tax salary; bequest desire uncertain → *above-average ability*.
    *   This is one of those dream scenarios that you hope shows up on the exam, because everything points to above-average ability to tolerate risk. Note that in cases like this, the individual's willingness is often above average, also, which makes your choice very easy.
        *   If willingness is below average, go with below average overall and recommend counseling to reconcile the difference.
        *   If willingness is average, go with average overall and recommend counseling to reconcile the difference.
        *   If willingness is above average, go with above average overall.

    Life insurance. Uncertain from data provided, but probably some demand for life insurance. Because of long time horizon, the correlation of human and financial capital is important as well as whether the client has dependents to protect. Also determine the client's utility from leaving an estate and willingness to tolerate risk.

4. Working individual; 5 years until retirement; $1 million portfolio; $150,000 annual expenses are approximately equal to after-tax salary; wishes to maintain current lifestyle in retirement; bequest desire uncertain → *average ability*.

    • The shortened time horizon changes the scenario dramatically. The individual has made no comments about a desired bequest, so we only assume he wishes to maintain the size of the portfolio (typical assumption for any morning case). However, the shortened time horizon reduces the individual's ability to tolerate risk, even though current expenses are being met by the salary. If the client was using the portfolio to meet part of his living expenses, the ability would be below average.

        ◆ If willingness is below average, go with below average overall. Probably no need to recommend counseling to reconcile the difference, because of the very short time horizon. (You should state that in risk tolerance objective.)

        ◆ If willingness is average, go with average overall.

        ◆ If willingness is above average, go with average overall and recommend counseling to reconcile the difference.

    Life insurance. With short time horizon, the demand for life insurance is uncertain, so look for correlation of human and financial capital as well as whether the client has dependents to protect. Look for statements about the client's utility from leaving an estate and willingness to tolerate risk.

5. Working individual; 15 years until retirement; $1 million portfolio; $150,000 annual expenses approximately equal to after-tax salary; wishes to maintain current lifestyle in retirement; strong bequest desire → *average ability*.

    • The individual now has a strong desire to leave a bequest, so we assume he wishes at a minimum to maintain the size of the portfolio. The lengthened time horizon reinforces the individual's ability to tolerate risk. If the client was using the portfolio to meet any or all living expenses, ability would probably be below average.

        ◆ If willingness is below average, go with below average overall and recommend counseling to reconcile the difference.

        ◆ If willingness is average, go with average overall.

        ◆ If willingness is above average, go with average overall and recommend counseling to reconcile the difference.

    Life insurance. Probably has a strong demand for life insurance, because of the strong bequest desire, long time horizon, and modest wealth.

6. Working individual; 15 years until retirement; $20 million portfolio; $200,000 annual expenses approximately equal to after-tax salary; wishes to maintain current lifestyle in retirement; strong bequest desire → *above average ability*.

    • This is similar to the third example, because everything points to above average ability to tolerate risk. Even if current expenses were being met by the portfolio, this client's ability would be no worse than average, because total expenses amount to less than 1.5% of the portfolio (this considers taxes at 30%, so total before-tax dollar return would have to be $200,000 / 0.7 = $285,714 or 1.429% of portfolio).

        ◆ Because of considerable portfolio size, if willingness is below average, go with average overall and recommend counseling to reconcile the difference. Notice that when the client has significant wealth, we can adopt an overall risk tolerance that is an average of the individual's willingness and ability.

        ◆ If willingness is average, go with average overall and recommend counseling to reconcile the difference.

        ◆ If willingness is above average, go with above average overall.

    Life insurance. Probably some demand for life insurance, because of the long time horizon and strong bequest desire.

7. Working individual; 15 years until retirement; $2 million portfolio; $150,000 annual expenses with $50,000 met by portfolio; will not reduce current lifestyle and wishes to maintain current lifestyle in retirement; strong bequest desire → *below-average ability*.
    *   The long time horizon and fairly large portfolio do not compensate for the liquidity needs and the desire to maintain the current lifestyle. The strong bequest desire only reinforces the decision of below average.
        *   If willingness is below average, go with below average.
        *   If willingness is average, go with below average overall and recommend counseling to reconcile the difference.
        *   If willingness is above average, go with below average overall and recommend counseling to reconcile the difference.

    Life insurance. Probably some demand for life insurance, because of the long time horizon and strong bequest desire.

We could go on and on dreaming up new and different scenarios, but this makes a great topic for group discussion. Meet with two or three fellow Level 3 candidates and think up possible exam scenarios. Make some of them complicated and others more straightforward with changing time horizons, liquidity needs, bequest desires, portfolio sizes, salaries, and amounts of liquidity needs met by the portfolio.

Objectives	Return Objective	**For the Exam:**
		Cash inflows for the coming year:

For the Exam:

Cash inflows for the coming year:

Salary	$150,000	

Cash outflows:

Taxes on salary	$49,500	(150,000 × 0.33)
Living expenses	100,000	
Allison's care	105,000	(100,000 × 1.05)
Ernie Jr. stipend	50,000	
Total outflows:	$304,500	

Net	($154,500)

Required after-tax **real** rate of return = $154,500 / $5,000,000 = 0.0309 = 3.1%

Required after-tax real rate of return	= 3.1%
Plus: Annual inflation rate	= 2.0%
Required after-tax **nominal** rate of return	= **5.1%**

Discussion:

Over the coming year, Marks will draw a salary of $150,000 and pay $49,500 in income taxes. Living expenses are given to us at $100,000 for the coming year, but the $100,000 cost of Allison's care was for the previous year. That means the cost of Allison's care for the coming year will be 5% higher ($105,000). This is the first year of Ernie Jr.'s stipend, so we use $50,000.

Total outflows for the coming year, including taxes, are estimated at $304,500 with the only inflow the $150,000 salary Ernie Sr. will draw. This leaves a shortfall of $154,500 that must be made up by the portfolio. To pay the $154,500, the $5,000,000 portfolio must earn 3.1% after-tax. To maintain the purchasing power of the portfolio principal (the $5,000,000), we must add inflation for a total after-tax nominal return of 5.1%.

Note 1: Alternatively, you could have compounded by the rate of inflation and arrived at a required after-tax nominal return of (1.031)(1.02) – 1 = 5.16%. Unless you are directed to present the answer in a specific form, either way would be acceptable on the exam.

Note 2: The vignette may or may not state that you must protect the principal (i.e., maintain purchasing power). To stress the point, I deliberately left out the statement in this case. On the exam, always assume you are to protect the principal unless you are specifically told otherwise.

Answer for Question 1-B

Constraints	Time Horizon	**For the Exam:** Long term consisting of two stages: (1) three years until retirement; (2) retirement years. A possible third stage relates to the daughter, Allison, whose care is to be funded by the portfolio as long as she lives. **Discussion:** Individuals usually have a two-stage time horizon; the years until retirement and the years of retirement. Note that unless stated otherwise, the estate becomes someone else's concern upon the death of the client. That is, the client's IPS, including time horizon, stops at death. In this case, the time horizon is somewhat uncertain, because Allison might outlive both parents and her care is to be paid by the portfolio. The portion of the estate that goes to Ernie Jr., however, becomes his portfolio with all constraints and objectives associated with his needs. Note: On the exam, you don't necessarily have to state whether a time horizon is long-term, intermediate-term, or short-term. If you can figure out the number of years, state that. For example, you could say the three years until retirement represents a short-term first stage of the time horizon, and that would be fine. Trouble starts, however, when you have stages of uncertain classification (e.g., eight years).
	Liquidity	**For the Exam:** In first year, portfolio must provide $154,500. **Discussion:** The Marks spend approximately $100,000 annually. They have expressed a desire to provide $100,000 annually for their daughter's care and $50,000 annually for their son's support. Since Marks' salary is only $150,000, the portfolio must provide $154,500 to cover living expenses.
	Legal/Regulatory	**For the Exam:** Marks should seek counsel to create a trust to care for the daughter and son. **Discussion:** There are no apparent legal or regulatory constraints. The Marks should seek legal counsel to create a trust that establishes care for their daughter and son.

Constraints	Taxes	**For the Exam:** The average tax rate is 33%, so tax aspects of investments should be considered. **Discussion:** The Marks are taxable investors. Tax aspects of investments should always be considered for individuals.
	Unique Circumstances	**For the Exam:** Support of the daughter and son. **Discussion:** Allison's care will presumably continue after the death of both parents and must be provided. There is some desire to leave 50% of the estate to the son, although no minimum amount is specified. Given their below-average risk tolerance, Ernie and Ellie probably hold some life insurance.

C. **For the Exam:**

For the calculation part of the question, your objective would be to simply provide the calculations as shown below. You should show your work on the exam in case you make a mathematical mistake. This provides you with the potential for receiving partial credit as long as your process for calculating the answer is correct.

The question also asks you to explain the information provided by the ratio, for which you would state: "The safety first ratio is the number of standard deviations by which the expected return exceeds the minimum acceptable return."

Discussion:

Roy's Safety First (RSF) rule is a measure of downside risk. The manager calculates the expected return and standard deviation of returns for the portfolio. Employing the empirical rule:

- ≈ 68% of all returns will fall within one standard deviation of the mean.
- ≈ 95% of all returns will fall within two standard deviations of the mean.
- ≈ 98% will fall within three standard deviations.

A safety first ratio is the number of standard deviations the portfolio expected return exceeds the minimum acceptable return. For example, with an expected return of 14%, a standard deviation of 8%, and a minimum acceptable return of zero, the safety first measure

is $\dfrac{0.14 - 0}{0.08} = 1.75$ standard deviations below the mean.

Professor's Note: Safety first rules were first introduced in the Level 1 curriculum, Investment Tools, Quantitative Methods section, and are in the Level 3 Portfolio Management material as Roy's Safety First measure. Basically, they tell us the probability of experiencing a return below some target. You're looking at the left hand side of the distribution's tail. A higher safety first ratio means that there is a smaller chance of the return less than the desired minimum.

In order to calculate the RSF ratios, we must first calculate the standard deviations for each allocation using its after-tax returns, Sharpe measures, and the T-bill rate. The calculations for each allocation are:

1. Determine standard deviation:

$$\text{Sharpe}_P = \frac{R_P - R_F}{\sigma_P} \Rightarrow \sigma_P = \frac{R_P - R_F}{\text{Sharpe}_P}$$

$$\sigma_A = \frac{\hat{R}_A - R_F}{\text{Sharpe}_A} = \frac{0.080 - 0.02}{0.46} = 0.1304$$

$$\sigma_B = \frac{\hat{R}_B - R_F}{\text{Sharpe}_B} = \frac{0.072 - 0.02}{0.60} = 0.0867$$

$$\sigma_C = \frac{\hat{R}_C - R_F}{\text{Sharpe}_C} = \frac{0.063 - 0.02}{0.75} = 0.0573$$

$$\sigma_D = \frac{\hat{R}_D - R_F}{\text{Sharpe}_D} = \frac{0.052 - 0.02}{0.88} = 0.0364$$

2. Determine RSF:

$$\text{RSF}_P = \frac{\hat{R}_P - \text{MAR}}{\sigma_P}$$

$$\text{RSF}_A = \frac{\hat{R}_A - \text{MAR}}{\sigma_A} = \frac{0.080 - (-0.02)}{0.1304} = 0.767$$

$$\text{RSF}_B = \frac{\hat{R}_B - \text{MAR}}{\sigma_B} = \frac{0.072 - (-0.02)}{0.0867} = 1.061$$

$$\text{RSF}_C = \frac{\hat{R}_C - \text{MAR}}{\sigma_C} = \frac{0.063 - (-0.02)}{0.0573} = 1.449$$

$$\text{RSF}_D = \frac{\hat{R}_D - \text{MAR}}{\sigma_D} = \frac{0.052 - (-0.02)}{0.0364} = 1.978$$

D. **For the Exam:**

Portfolio D is best:
*   Return exceeds the required return.
*   Highest safety first criterion.

Discussion:

Portfolio D is the most appropriate portfolio for the Marks.

Return: The expected portfolio total return is 5.2%, which exceeds the return required (5.1%) to meet the liquidity needs of the Marks and the expected rate of inflation.

Risk: The ability of Marks to tolerate risk is average, but his willingness is low and he does not want the portfolio value to decline more than 2% in any year, thus overall both his ability and willingness are below average. This is clearly the portfolio that best meets the client's safety first criterion. The safety-first ratio indicates that there is less than a 3% chance that returns will be worse than −2%, assuming portfolio returns are normally distributed.

Professor's Note: How did we arrive at less than a 3% chance? Using a one-tailed test (we're only worried about the downside here), at a critical value of 1.98, less than 3% of the distribution lies to the left. Or if you want to be more precise, look up 1.98 in a z-table and you will find that only 2.39% lies in the tail.

Liquidity: The portfolio must meet a required spending shortfall of $154,000 in the first year, which is expected to grow at an average rate of inflation of 2%. Adjusted for inflation, this translates to a required return of 5.1%. All the portfolios meet this requirement.

Time horizon: The portfolio meets the return requirement and covers inflation, so Allison's continuing care is funded in perpetuity.

Tax: The tax advantages to the portfolios are small, as almost all returns are currently taxable. Portfolio D is acceptable from a tax standpoint.

Unique: The bequest for the son and the continuing care of the daughter are both assured at levels higher than anything anticipated or desired by the Marks.

Overall: There is no reason given in the case to take more risk or seek a higher return than that generated by Portfolio D. The Marks state no other bequest motive other than what we have addressed. Do not misinterpret the issues here—the Marks' needs are covered by a good margin, and the bequest to the son is a maximum, not a minimum, and is not defined in dollar terms.

Sample Scoring Key:
A. 6 points each for addressing the two objectives.
B. 3 points each for time horizon and liquidity, 2 points for addressing the unique considerations, 1 point each for tax and legal.
C. 2 points for ratio formula, 2 points for interpretation, 2 points for correct calculations.
D. 4 points for selecting and justifying the correct portfolio.

QUESTION 2

Reference: Book 2, Study Session 5, LOS 20.i,j,l

Cross-reference to CFA Institute assigned reading: Reading 20

Answer for Question 2-A

	Investment Policy Statement for Unilife Portfolio Segments
Objectives	**Return Objectives** **For the Exam:** Short-term portfolio: return should meet the return for 90-day high-grade commercial paper. Long-term bond portfolio: return should exceed the crediting rate + operating expenses = 7% (5% + 2%). Stock portfolio: returns should meet or exceed the returns for the benchmarks S&P midcap and S&P 500 to grow the surplus. **Discussion:** Short-term portfolio: Returns of the short-term portfolio should meet the returns for Moody's or Standard and Poor's 90-day benchmark commercial paper. Investment returns from U.S. Treasuries are acceptable, but somewhat higher returns are desirable for competitive positioning. Long-term bond portfolio: Since the purpose of this portfolio is to cover crediting rates and operating expenses, the required return of this segment is 7% plus the desired spread (i.e., 5% + 2% + spread). Attention to opportunities in 10-year or longer A-rated corporate instruments should be directed to attaining the required after-tax return. Stock portfolio: Returns to the stock portfolio should meet or exceed the total returns to the designated benchmarks, the S&P MidCap and S&P 500. The focus should be on growing the surplus and providing a competitive advantage. *Professor's Note: This answer is a good example of situations where you should not be afraid to state the obvious, even when it means more or less repeating what is stated in the vignette.*
	Risk Tolerance **For the Exam:** Short-term portfolio: risk should not exceed the risk for 90-day high-grade commercial paper. Long-term bond portfolio: risk should not exceed that for A1-rated corporate bonds. Stock portfolio: can accept market to above market levels of risk. The portfolio should be well diversified including the maximum 5% international allocation. **Discussion:** Short-term portfolio: The quality of commercial paper instruments should not be sacrificed. The minimum acceptable quality for this portfolio is that at 90-day high-grade commercial paper. Long-term bond portfolio: A1-rating is the lowest quality corporate instruments that can be held in this portfolio. Although UniLife seeks higher return from extending maturity, minimum acceptable credit quality instruments are required to meet the liability structure.

	Stock portfolio: The stock portfolio can accept market to above market levels of risk. Growing the surplus is the focus. Maintaining a well-diversified portfolio is required, including the maximum 5% international allocation, because adding international equities to a diversified holding of domestic equities has been shown to shift the efficient frontier upward (i.e., increased return for given risk).
	Notice that the investment portfolio is effectively segmented into three separate portfolios, each with a specific goal. The goals for the three portfolios, as stated in the statements by UniLife management, are typical.

Answer for Question 2-B

Constraints	**Time Horizon**
	For the Exam:
	Short-term portfolio: 30 days to 1 year.
	Long-term bond portfolio: 10 to 20 years. A laddered maturity portfolio is appropriate.
	Stock portfolio: Perpetual due to capital gains (i.e., growth) preference.
	Discussion:
	Since the investment portfolio is segmented according to goals, each segment has its own time horizon.
	Short-term portfolio: Very liquid, low-risk, low-return assets. The targeted time horizon for the short-term portfolio is as short as 30 days and no longer than one year.
	Long-term bond portfolio: The targeted time horizon for the long-term portfolio is 10 to 20 years. To minimize sensitivity to interest rates, a laddered maturity portfolio is appropriate. This laddered maturity structure represents a pseudo-cash flow matching strategy, in that bonds sequentially mature to meet liquidity needs. Maturing short term bonds are replaced with bonds of maximum maturity within the IPS guidelines.
	Stock portfolio: The time horizon for the stock portfolio is perpetual. Insurance companies are taxable entities, so attention to investments with potential for capital gains is encouraged.
	Liquidity
	For the Exam:
	Short-term portfolio: Liquidity requirements are high to provide cash as needed to cover liability payments.
	Long-term bond portfolio: Liquidity required to meet credited rates and net interest margin and can be met from the laddered maturities.
	Stock portfolio: Liquidity requirements are low and focus is on long-term growth.
	Discussion:
	Short-term portfolio: Liquidity requirements for this portfolio are high. Access to cash when needed to cover liability payments is paramount.
	Long-term bond portfolio: Liquidity requirements (i.e., the credited rates and net interest margin) of the long-term portfolio are expected to be met from the laddered maturity schedule inherent in the instruments selected. Periodic income payments generated by instruments in the portfolio can be used to meet shorter term liquidity needs.
	Stock portfolio: The liquidity requirements for the stock portfolio are low. Liquidity will be provided by the short term portfolio and to a lesser extent, the long-term bond portfolio.

Constraints	**Legal/Regulatory**
	For the Exam: State regulations and NAIC should be considered. **Discussion:** Numerous state regulations and general provisions of the NAIC govern the activities of insurance companies. Therefore, operating divisions should meet with appropriate counsel for advice on regulatory matters. Exam questions are getting more specific; they tend to ask for parts of the objectives and constraints. If asked for the legal/regulatory constraint for an insurance company, this "canned" answer will suffice in addition to anything specifically mentioned in the case (e.g., outstanding lawsuits).
	Taxes **For the Exam:** State and federal taxes apply so investments should be considered on an after-tax basis. **Discussion:** Operations are taxable at both the state and federal level. Within risk objectives, investments in instruments that generate the highest after-tax total return are encouraged.
	Unique Considerations **For the Exam:** None. **Discussion:** *Professor's Note: No unique circumstances are apparent in the case. An answer of "none" would suffice because even though UniLife finds itself facing steep competition, this is not unique to UniLife. Had UniLife faced large, uncertain losses due to a hurricane, for example, that could be listed as a unique circumstance.*

Sample Scoring Key:
A. 2 points for each of the three portfolio segment return objectives and 2 points for each of the three portfolio segment risk objectives.
B. 2 points for each of the three time horizons, 2 points for each of the three liquidity constraints, and 2 points each for the legal, tax, and unique consideration statements.

QUESTION 3

Reference: Book 1, Study Session 3, LOS 7, 9.a, 11.b, 13.a

Cross-reference to CFA Institute assigned reading: Readings 7, 9, 11, and 13

Answer for Question 3

Comment	Identify the behavioral concept	Briefly describe the behavioral concept
"Pension plan participants currently have 90% of their investments in traditional asset classes. Our portfolio management firm has had difficulty getting investors to consider the non-traditional investments that are available through newly introduced exchange traded funds."	Status quo bias	**For the Exam:** This refers to defined contribution pension plan participants' tendency to make an original allocation and not change it despite changing conditions. **Discussion:** The speaker's statement is descriptive of the status quo bias concept. Status quo bias refers to defined contribution pension plan participants' tendency to make an original allocation and not change it. Lacking an understanding of the interaction of fund characteristics and macroeconomic variables, participants can fail to recognize the opportunity or need to change their allocations in response to changing conditions. Also, participants can be overwhelmed by the number of alternative fund choices, particularly as the number increases. The result is that, without being forced to regularly evaluate their allocation, investors tend toward a buy and hold (do nothing) strategy.
"Despite the recent increase in the CBOE volatility index (VIX) and increasing credit spreads, I have not increased the expected risk premium for stock investments beyond the 4.5% I forecasted earlier this year."	Anchoring	**For the Exam:** This is the inability to fully incorporate the impact of new information on projections. **Discussion:** The speaker's statement is descriptive of the anchoring concept. Anchoring refers to the inability to fully incorporate (adjust) the impact of new information on projections. For example, an analyst may have already made a forecast for the performance of a stock, when the firm releases new information that can have a material effect on the stock price. The analyst, being *anchored* by his prior projection, will tend to not fully reflect the full value of the new information in his revised projection. Overconfidence could also describe the behavioral concept. In that case the individual might feel he or she is better at interpreting information than the market. Also related to biased expectations.

"The recent bubble in technology stock prices resulted in stock valuations not justifiable by even the most optimistic fundamental analysis. However, it was difficult to exploit the stocks' mispricing because individual investors kept bidding up prices as they expected the trend to continue."	Representativeness	**For the Exam:** Investors saw the upward trend as representative of future performance. **Discussion:** Representativeness is indicated by an "if-then" relationship. In this case, the investors expect the trend to continue. "If the market did well this quarter, then it will do well next quarter." Representativeness can be indicated in many situations. The key to identifying it is that investors see some action or price movement that implies another.

Sample Scoring Key: 3 points for discussing each behavioral concept.
1 point for proper identification of each behavioral concept.
2 points for discussing each behavioral concept, but only if identification is correct.
0 points possible if identification is wrong.

QUESTION 4

Reference: Book 5, Study Session 18, LOS 48.d,e,g,h,i,l

Cross-reference to CFA Institute assigned reading: Reading 48

Answer for Question 4

Knight's statements	Accurate/inaccurate representation of CFA Institute GIPS (circle one)	Reason(s) for inaccuracy
"All composites will have the same beginning and ending annual dates. We will apply accrual accounting to all interest generated by the bonds in our portfolios. Until 2010 we will calculate time-weighted returns that approximate the effect of daily cash flows. All discretionary, fee-paying portfolios will be included in at least one composite and composites will be defined according to investment strategy and/or objectives."	Accurate	**For the Exam:** Not required. **Discussion:** All these statements are directly out of the GIPS standards. In addition, starting 2010, portfolios must be valued with each significant cash flow.
"My firm is approximately seven years old. Since GIPS only requires five years of annual investment performance, I can easily meet that requirement. Since my reporting systems are so effective, I also will have no problem maintaining the 5-year reporting requirement into the future."	Inaccurate	**For the Exam:** Five years is minimum report (unless the firm is less than five years old). Must add additional year each year until ten compliant years reported. **Discussion:** GIPS requires at least five years of compliance, or from firm inception. Each year the firm must add an additional year until ten compliant years are reported.

"My effective electronic systems will have no trouble capturing and maintaining cost and market values for portfolio valuations. My system automatically generates return information every quarter and, for my international composites, uses the same exchange rate sources for the portfolios and the benchmark."	Inaccurate	**For the Exam:** Portfolio returns must be calculated monthly. **Discussion:** Beginning January 1, 2006, composite returns must be calculated at least quarterly using asset-weighted portfolio returns.
"All of my fee-paying portfolios will be included in at least one composite. When clients decide they no longer need my services, my system automatically recalculates previous portfolio performance to reflect the removal of the portfolios from relevant historical performance presentations."	Inaccurate	**For the Exam:** Composite performance should reflect the historical performance of removed portfolios. **Discussion:** All fee-paying discretionary portfolios need to be included in at least one composite. When clients ask for their funds, however, prior portfolio performance should not be adjusted for the removal of the portfolio.

Sample Scoring Key:
1 point for proper selection of accurate or inaccurate.
2 points for reason(s) provided, but only if accurate/inaccurate choice is correct.
0 points possible if accurate/inaccurate decision is wrong.

QUESTION 5

Reference: Book 3, Study Session 11, LOS 32.i,l,r,s,u

Cross-reference to CFA Institute assigned reading: Reading 32

A.   **For the Exam:**

Your objective in this type of question would be to provide the calculations as shown below (without our accompanying verbiage). You should show your work on the exam in case you make a mathematical mistake. This provides you with the potential for receiving partial credit if your process for calculating the answer is correct.

Discussion:

The expected active return and risk for this subset of managers is determined using the allocations to the managers. Note that to calculate the portfolio active risk, we assume that the correlations between the managers' active returns are zero. Note that active return and active risk are labeled alpha and tracking error in the table.

The expected active return is calculated as a weighted average:

expected active portfolio return = $(0.10 \times 2.8\%) + (0.20 \times 0\%) + (0.25 \times 2\%) +$
$(0.05 \times 3.5\%) + (0.40 \times 1.1\%) = 1.40\%$

The expected active risk is calculated as:

portfolio active risk
$$= \sqrt{(0.10)^2(0.052)^2 + (0.20)^2(0)^2 + (0.25)^2(0.031)^2 + (0.05)^2(0.068)^2 + (0.40)^2(0.0162)^2}$$
$$= \sqrt{0.000141} = 0.01187 = 1.19\%$$

The investor's expected information ratio is then 1.40% / 1.19% = 1.18.

> Sample Scoring Key:
> 3 points for the calculation of the expected active return.
> 4 points for the calculation of the expected active risk.
> 2 points for the calculation of the information ratio.

Answer for Question 5-B

Comment	Correct or incorrect? (circle one)	Explanation
"From your data it appears that your core investment is Hoke associates. Hoke should mitigate the overall risk of your strategy, while the four satellites should provide an active return component."	Incorrect	**For the Exam:** Hoke Associates and Wrightsville Managers constitute the 60% core. **Discussion:** Hoke's expected 0% active return indicates a passive indexing style. Wrightsville Managers utilizes an enhanced indexing style, which is not classified as active management, so Wrightsville is also part of the core. The strategy behind a core and satellite approach entails using indexed and/or enhanced indexed portfolios as a core to generate a fairly stable return. The satellites are actively managed portfolios and can have both a true active return (alpha) and risk (tracking error) and misfit active return and risk. The strategy in a core-satellite approach is attaining a fairly stable return (managed within desired risk parameters) and adding potential for added return through active management of the satellites.
"The portfolio of Diamond Management is likely weighted towards utility and financial stocks."	Correct	**For the Exam:** Not required. **Discussion:** Value managers tend to have greater representation in the utility and financial industries. Because Diamond Management is value-oriented, it is likely to have greater representation in the utility and financial industries. These industries typically have higher dividend yields and lower valuations. Growth managers tend to have higher weights in the technology and health care industries because these industries often have higher growth.

"I expect that investors who pursue an investment approach similar to Hoke Associates will generally have higher information ratios than other investment approaches."	**Incorrect**	**For the Exam:** Enhanced indexing usually has the highest information ratios. Hoke Associates is using a passive investment strategy. **Discussion:** Hoke Associates is using a passive investment strategy approach, Wrightsville is using an enhanced indexing (also known as semiactive) approach, and the other managers are using active approaches. Generally, semiactive managers have the highest information ratios. That is also the case in this specific example. The expected information ratio (active return divided by active risk) for Wrightsville is 1.10 / 1.62 = 0.68, the highest of any other managers.
"We should carefully monitor the style of SRI Advisors because they likely have a bias towards value stocks, given their investment emphasis."	**Incorrect**	**For the Exam:** SRI uses a socially responsible investing approach, which is usually tilted towards growth and small-cap stocks. **Discussion:** SRI Advisors uses a socially responsible investing approach, which typically excludes basic industries and energy companies. These industries tend to contain value stocks, so socially responsible portfolios are usually tilted towards growth stocks. They also usually have a bias towards small-cap stocks. Investors should, however, monitor style biases from socially responsible investing so the appropriate benchmark can be chosen and so that unintended style biases can be curtailed.

Sample Scoring Key:
1 point for identifying whether the statement is correct or incorrect.
2 points for the explanation of why each is correct or incorrect.

Answer for Question 5-C

Comment	Correct or incorrect? (circle one)	Explanation
"Our proposed plan should contain high water mark provisions. These provisions state that managers will be paid no less than a certain amount during bear markets. This will prevent us from losing good managers during market downturns and, at the same time, help us avoid paying excess performance fees."	Incorrect	**For the Exam:** High water mark provisions require a manager to recoup underperformance in previous years before they receive future performance-based fees. **Discussion:** Dumas is inaccurate regarding her description of high water mark provisions. High water mark provisions require a manager to generate excess returns above underperformance in previous years before they receive their performance-based fee this year. The inclusion of high water mark provisions facilitates symmetric compensation (rewards for good performance and punishment for bad performance), which increases the incentive for the manager to generate excess returns.
"Your proposal to cap performance fees is illogical. The cap would discourage your managers from taking the risks necessary to obtain higher returns. Rather than aligning the managers' goals with your own, this could have a very negative effect."	Incorrect	**For the Exam:** Fee caps are used to discourage managers from taking too much risk and to align the managers' goals with the sponsor (investors). **Discussion:** Performance-based fees are a common component of the total fees paid to portfolio managers. They are usually included as an incentive for managers to pursue alpha-generating strategies, rather than rely solely on an assets-under-management (AUM) fee. AUM fees are based on the size of the portfolio, where performance fees are based on performance. The proportion of total fees represented by the two components depends on the managers' track record and the size of the portfolio (which tend to be highly positively correlated). Generally, the better the track record, the larger the portfolio, and the smaller the AUM fee as a proportion of total fees. That is, the better the track record and the larger the portfolio, the more the manager is willing to accept a small AUM fee and a larger performance-based fee. Note, however, that performance fees provide an incentive for the manager to take greater and greater risks in the hopes of generating larger and larger performance fees. In response, investors and sponsors tend to place caps on the overall performance fee. Since the manager no longer has unbounded fee potential, he will take only the risk necessary to maximize portfolio performance and resulting fees. Since the cap is jointly established by the manager and the sponsor, the cap effectively aligns the interests of the two.

Sample Scoring Key:
1 point for identifying whether the statement is correct or incorrect.
2 points for the explanation of why each is correct or incorrect.
0 points possible if correct/incorrect decision is wrong.

QUESTION 6

Reference: Book 5, Study Session 17, LOS 46.k,l

Cross-reference to CFA Institute assigned reading: Reading 46

For the Exam:

A.   Pure sector allocation effect:

$$R_{agric,PS} = \left(w_{agric,P} - w_{agric,B}\right)\left(R_{agric,B} - R_B\right)$$
$$= \left(0.1055 - 0.0645\right)\left(0.0135 - 0.0056\right)$$
$$= \left(0.041\right)\left(0.0079\right) = 0.000323 = 0.032\%$$

B.   Within-sector selection effect:

$$R_{agric,WS} = w_{agric,B}\left(R_{agric,P} - R_{agric,B}\right)$$
$$= 0.0645\left[-0.0082 - \left(0.0135\right)\right]$$
$$= 0.0645\left(-0.0217\right) = -0.001399 = -0.14\%$$

C.   Allocation-selection effect:

$$R_{agric,AS} = \left(w_{agric,P} - w_{agric,B}\right)\left(R_{agric,P} - R_{agric,B}\right)$$
$$= \left(0.1055 - 0.0645\right)\left(-0.0082 - 0.0135\right)$$
$$= \left(0.041\right)\left(-0.0217\right) = -0.000889 = -0.09\%$$

Discussion:

The pure sector allocation effect measures the ability of the manager to identify sectors that will out-perform and over-weight them in the portfolio (relative to the benchmark). When the manager over-weights an out-performing sector or under-weights an underperforming sector, the effect is positive. Roberts added 3.2 bps by over-weighting an out-performing sector.

The within-sector selection effect (a.k.a. security selection effect or selection effect) measures the manager's ability to identify and select superior securities (relative to those in the benchmark) to represent each sector. When the manager is able to do this, the sector return in the portfolio is greater than the same sector return in the benchmark. Roberts lost 14 bps by selecting different securities to represent the agriculture sector in his portfolio than those in the benchmark.

The allocation/selection effect (a.k.a. allocation/selection interaction effect) measures the combination of the manager's ability to identify superior securities in each sector and his ability to over- or under-weight sectors according to their expected performance. Note that the weight of a sector in the portfolio is affected by the manager's feelings about the overall sector as well as individual securities in the sector. Over-weighting expected outperformers and under-weighting expected underperformers may not offset each other and hence the portfolio weight for the sector can end up different from the benchmark. In other words, the manager can overweight a sector in the portfolio by simply holding more of the same securities as held by the benchmark or by changing the selection and weighting of individual securities in the sector. The combination of over-weighting the agriculture sector with Roberts' selection of under-performing securities in the agriculture sector produced a negative allocation/selection effect.

When you see a question like this on the exam, look at the numbers quickly to get an overall impression of the how the manager's return relative to the benchmark was produced. For example, by comparing the return for the agriculture sector in the benchmark to the overall benchmark return, you know that agriculture outperformed over the period. Since the manager over-weighted the sector in the portfolio, you know his pure sector allocation effect must be positive. He must have generated excess return (alpha) by over-weighting the agriculture sector.

Likewise, you know by comparing the manager's agriculture sector return (i.e., the agriculture sector return in the portfolio) to the agriculture sector return in the benchmark, that the manager's within-sector selection effect must be negative.

The allocation-selection (AS) interaction effect is harder to judge by simply looking at the data. This return measures the overall impact on the portfolio return of changing the weights of the sectors and selecting different securities to represent the sectors. The AS effect is positive only when the two effects have the same sign. For example, if he over-weights a sector in which he has selected out-performers, the AS effect is positive. Likewise, if he under-weights a sector in which he selects poorly, the AS effect is positive. Anytime the signs are different, as in this case, the effect is negative. Roberts over-weighted the sector but selected poorly (i.e., negative selection effect).

Sample Scoring Key:
2 points for each correct equation.
2 points for each successful calculation.
2 points for each correct explanation.

QUESTION 7

Reference: Book 2, Study Session 5, LOS 21.c
Book 3, Study Session 9, LOS 28.j
Book 3, Study Session 10, LOS 30.d,e
Book 4, Study Session 15, LOS 42.c

Cross-reference to CFA Institute assigned reading: Readings 21, 28, 30, and 42

A. **For the Exam:**

   i.   Buy the interest rate puts.

   ii. A decrease in interest rates results in higher values of the puts, which helps offset the higher value of the liabilities.

   iii. The present value of the liabilities (pension obligations) is based on long-term rates while interest rate puts are written on short-term rates, so this is not the preferred strategy.

Discussion:

The present value of plan liabilities increases as interest rates decrease. Exchange-traded interest rate put options will increase in value if rates decline below the put strike rate. The increased value of the put will offset to some extent an increase in plan liabilities.

The payoff to an interest rate put is calculated as:

payoff = notional principal [max (0, strike rate – LIBOR)(D/360)]

As interest rates (e.g., LIBOR) fall, the payoff increases.

The premium paid to purchase the interest rate put could be thought of as an insurance premium. The insurance (i.e., payoff from the put) offers protection against even greater funding requirements from the plan sponsor if interest rates fall in the future.

Note: Some might argue for the sale of interest rate call options to generate income (i.e., premiums). If interest rates should increase, however, the calls would go in the money at the same time that liabilities (inflation-indexed pension payments) increase.

The main disadvantage to the put strategy, and the reason it is not recommended, is that exchange-traded interest rate options are on short-term interest rates, whereas the liabilities of the plan have a long duration. If the short end of the yield curve does not fall, while the long end does, the strategy provides no protection, and they are out the premium. For this reason, they will not necessarily achieve the stated goals. In other words, the potential remains for the underfunding of the plan to worsen.

B. **For the Exam:**

   i.   Buy call options on Treasury bonds.

   ii. A decrease in interest rates results in a higher value of the calls which offsets the higher present value of the liabilities.

   iii. The duration of the liabilities should be similar to that of the hedge and unlike going long in Treasury bond futures, the option does not result in losses if interest rates increase as expected, so this is the preferred hedge.

Discussion:

Purchasing call options on Treasury bonds is the strategy that will most likely achieve the stated goals. Call options on long maturity bonds will spread the cash flows on the underlying over the yield curve to best match the liability cash flows, and the duration of the bonds can be matched to the duration of the liabilities. This should offer a fairly good hedge against future funding requirements arising from a downward shift of the yield curve. This strategy provides the best protection against further underfunding of the plan, because it also does not result in losses (except for the cost of the option premium) if interest rates increase as expected.

Since exchange-traded Treasury bond options are thinly traded, these call options will likely be OTC options so counterparty risk is a concern. If exchange traded options are used, the terms will not be as flexible as OTC options, and they may have to be rolled over. OTC options are less liquid and more expensive. American style options would offer some flexibility.

C. **For the Exam:**

  i.   Go long Treasury bond futures.

  ii. A decrease in interest rates results in a higher value of the Treasury bond futures, which helps offset the higher value of the liabilities.

  iii. However, an increase in interest rates would produce losses, so this is not the preferred hedge. The option in Part B provides flexibility that the Treasury bond futures does not.

Discussion:

A long position in Treasury bond futures will hedge the risk of increasing liabilities due to interest rate decreases, and the duration and cash flow arguments from above support this. The use of futures, however, is inappropriate because they also hedge upward shifts in the yield curve. If rates rise (as they expect), Matrix will have losses (and negative cash flows from marking to market) on the futures position.

In other words, Matrix prefers an asymmetric hedge, (i.e., one that only hedges against falling interest rates). With the option in Part B, an asymmetric hedge, the put provides protection when interest rates fall. If interest rates rise as expected, however, Matrix lets the option expire worthless.

Sample Scoring Key:
A. 3 points for describing the purchase of puts, 3 points for rejecting the strategy because the puts are on short term rates.
B. 3 points for buying call options on Treasury bonds, 3 points for recommending the strategy because a good duration/cash flow match is possible.
C. 3 points for buying the futures and the duration match argument, 3 points for rejecting the strategy because of the poor outcome if their expectation of rising rates turns out to be true.

QUESTION 8

Reference: Book 1, Study Session 4, LOS 14.n

Cross-reference to CFA Institute assigned reading: Reading 14

Answer for Question 8

Statement	Agree or disagree (circle one)	Explanation
"Since all has gone according to plan since our first meeting a year ago, I think it is time we focus efforts on your retirement. The most important objective is to determine an exact future value goal for your portfolio, integrating an expected rate of return, inflation, and your tax position to produce your retirement profile."	Disagree	**For the Exam:** • Single estimates do not account for the range of potential outcomes. • Investors need to see the range of potential outcomes so that they understand the risks involved. **Discussion:** Although single (deterministic) estimates of retirement portfolio value are useful as a starting point, they are not the most important objective in retirement planning because they do not account for the probabilistic nature of future outcomes. Portfolio values generated by the deterministic procedures do not allow either the investor or professional to see the range of outcomes that can potentially occur. Hence, single values are not the most informative retirement profile figure. Investors need to see the range of potential outcomes so that they understand the risks involved in retirement planning. (See Book 1 page 303 of the SchweserNotes for more information.)

"Once we have generated the single point estimate for the value of your retirement portfolio, we can apply some Monte Carlo techniques to see various other outcomes. Monte Carlo techniques will generate various portfolio values at retirement but, unfortunately, will not account for the risks inherent in our investment decisions. So, we will just have to pay a little more attention to the various portfolio levels."	**Disagree**	**For the Exam:** Monte Carlo techniques allow managers to use various return and risk assumptions as inputs. **Discussion:** Monte Carlo techniques allow managers to incorporate not only return expectations, but also risk factors such as inflation, changes in interest rates, and the correlation between portfolio assets. Because of the dynamic nature of Monte Carlo simulations, investors not only see potential portfolio values, they also see potential risk situations along the path to retirement. For example, the investment advisor can run a Monte Carlo simulation analysis using a 60/40 allocation to stocks/bonds. The advisor can run it again using a 70/30 allocation. Each simulation will produce its own distribution of returns, given the inputted model assumptions. By comparing the distributions and the associated probabilities of meeting some retirement goal, the Monte Carlo simulations provide a more complete picture of the risk involved with investment decisions. (See Book 1 page 303.)
"Think of the various portfolio levels as a range of potential outcomes your portfolio can achieve in ten years. The primary focus when evaluating those outcomes, however, will still be on the risks you wish to avoid in the present, and not necessarily any risks that may occur along the way."	**Disagree**	**For the Exam:** Monte Carlo shows the tradeoff between short-term and long-term risk exposures. **Discussion:** One of the most beneficial outcomes of using Monte Carlo in retirement planning is having the ability to see the tradeoff of short-term risk with the risk of not meeting retirement objectives. Although one can focus on short-term risk, seeing the ultimate risk of not meeting retirement goals as well as potential value paths the portfolio could take on the way to retirement are two of the primary benefits of using Monte Carlo. For example, clients may say that they only want to invest in bonds because they think that stocks are too risky. The investment advisor can use Monte Carlo analysis to show the clients that a focus on bonds increases their risk of falling short of the long-term retirement objective. (See Book 1 page 303.)

"Although we can incorporate taxes in our Monte Carlo techniques, the compounding assumptions we made when we calculated the single point estimate of portfolio value are just fine. Compounding does not play that much of a role with Monte Carlo, which simplifies the application of the procedure."	Disagree	**For the Exam:** Monte Carlo does a better job of incorporating the compounding effects of reinvestment, which can have a large impact on future portfolio values. **Discussion:** The compounding assumptions used in the deterministic approach to retirement planning are too simplistic. Monte Carlo does a much better job of incorporating the compounding effects of reinvestment, which can have a large impact on future portfolio values. For example, using an assumed reinvestment rate of 3% will lead to much different terminal values than a 5% reinvestment rate assumption. Or a client who starts using portfolio income for living expenses at age 62 will have a much lower portfolio value to work with than another who waits until age 70.

Professor's Note: This material is drawn from the discussion of Monte Carlo analysis in Study Session 4, Private Wealth Management. Be aware, however, that Monte Carlo analysis is also discussed in Study Session 8, Reading 26, Asset Allocation; and Study Session 14, Reading 39, Risk Management. You should be ready to answer a question on it given its frequency of appearance in the curriculum.

Sample Scoring Key:
1 point for correctly agreeing or disagreeing.
2 points for justification.
0 points possible if agree/disagree decision is wrong.

QUESTION 9

Reference: Book 2, Study Session 6, LOS 23.h,n,o,p
Book 2, Study Session 7, LOS 24.b,e,f

Cross-reference to CFA Institute assigned reading: Readings 23 and 24

Answer for Question 9-A

Comment	Correct or incorrect? (circle one)	Explanation, if incorrect
"Using the Taylor rule, I expect the Canadian central bank to target an interest rate of about 6.0%."	Incorrect	**For the Exam:** Your objective in this type of question would be to provide the calculations as shown below (without our accompanying verbiage). You should show your work on the exam in case you make a mathematical mistake. This provides you with the potential for receiving partial credit if your process for calculating the answer is correct. **Discussion:** Given this information, the interest rate the central bank should target using the Taylor rule is: $$r_{target} = 4.0\% + [0.5 \times (6.5\% - 4.5\%) + 0.5 \times (7.5\% - 3.5\%)]$$ $$= 4.0\% + [1.0\% + 2.0\%] = 7.0\%$$ The higher than targeted growth and higher than targeted inflation argue for a targeted interest rate of 7%. This rate is intended to slow down the economy and inflation.
"Based on the information I have gathered, we should be advising clients interested in the Canadian economy to invest in Canadian cash instruments, rather than stocks or bonds."	Correct	**For the Exam:** Not required. **Discussion:** Hoey's advice is correct because when expected inflation is high (here 7.5%), the return on cash instruments increases and it is likely that the central bank will raise rates to curb inflation. The return on cash instruments will increase as the bank's targeted rate increases. Although stocks can sometimes provide an inflation hedge, prices often fall when the central bank raises rates, as is predicted here. Inflation above 3% can be negative for stocks, because it increases the likelihood that the central bank will raise rates. Bonds are a poor inflation hedge and are adversely affected by increases in interest rates.

Sample Scoring Key:
1 point for identifying whether the statement is correct or incorrect.
2 points for the explanation if incorrect.
0 points possible if correct/incorrect decision is wrong.

Answer for Question 9-B

Comment	Correct or incorrect? (circle one)	Explanation, if incorrect
"The European Central Bank has been cutting interest rates. One potential impact on the euro is to decrease its value because investors will seek higher returns elsewhere. Unlike most analysts, however, I use a capital flows approach which projects that the euro will actually increase in value."	Correct	**For the Exam:** Not required. **Discussion:** Nurnberg is correct in stating that in a capital flows approach, the euro would actually increase in value. In this approach, it is the flow of long-term funds that influences the value of a currency. Under this approach, a cut in interest rates could stimulate the European economy, which would result in higher stock returns, thus making Europe a more attractive place to invest. This process would increase the value of the euro.
"Short-term interest rates on government bonds in Great Britain are 3.2% and 10-year rates are 5.9%. This indicates that, for an investor considering investing in Britain, British corporate bonds would be a better investment than British stocks."	Incorrect	**For the Exam:** The yield curve is upward sloping, indicating that the economy will expand. This is more favorable for stock investments. **Discussion:** Nurnberg is incorrect. Given the stated interest rates, the yield curve in Britain is upward sloping, and the upward-sloping yield curve indicates that the British economy is likely to expand in the future. When an economy expands, stocks are typically better investments than bonds. Stocks benefit from the increased business activity. Inflation and interest rates often increase in an expansion, resulting in decreased bond prices. Relationships between asset prices and returns, inflation, stages of the business cycle, and shapes of the yield curve are important for the exam. (See LOS 23.e, f, and g, Book 2, pages 86–91.)

"Mexico's largest trading partner is the United States. Given that the United States is in the early stages of an economic expansion, Mexican stocks would be attractive investments."	Correct	**For the Exam:** Not required. **Discussion:** Nurnberg is correct. The returns for emerging market stocks are positively correlated with the business cycles of developed economies. The correlation is due to trade and capital flows between countries. If the United States is in an early expansion, Mexican businesses and stocks should benefit from the increased economic activity.
"Economists project that in the coming months, business confidence in Japan will increase. The Bank of Japan will continue to accommodate growth by keeping interest rates low. Japanese government spending will increase as Japan puts a renewed emphasis on defense spending. Inflation in Japan will fall or remain stable. Given this outlook, I suggest that for an investor with a time horizon of a few years, an allocation to Japanese bonds is warranted."	Incorrect	**For the Exam:** Japan is in the initial recovery phase, which is followed by the early expansion phase with rising interest rates. Bonds are poor investments while stocks do better in these phases. **Discussion:** Nurnberg is incorrect. The scenario of increasing business confidence, low interest rates, increased government spending, and falling inflation is consistent with the initial recovery phase of an economy. This phase of the economy usually lasts a few months and is typically followed by the early expansion phase, which usually lasts a year to several years. In both these phases, stock prices increase while bonds are stagnant or falling in price. Thus, an investor with a time horizon of a few years should be invested in Japanese stocks.

Sample Scoring Key:
1 point for identifying whether the statement is correct or incorrect.
2 points for the explanation if incorrect.
0 points possible if correct/incorrect decision is wrong.

C. **For the Exam:**

Your objective in this type of question would be to provide the calculations shown below (without our accompanying verbiage). You should show your work on the exam in case you make a mathematical mistake. This provides you with the potential for receiving partial credit if your process for calculating the answer is correct.

Discussion:

Using the earnings multiplier approach, we multiply the earnings multiplier (the justified P/E ratio) by the expected earnings to get an expected future price. Adding in the expected dividend, we can then estimate an expected rate of return. To calculate the earnings multiplier, we first need the growth rate for the market, which is the retention ratio times the return on equity (ROE). The dividend payout is $1.50 out of $5.00 in earnings so the retention ratio is
$3.50/$5.00 = 70%. Using DuPont analysis, the ROE is the net profit margin times the total asset turnover ratio times the financial leverage: 6% × 1.30 × 1.25 = 9.75%. The growth rate is then 70% × 9.75% = 6.83%.

We will also need the dividend payout ratio and the required return on stock. The former is just one minus the retention ratio (1 − 0.70 = 30%) or $1.50/$5.00 = 30%. The required return on equity is the government bond rate plus the equity risk premium: 4% + 6.5% = 10.5%.

The earnings multiplier is the dividend payout ratio (30%) divided by the required return on equity (10.5%) minus the growth rate (6.83%): 0.30 / (0.1050 − 0.0683) = 8.17.

The expected future price of the series is the earnings multiplier times the future earnings: 8.17 × $5.00 = 40.85. The expected return is the expected dividend plus the price change in the series divided by the original price: ($1.50 + $40.85 − $40.00) / $40.00 = 5.88%.

Your answer may differ by a few tenths of a percent depending on how many decimal places you used in intermediate calculations. If you used your calculator's memory throughout, the return would have been calculated as 5.79%.

Sample Scoring Key:
2 points for the calculation of the growth rate.
4 points for the calculation of the earnings multiplier.
4 points for the calculation of the expected rate of return.

EXAM 1
AFTERNOON SESSION ANSWERS

To get detailed answer explanations with references to specific LOS and SchweserNotes content, and to get valuable feedback on how your score compares to those of other Level 3 candidates, use your Username and Password to gain Online Access at *www.schweser.com* and choose the left-hand menu item "Practice Exams Vol. 1."

10.1.	B	14.1.	A	18.1.	B
10.2.	B	14.2.	C	18.2.	C
10.3.	A	14.3.	A	18.3.	C
10.4.	B	14.4.	A	18.4.	A
10.5.	C	14.5.	B	18.5.	B
10.6.	A	14.6.	C	18.6.	C
11.1.	A	15.1.	B	19.1.	C
11.2.	C	15.2.	B	19.2.	B
11.3.	C	15.3.	B	19.3.	C
11.4.	C	15.4.	C	19.4.	C
11.5.	C	15.5.	A	19.5.	C
11.6.	C	15.6.	B	19.6.	B
12.1.	C	16.1.	B		
12.2.	C	16.2.	B		
12.3.	B	16.3.	A		
12.4.	C	16.4.	C		
12.5.	A	16.5.	A		
12.6.	C	16.6.	C		
13.1.	B	17.1.	A		
13.2.	B	17.2.	B		
13.3.	B	17.3.	C		
13.4.	C	17.4.	B		
13.5.	C	17.5.	B		
13.6.	C	17.6.	A		

Exam 1
Afternoon Session Answers

QUESTION 10

Reference: Book 1, Study Session 1

Cross-reference to CFA Institute assigned reading: Readings 1 and 2

10.1. **B** Standard II(B) Market Manipulation prohibits members and candidates from misleading investors through manipulated securities prices or volume. BIC's principals have suggested to Bair that she artificially inflate the Quaker Fund's price to alter the market's perception of the fund and mislead investors. (Study Session 1, LOS 1.b)

10.2. **B** Standard I(A) Knowledge of the Law requires members and candidates to know and comply with rules, laws, and regulations that apply to their professional activities. If there is a conflict, members and candidates are expected to adhere to the stricter of applicable laws, rules, and regulations or the Code and Standards. Because the Quaker Fund is located in Holland, which does not allow crossing trades (a law that is stricter than the Code and Standards), the fund is not allowed to utilize such a practice even for clients that live in countries with less strict regulations. Thus, the policy for clients in Norway violates Standard I(A). In the case of the policy for clients located in Denmark, no violation has occurred since the fund is going to comply with Denmark's law, which is stricter than the Code and Standards. (Study Session 1, LOS 1.b)

10.3. **A** According to Standard III(B) Fair Dealing, members and candidates are allowed to offer different levels of service but must offer all levels of service to all clients and must disclose the existence of different levels of service to all clients and prospects. By not disclosing the levels of service to Swedish investors, Bair is adhering to local law, which is less strict than the Code and Standards and thus is in violation of Standard I(A) Knowledge of the Law, which requires she adhere to the stricter of the two. She also violated Standard III(B) by not disclosing the service levels. (Study Session 1, LOS 1.b)

10.4. **B** According to Standard II(A) Material Nonpublic Information, it is appropriate procedure for the member or candidate who possesses material nonpublic information to first attempt to have the subject company disclose the information publicly themselves. If this is not possible, then the appropriate supervisor and/or compliance officer should be made aware of the situation. (Study Session 1, LOS 1.b)

10.5. **C** Standard II(A) Material Nonpublic Information prohibits trading on material nonpublic information in all situations. The investment bankers should have known that the information was material and nonpublic and have thus violated Standard II(A) by trading on the information. (Study Session 1, LOS 1.b)

10.6. **A** The large earnings restatement is certainly material information. Disclosing the information before the conference call does not make the information public even if several analysts overheard the information. Disclosing the information to her compliance officer also does not make the information public. Therefore, Bair has traded on the basis of material nonpublic information and is in violation of Standard II(A). (Study Session 1, LOS 1.b)

Sample Scoring Key: 3 points for each correct response.

QUESTION 11

Reference: Book 1, Study Session 1

Cross-reference to CFA Institute assigned reading: Readings 1 and 2

11.1. **A** Mackley has appropriately disclosed the referral arrangement to clients and prospects but the nature of the arrangement itself is a violation of Standard VII(A) Conduct as Members and Candidates in the CFA Program. According to this Standard, members and candidates are prohibited from activities that compromise the integrity of CFA Institute. Mackley has misused her authority to select companies to make presentations to her local society. She only selects Kern & Associates to make presentations and excludes their competitors in order to generate referrals for her business. This reflects poorly on the local society and CFA Institute. Mackley may have also violated Standard I(D) Misconduct by engaging in behavior that reflects poorly on her professional reputation. (Study Session 1, LOS 1.b)

11.2. **C** Welch violated Standard V(C) Record Retention by failing to maintain adequate records to support his investment recommendations. In the absence of other regulation, CFA Institute recommends keeping such records for a minimum of seven years. Certainly, one week is not an adequate record retention policy. Mackley violated Standard III(C) Suitability by purchasing the stock for all clients with a net worth greater than $6 million. It does not matter that the clients are later happy with the stock performance. Mackley should have evaluated the stock purchase for all of her accounts, not just the larger ones, in terms of each account's objectives and constraints as stated in their investment policy statements. (Study Session 1, LOS 1.b)

11.3. **C** According to Standard IV(B) Additional Compensation Arrangements, members and candidates are not to accept additional compensation (monetary or non-monetary) unless they obtain written consent from all parties, including their employer. The use of the condo, however, can be considered additional compensation and presents a potential conflict of interest, if Mackley agrees to the arrangement. Thus, it must be disclosed to the employer and written consent must be obtained from the employer. Standard I(B) Independence and Objectivity notes that client gifts must be disclosed to the employer before being accepted. (Study Session 1, LOS 1.b)

11.4. **C** According to Standard VII(B) Reference to CFA Institute, the CFA Designation, and the CFA Program, proper use of the designation would stipulate that CFA and Chartered Financial Analyst always be used as adjectives. Also, the designation may not be written in bold type. (Study Session 1, LOS 1.b)

11.5. **C** Mackley violated Standard VII(B) Reference to CFA Institute, the CFA Designation, and the CFA Program by linking her future investment performance to her status as a CFA charterholder. Mackley has not, however, violated the standard with her references to the CFA program and the examinations. (Study Session 1, LOS 1.b)

11.6. **C** According to Standard III(E) Preservation of Confidentiality, Mackley has a duty to keep information about her clients confidential, unless it involves illegal activities, in which case she may need to disclose the information to her supervisor, compliance officer, or regulatory authorities as is appropriate. She should not have divulged the inheritance to an outside contractor, especially since that individual has contacts with other management firms. (Study Session 1, LOS 1.b)

> Sample Scoring Key: 3 points for each correct response.

QUESTION 12

Reference: Book 5, Study Session 18
Book 2, Study Session 5

Cross-reference to CFA Institute assigned reading: Readings 22 and 48

12.1. **C** Firm B and Firm C both have a plan surplus. Both Firm A and Firm D are underfunded by $160 million, which represents 11% for A and over 18% for D.

Pension plan liabilities are similar to debt securities in that their present values fluctuate with interest rates. Plan D has only 25% of assets invested in fixed income securities. (75% in equities), so the plan assets of Firm D are sensitive to the systematic risk of equity markets to a greater degree than those of the other firms. (Study Session 5, LOS 22.a)

12.2. **C** Both of the statements have correct and incorrect portions, so the answer is C, neither is correct. Rose starts off with a correct statement, when he says that pension assets should be included in the firm's overall weighted average cost of capital (WACC). Since we use asset betas, however, the WACC usually decreases when we calculate the firm's overall WACC. The equity securities held as assets by the pension plan can have an average beta that is higher than the beta of the sponsoring firm's assets. However, the weighted average asset beta for the plan, assuming debt securities have zero betas, is usually less than that for the sponsoring firm's operating assets, so combining the firm's and plan's assets usually produces a lower WACC.

Boatman also starts out with a true statement when he says that pension plans usually hold long term bonds to match their pension liabilities. However, it is the proportion of equity securities in the plan's assets that drives the risk of the plan assets, not the proportion of debt (fixed income). The rest of his statements are correct.
(Study Session 5, LOS 22.b)

12.3. **B** Scenario B is the most likely scenario. Using an expanded balance sheet format, it can be seen that as pension plan risk increases, so does the total asset beta.

Under the assumption that the firm would like to keep its cost of equity capital constant, the firm must make changes in its capital structure on the right hand side of the balance sheet to accommodate the pension plan's increased allocation to equity. More specifically, to keep the equity beta constant, the firm must reduce its risk to its shareholders by reducing its financial leverage (debt). Thus it must use more equity capital, thereby decreasing its debt-to-equity ratio. (Study Session 5, LOS 22.c)

12.4. **C** To obtain the capital and income return, we must first calculate the capital employed (C_E), which utilizes the capital at the beginning of the period (C_0), the capital contribution, and the capital disbursement. If the capital contribution came at 0.52 into the quarter, then the manager had use of those funds for 0.48 of the quarter. We weight the capital contribution of $2,300,000 by this portion.

If the capital disbursement came at 0.74 into the quarter, then the manager lost use of these funds for 0.26 of the quarter. We weight the capital disbursement of $850,000 by 0.26 and subtract it as follows.

$$C_E = C_0 + \sum_{i=1}^{n}(CF_i \times w_i)$$

$$C_E = \$18,000,000 + \$2,300,000(0.48) - \$850,000(0.26) = \$18,883,000$$

To determine the capital return (R_C), we examine the capital gain or loss, capital expenditures, and sale of properties. Capital expenditures (E_C) are those used for improving a property and are subtracted because they will be reflected in the property's ending value and the manager should not receive credit for this additional value.

The proceeds from the sale of properties (S) are added in because the drop in ending property value from a sale should not be counted against a manager.

Using the provided figures:

$$R_C = \frac{MV_1 - MV_0 - E_C + S}{C_E}$$

$$R_C = \frac{\$20,200,000 - \$19,100,000 - \$1,000,000 + \$1,820,000}{\$18,883,000} = 10.2\%$$

To determine the income return (R_i), we use the investment income (INC) minus the non-recoverable expenses (E_{NR}) minus debt interest (INT_D) minus property taxes (T_P). Essentially we subtract the cost of doing business on a periodic basis from investment income as below.

$$R_i = \frac{INC - E_{NR} - INT_D - T_P}{C_E}$$

$$= \frac{\$58,000 - \$178,000 - \$152,000 - \$219,000}{\$18,883,000} = -2.6\%$$

The total return for the quarter is the sum of the capital return and the income return:

$$R_T = R_C + R_i = 10.2\% - 2.6\% = 7.6\% \text{ (Study Session 18, LOS 48.p)}$$

12.5. **A** Comment 1 is correct. The general provisions require that valuations take place monthly until 2010. After 2010, valuations must also occur anytime a large external cash flow occurs. For real estate, valuations should take place annually until 2008, after which quarterly valuations are required. For private equity, valuations should take place annually.

Comment 2 is incorrect. The performance standards in the general provisions allow either gross or net of fees returns to be presented. The standards for real estate do not differ from the general provisions in this regard. For private equity, both net-of-fees and gross-of-fees returns must be presented in the case of the composite since-inception internal rate of return. (Study Session 18, LOS 48.q)

12.6. **C** Comment 1 is incorrect. It is true that the general provisions for GIPS make the verification of GIPS compliance by an outside third party voluntary and that real estate must be valued by an outside trained professional at least every three years.

However, there is no requirement that the valuation of private equity be performed by an outside third party. It is the case that the valuation must be performed in a professional manner by experienced individuals under the supervision of senior management.

Comment 2 is incorrect. Although both income and capital gains are required in the *calculation* of returns under all GIPS provisions, *presentation* of both is not required under the general provisions. For real estate, it is required that both the capital return and income return be disclosed. Note that they must sum to the total return.

In the case of private equity, the income return per se is not required to be disclosed, but the firm must present the values for the following: paid-in-capital; total invested capital; and cumulative distributions to date. The following multiples must also be presented: total value to paid-in-capital; cumulative distributions to date to paid-in-capital; and residual value to paid-in-capital. (Study Session 18, LOS 48.q)

Sample Scoring Key: 3 points for each correct response.

QUESTION 13

Reference: Book 3, Study Sessions 9 and 10
Book 4, Study Session 15

Cross-reference to CFA Institute assigned reading: Readings 28, 30, and 43

13.1. **B** Price of bond in one year: N = 19 × 2 = 38; PMT = 7 / 2 = 3.5; I/Y = 8 / 2 = 4;
FV = 100; CPT → PV = −90.32

Value of coupons at end of one year: N = 1 × 2 = 2; PMT = 7 / 2 = 3.5; I/Y = 8 / 2 = 4;
PV = 0; CPT → FV = −7.14

The semiannual return is the rate of return between today and the accumulated value one year from now:

N = 2; PMT = 0; PV = −100; FV = (90.32 + 7.14) = 97.46; CPT → I/Y = −1.28%

The bond equivalent yield is −1.28% × 2 = −2.56%. (Study Session 9, LOS 28.e)

13.2. **B** In the first sentence of the first statement, two of the three statements are correct. The repo rate is directly related to the maturity of the repo (the repo term) and inversely related to the quality of the collateral. The longer the repo term, the higher the repo rate and as the quality of the collateral increases, the repo rate decreases. Although the maturity of the collateral is considered in determining the quality of the collateral, however, it does not act as a separate factor in determining the repo rate. The last part of the first statement is correct.

The first sentence in the second statement is correct, but the second sentence is incorrect. If the availability of the collateral is limited, the repo rate will be lower, not higher. This is because the lender may be willing to accept a lower rate in order to obtain a security they need to make delivery on another agreement. (Study Session 10, LOS 30.b)

13.3. **B** The gross profit on the portfolio is: $200 million × 8% = $16 million.

The cost of borrowed funds is: $60 million × 3% = $1.8 million.

The net profit on the portfolio is: $16 million − $1.8 million = $14.2 million.

The return on the equity invested (i.e., the portfolio) is thus: $14.2 / $140 = 10.14%.

Alternatively, the problem can be solved using:

$$R_p = R_i + [(B / E) \times (R_i - c)]$$

where:
R_p = return on portfolio
R_i = return on invested assets
B = amount of leverage
E = amount of equity invested
c = cost of borrowed funds

Using the figures above: 8% + [(60 / 140) × (8% − 3%)] = 10.14%. (Study Session 10, LOS 30.a)

13.4. **C** The duration is calculated with the following formula:

$$D_p = \frac{D_i I - D_B B}{E}$$

where :
D_p = duration of portfolio
D_i = duration of invested assets
I = amount of invested funds
B = amount of leverage
E = amount of equity invested

Using the values in the problem:

$$D_p = \frac{(7.2)200 - (0.8)60}{140} = 9.9$$

(Study Session 10, LOS 30.a)

13.5. **C** Both statements are incorrect. It is true that portfolio managers, especially active managers, complain that using variance and standard deviation to calculate Sharpe ratios biases the results, because the variance includes returns in excess of the hurdle rate (i.e., positive outcomes). The only false part of the first statement is that semi-variance is easy to calculate. Because of the difficulties of calculating all the variances and correlations, neither regular variance nor semi-variance is easily calculated for large bond portfolios.

Although much of the second statement is true, shortfall risk is effectively the same thing as VAR (sort of). The output from a VAR calculation is the maximum loss at a given probability. In other words, you specify the probability and VAR provides the amount of loss. With shortfall risk, you provide the amount of loss (or other target amount or return) and shortfall risk provides the probability. They are both deficient in that they do not provide a measure of the magnitude of potential catastrophic losses. To help compensate for this deficiency in VAR, managers sometimes calculate tail value at risk (TVAR) which is VAR plus the expected value in the lower tail. (Study Session 10, LOS 30.c)

13.6. **C** Castillo is incorrect. To synthetically refinance Shaifer's fixed rate euro debt of 9.5%, Shaifer should buy a receiver swaption. If Euribor falls below the swap fixed rate of 7.60%, Shaifer will exercise the swaption and pay the lower floating rate while receiving 7.60%. In net, they would pay Euribor plus 1.9% (9.5% + Euribor – 7.6%). In net, they would pay a floating rate, which would be 7.8% in one year, given the projected Euribor of 5.9% in one year. Note: The terms "receiver" and "payer" refer to the pay fixed arm of the swap. A receiver swaption, therefore, is an option to enter a swap as the receive-fixed counterparty.

So Diaz is incorrect because the effective rate is not 7.5% in one year. In essence, Shaifer has called in the old debt at 9.5% and synthetically refinanced its debt to a floating rate, which will be 7.8% in one year. (Study Session 15, LOS 43.h)

Sample Scoring Key: 3 points for each correct response.

QUESTION 14

Reference: Book 3, Study Sessions 9 and 10

Cross-reference to CFA Institute assigned reading: Readings 28, 29, and 30

14.1. **A** Truxel is correct as international bond portfolio duration management has been made easier through the increasing availability of fixed income derivatives. Timberlake is also correct in saying that the European Monetary Union has made it easier to rotate across sectors, because there are now more non-governmental bonds available internationally. (Study Session 10, LOS 30.h)

14.2. **C** Any duration mismatch is considered a large factor mismatch, so Truxel is incorrect. Timberlake is correct as credit analysis is the most important determinant of relative bond performance. (Study Session 9, LOS 28.b)

14.3. **A** If there is a parallel shift in the yield curve of 60 basis points for Treasury yields, the approximate percent change is the modified duration of the portfolio times 0.6%. The modified duration of the portfolio is a weighted average of the individual sector durations: $(0.12 \times 5.3) + (0.3 \times 5.4) + (0.3 \times 5.5) + (0.28 \times 5.0) = 5.3$. The modified duration of $5.3 \times 0.6\% = 3.2\%$ change in the portfolio value. (Study Session 9, LOS 28.g)

14.4. **A** The spread durations for non-Treasuries are the same as their effective durations. The calculation and resulting change from a uniform widening of 60 bps in all spreads is the same as if the yield curve had shifted 60 bps with no change in the spreads. (Study Session 9, LOS 28.h)

14.5. **B** To determine which sector could generate the greatest tracking error, calculate the contribution to the portfolio's duration for each sector and do the same for the index. The sector whose duration contribution deviates the most from the benchmark will contribute the most to potential tracking error. The contribution to duration is just the proportion invested in each sector times the sector's duration. For example, for AAA bonds in the portfolio, it is $0.12 \times 5.3 = 0.636$. For AAA bonds in the index, it is $0.35 \times 5.3 = 1.855$. The discrepancy between the portfolio and the index for this sector is $0.636 - 1.855 = -1.219$. This is the largest absolute difference of all the sectors. The calculations for all the sectors are as follows:

Contribution to Effective Duration			
	Portfolio	Index	Difference
AAA	0.636	1.855	−1.219
AA	1.620	1.620	0.000
A	1.650	1.375	0.275
BBB	1.400	0.500	0.900
TOTAL	5.306	5.350	

(Study Session 9, LOS 28.h)

14.6. **C** The following are rationales for trading in the secondary bond market:
- Yield/spread pickup trades.
- Credit-upside trades.
- Credit-defense trades.
- New issue swaps.
- Sector-rotation trades.
- Curve-adjustment trades.
- Structure trades.
- Cash flow reinvestment.

Seasonality is a secondary trading constraint (i.e., reason for not trading). (Study Session 10, LOS 29.e)

> Sample Grading Key: 3 points for correct response.

QUESTION 15

Reference: Book 3, Study Session 10

Cross-reference to CFA Institute assigned reading: Reading 30

15.1. **B** Because interest rates are higher in Great Britain, we know by covered interest rate parity that its currency must trade at a forward discount. To determine the exact forward discount, we calculate a simple percentage change using the formula:

$$f_{d,f} = \frac{F - S_0}{S_0}$$

where :
$f_{d,f}$ = forward premium or discount for currency f in terms of d
F = forward rate
S_0 = spot rate

In the formula, be sure to put the currency that you want to make a statement about (whether it is at a premium or discount) in the denominator. Here we are discussing the £.

$$f_{d,f} = \frac{C\$1.60 - C\$1.75}{C\$1.75} = -8.57\%$$

So the British pound is trading at an 8.57% forward discount relative to the Canadian dollar. Note: Since the current 1-year rates in Great Britain and Canada are 11% and 4%, respectively, we would expect the £ to depreciate relative to the $C. (Study Session 10, LOS 30.j)

15.2. **B** Covered interest arbitrage will assure that the forward rate given by the interest rate parity relationship will prevail. The interest rate parity condition that expresses the relationship between the Canadian dollar and the British pound is expressed as follows:

$$F = S_0 \times \frac{(1 + c_d)}{(1 + c_f)}$$

where:
F = forward exchange rate between the Canadian dollar and British pound
S_0 = spot exchange rate between Canadian dollars and the British pound
c_d = the cash rate in the domestic currency (here the Canadian dollar)
c_f = the cash rate in the foreign currency (here the British pound)

Using the information provided and covered interest rate parity, the forward exchange rate between C$ and £ must be:

$F_{C\$,£}$ = 1.75 [(1 + 0.04) / (1 + 0.11)] = 1.6396 C$/£

(Study Session 10, LOS 30.j)

15.3. **B** Rolle should recommend investment in the Tatehiki bond if a hedged position will be taken. The easiest way to make this determination is to examine their excess returns, which is the bond return minus the risk-free rate in the foreign country.

The Knauff company bond return: 8.0% – 5.0% = 3.0%.

The Tatehiki company bond return: 6.0% – 2.0% = 4.0%.

Note that we assume both bonds have similar risk and maturities so the decision is based solely on the returns. (Study Session 10, LOS 30.j)

15.4. **C** The Knauf bond promises a return of 8% in euros. Since you hedge using current forward rates, which would incorporate the expected 0.2% depreciation in the euro relative to the dollar (the euro will be trading at a forward discount of 4.8 – 5 = –0.2%), you effectively lock in the current forward discount. The expected return to U.S. investors would be 7.8%, the expected return on the bond (8%) less the forward currency differential (–0.2%).

The unhedged return for the Tatehiki bond is its return in yen of 6.0% plus the expected 2.0% appreciation in the yen geometrically linked which equals (1.06)(1.02) – 1 = 8.1%. (Study Session 10, LOS 30.j)

15.5. **A** The hedge is best described as a currency proxy hedge. In a proxy hedge the manager enters a forward contract between the domestic currency and a second foreign currency that is correlated with the first foreign currency. Proxy hedges are utilized when forward contracts on the first foreign currency are not actively traded or hedging the first foreign currency is relatively expensive. Notice that in currency hedging, the proxy hedge is what we would usually refer to as a cross hedge in most other financial transactions. (Study Session 10, LOS 30.j)

15.6. **B** The best hedge of the Crawfordville floating rate CD is an interest rate cap. An interest rate cap is a series of interest rate calls that put a cap on the cost of a liability. If interest rates rise above the cap strike rate, the cap will provide a payment to the bank that mitigates their increased cost of paying out interest on the CD. If interest rates fall, the bank will let the cap expire worthless and benefit from the lower rate. The floor provides a minimum return on a held loan and would not hedge the bank's floating rate CD liability.

The best hedge for Ryder's portfolio of fixed coupon rate bonds would be a protective put on the T-bond futures contract. The purchase of a put hedges a bond investment because the put will rise in value when interest rates rise. If interest rates fall, the bond investment will increase in value and the manager will let the put expire worthless. The cost of the put will however reduce the manager's return.

In a covered call, the manager sells a call to earn extra income. If interest rates rise, the loss on the bond will be buffered by the income from the sale of the call. However, the call does not provide downside protection as strong as that from the protective put. (Study Session 10, LOS 30.e)

Sample Scoring Key: 3 points for each correct response.

QUESTION 16

Reference: Book 4, Study Session 13

Cross-reference to CFA Institute assigned reading: Reading 36

16.1. **B** A representative set of checkpoints for selecting an alternative investment manager would include assessing the market opportunity, the investment process, the organization, the people, the terms and structure, the ancillary service providers, and the documents. Low market efficiency is a common feature of many alternative investments. In fact, the reason that alternative investments present market opportunities is that their markets are not efficient. (Study Session 13, LOS 36.b)

16.2. **B** Historically, private equity returns have generally been higher than stock returns over most periods. Since a source of the return is often associated with IPOs and other market activity, the returns tend to be correlated with stock returns. This lowers the amount of diversification private equity can offer a standard stock and bond portfolio. (Study Session 13, LOS 36.d)

16.3. **A** The portfolio allocation to this class should be 5% or less with a plan to keep the money invested for 7–10 years and not 5 years as stated in the vignette. Five to ten investments is a recommended range to achieve diversification within the private equity investments. Since five investments times $5 million is less than $30 million (5% of the portfolio), the recommended size is appropriate. (Study Session 13, LOS 36.d)

16.4. **C** They were both correct. It is true that private equity benchmarks suffer from infrequent repricing. It is also true that many private equity investors create their own benchmarks. (Study Session 13, LOS 36.e)

16.5. **A** In contrast to VC funds, buyout funds usually have higher leverage, earlier and steadier cash flows, less error in the measurement of returns, less frequent losses, and less upside potential. These differences are the natural consequence of the buyout funds purchasing entities in later stages of development or even established companies where the risks are lower. (Study Session 13, LOS 36.i)

16.6. **C** Farmington indicated that the clients have not expressed a concern even when the market and portfolio have not performed well. This indicates that decision risk, the risk of the client irrationally requesting a change in strategy because of recent investment losses, may not be an issue. Tax issues are always important. Since Carnegie will be investing in private equity, he certainly needs to find out about other closely held investments the Lewis family holds. Finally, the horizon is important, and it is especially important because Farmington indicated a five-year horizon for the private equity investments. That is too short for this category of asset. (Study Session 13, LOS 36.c)

> Sample Scoring Key: 3 points for each correct response.

QUESTION 17

Reference: Book 1, Study Session 4

Cross-reference to CFA Institute assigned reading: Reading 15

17.1. **A** A flat tax structure on income, dividends, and capital gains can be best classified as a flat and heavy tax regime. Note that a common feature of this type of regime is the favorable treatment of interest income. A flat and light regime would extend the favorable treatment to dividends and capital gains. (Study Session 4, LOS 15.a)

17.2. **B** Given a pretax return of 7%, an annual tax rate of 25%, and annual compounding:

$$FV = 1,000,000 \, [1 + 0.07 \, (1 - 0.25)]^{15} = 2,154,426$$

(Study Session 4, LOS 15.b)

17.3. **C** The reduction in portfolio risk can be expected to reduce expected returns. Since her investment objective is to accumulate assets that will generate income equal to her wage income, the investment horizon will increase. When taxes are paid periodically during the holding period, a longer investment horizon will increase tax drag, and the tax drag will exceed the applicable tax rate. (Study Session 4, LOS 15.e)

17.4. **B** Given a pretax return of 12%, a 10-year holding period, a tax rate of 35%, and a cost basis of $250,000:

$$FV = 250,000 \, [(1 + 0.12)^{10} \, (1 - 0.35) + 0.35] = 592,200$$

$$gain = 592,200 - 250,000 = 342,200$$

Note that solution A is approximately the value that would be derived if the last term in the brackets were left out. Solution C ignores the cost basis in calculating the gain. (Study Session 4, LOS 15.b)

17.5. **B** The gross sale proceeds, tax, $ tax drag, and % tax drag are:

$$FV = 250,000[(1 + 0.12)^{10}] = 776,462$$

$$Tax = (776,462 - 250,000)0.35 = 184,262$$

$$TaxDrag = \left(\frac{184,262}{(776,462 - 250,000)} \right) = 0.35$$

Because this is an accrual tax situation, the tax drag is equal to the tax rate of 35%. (Study Session 4, LOS 15.b)

17.6. **A** The accrual equivalent after tax return is: $R_{AE} = \sqrt[9]{\dfrac{150,000}{60,000}} - 1 = 0.1071$

Note that 17.7% is the accrual equivalent tax rate (=1-(10.7/13.0)), but this is not the value that we are looking for in the question. (Study Session 4, LOS 15.c)

Sample Scoring Key: 3 points for each correct response.

QUESTION 18

Reference: Book 4, Study Sessions 14 and 15

Cross-reference to CFA Institute assigned reading: Readings 39 and 42

18.1. **B** Reneau is correct. Reneau is describing a bull call strategy which profits when the stock market rises. The bull call strategy involves purchasing one call with a low exercise price and selling the other with a high exercise price. The beginning stock price is usually below the two call strike prices. The maximum loss is the price of the low exercise price call minus the price of the high exercise price call.

Belanger is incorrect. Although a put and call of the same maturity and same exercise price could be used here, the correct strategy would be to sell the two options, not purchase them. Belanger is suggesting a long straddle where the better strategy in a flat market is a short straddle. However, if the stock market does rise, this strategy would have potentially unlimited losses, due to the call that was sold. An alternative strategy to exploit expectations of a stable stock market would be a long butterfly strategy. (Study Session 15, LOS 42.b)

18.2. **C** Reneau's intended strategy is a bull call spread. She should buy the 35 call and sell the 40 call for a net cost of $3.00. The maximum loss for a bull call spread is when it expires out of the money. In that case, the investor loses the initial investment, in this case $3.00. The breakeven for a bull call spread can be expressed as $X_L + C_L - C_H = \$35.00 + \$4.50 - \$1.50 = \$38.00$. If the stock closes at $38.00, the investor gains $3.00 on the call with the low exercise price; the call with the higher exercise price expires worthless. The $3.00 profit on the low exercise price call offsets the initial cost of $3.00. (Study Session 15, LOS 42.b)

18.3. **C** The option strategy Belanger is describing is a long straddle. Since the stock price will likely increase or decrease by a relatively large amount, the strategy would be to buy a straddle (i.e., a put and a call of the same strike price). The 40 put/calls offer the lowest cost straddle at a total cost of $5. At a stock price of $45, the call payoff is $5 and the strategy breaks even. (Study Session 15, LOS 42.b)

18.4. **A** The option strategy Reneau is describing is a butterfly spread. In this case, a butterfly spread is constructed by buying the 35 call and the 45 call, and selling two 40 calls for a net cost of 2.50. The maximum gain is calculated as $X_M - X_L - C_L + 2C_M - C_H = \$40.00 - \$35.00 - \$4.50 + 2(\$1.50) - \$1.00 = \$2.50$. Note that this is when the stock price is equal to the middle exercise price ($40.00). The maximum loss is calculated as $C_L - 2C_M + C_H = \$4.50 - 2(\$1.50) + 1.00 = \$2.50$. The maximum is incurred if the stock price closes below X_L (i.e., $35.00) or above X_H (i.e., $45.00). (Study Session 15, LOS 42.b)

18.5. **B** Reneau is correct and Belanger is incorrect. Reneau is describing a binary credit option (not a credit spread option as Belanger states) with a predetermined payout. Binary credit options can take the form of either puts or calls. (Study Session 14, LOS 39.k)

18.6. **C** Reneau and Belanger are both correct. Credit options written on an underlying asset directly protect against declines in the value of the asset. Credit spread options protect against adverse movements of the credit spread over a referenced benchmark, such as a Treasury security. (Study Session 14, LOS 39.k)

> Sample Scoring Key: 3 points for each correct response.

QUESTION 19

Reference: Book 5, Study Session 16

Cross-reference to CFA Institute assigned reading: Reading 45

19.1. **C** In a market expected to increase in relatively constant fashion, constant proportion portfolio insurance will outperform the other strategies. In a constant proportion strategy, a fixed proportion (m) of the cushion (= assets – floor value) is invested in stocks. CPPI refers to a constant proportion strategy with m > 1. Buy and hold is equivalent to the constant proportion strategy with m = 1, so its performance would be good, but not as good. (Study Session 16, LOS 45.h)

19.2. **B** In a market expected to oscillate, constant mix strategies (fixed percentage allocation to stocks) outperform the others, since they involve buying/selling stocks when prices fall/ rise. (Study Session 16, LOS 45.h)

19.3. **C** Although CPPI strategies offer downside protection, it is their convex nature that provides it. Statements A and B are correct. (Study Session 16, LOS 45.h)

19.4. **C** The portfolio has increased from $1,000,000 to $1,150,000, representing a 20% increase ($120,000) in equities and a $30,000 increase in debt and cash ($1,150,000 – $720,000 = $430,000). Since equities now represent 62.6% (= 720,000 / 1,150,000) of the portfolio and their strategic allocation is 60%, Tratman should take no action. (Study Session 16, LOS 45.f)

19.5. **C** This statement is too general. The need to rebalance is determined by several factors, including the volatility of the assets and the correlations among the classes. For example, if the assets in the portfolio are not overly volatile and are fairly highly correlated, monitoring more frequently than on an annual basis may be a waste of time and money. (Study Session 16, LOS 45.e)

19.6. **B** Illiquid assets generally have higher costs associated with buying and selling. In that case, too tight of a tolerance band (i.e., corridor) could require high costs. The investor should always strive for a happy medium between the need to rebalance and the associated costs. Answers A and C would support wider corridors. (Study Session 16, LOS 45.f)

Sample Scoring Key: 3 points for each correct response.

Exam 2
Morning Session Answers

QUESTION 1

Reference: Book 1, Study Session 4, LOS 14.j,k

Cross-reference to CFA Institute assigned reading: Reading 14

Answer for Question 1

		Investment Policy Statement for the Smythes
Objectives	Risk Tolerance	**For the Exam:** Ability: Below average. Willingness: Below average. Overall: Below average. **Discussion:** For either ability or willingness start at average and then adjust according to statements or circumstances. In this case the ability for the portfolio to tolerate risk is rather straight forward. Of their total annual expenses (including taxes on Barney's salary) of $165,188, the portfolio must provide $116,438. This means the portfolio has significant liquidity needs so we drop its ability to tolerate risk a "notch" to below average. When the client makes statements about risk, regardless of the statement, this usually indicates a focus on risk and below average willingness. This is confirmed by their desire for no debt. Also, if the client makes statements about prior risky investments, this would indicate below average tolerance. Take the client's actions into consideration, however. For example, you can almost totally ignore direct statements about their own risk aversion, because they will often say one thing and do another. You might see them say something like, "I have average risk aversion," but you notice that they have made regular speculative investments in the past. In this case the client's actions speak much louder than his words. In this case the clients' willingness and ability agree, so the overall risk tolerance is easy. Whenever there is a discrepancy between willingness and ability, however, always select the more conservative for the overall risk tolerance and suggest counseling to reconcile the difference. For example, assume the Smythes had above average willingness to tolerate risk and their ability was below average. You would still have selected below average for the overall statement. You would have also written, "Counseling is suggested to reconcile the difference." Never, however, assume anything that has not been stated or implied in the case vignette. For example, even if the client's risk aversion is greater than their ability to tolerate risk, do not assume the counseling has already occurred and they have agreed to the higher level of risk.

Objectives	Return	For the Exam:
		Cash inflows for the coming year: Salary $48,750 Cash outflows: Taxes on salary $12,188 Living expenses $153,000 Total outflows: ($165,188) Net ($116,438) Required after-tax **real** rate of return = $116,438 / $3,750,000 = 0.02117 = 3.1% Required after-tax real rate of return = 3.1% Plus: Annual inflation rate = 2.0% Required after-tax **nominal** rate of return = 5.1% **Discussion:** Over the coming year, Smythe will draw a salary of $48,750 and pay $12,188 in income taxes. Living expenses are given to us at $150,000 for the previous year, so for the coming year they should be 2% higher at $153,000. Total outflows for the coming year, including taxes, are estimated at $165,188 and their only inflow is Smythe's $48,750 salary. This leaves a shortfall of $116,438 that must be made up by the portfolio. To pay the $116,438, the $3,750,000 portfolio ($1,250,000 + $2,500,000) must earn 3.1% after-tax. To maintain the purchasing power of the portfolio principal (the $3,750,000), we must add inflation for a total after-tax nominal return of 5.1%. Note 1: Alternatively you could have compounded by the rate of inflation and arrived at a required after-tax nominal return of $(1.031)(1.02) - 1 = 5.16\%$. Unless you are directed to present the answer in a specific form, either way would be acceptable on the exam. Note 2: The vignette may or may not state that you must protect the principal (i.e., maintain purchasing power). To stress the point, I deliberately left out the statement in this case. On the exam, always assume you are to protect the principal unless you are specifically told otherwise.

| Constraints | Time Horizon | **For the Exam:**

Long-term, 2-stage time horizon: pre-retirement 25 years; retirement 15 to 20 years. There could be another stage consisting of the children's college years.

Discussion:

The most common time horizon statement for individual investors is: "Long-term time horizon consisting of two stages, pre-retirement and retirement." You will probably be able to note the number of pre-retirement years based on the client's current age and desired retirement age. In this case, we are told Barney is 40 and plans to retire at 65, so the pre-retirement stage is 25 years. The number of retirement years is only a guess, so putting a likely range is appropriate by assuming the client will live to 80 or 85.

The children provide a bit of a twist, in that we are not given any costs for college or even the number of college years. It is usually acceptable to state that another stage coinciding with the college years is possible. In our scenario, the children will complete college before the Smythes retire, so their college years will actually divide Barney and Heather's pre-retirement stage into three stages. The first stage lasts about six years until the first child starts college. The second stage consists of about six years until both children have finished college. The third stage consists of about 13 years until retirement. In this way, the children's college years could actually divide the Smythes' overall time horizon into four stages. To avoid this situation, prior exam questions have had the children graduating at the same time as the clients retire. |
| | Liquidity | **For the Exam:**

$116,438 of the Smythes' living expenses in the coming year and sufficient cash for emergencies.

Discussion:

For the liquidity portion of the IPS, include only those items that the portfolio must pay. Here, the Smythes' portfolio must meet a large portion of their living expenses ($116,438 of $165,188), so you state that. Also, you should probably list that a certain minimal amount should be held in cash or cash equivalents to meet emergency needs. This is usually six months living expenses. (That is obviously more important when the client's salary pays most or all of the annual expenses.)

This would also be the place to mention any charitable gifts the clients would like to pay out during the coming year. (None in this case.) |

Constraints (cont.)	Legal/ Regulatory	**For the Exam:** There are no special legal or regulatory issues. **Discussion:** Even though there are dependents/heirs, there is no indication in the case that the Smythes have a desire to establish trusts or engage in other succession planning issues. Consequently, you do not have to address any. Doing so would be an example of adding material that will not increase your score, and could cost you points if incorrect.
	Taxes	**For the Exam:** The Smythes are taxed as individuals, so all investment decisions should consider tax effects. **Discussion:** • We are not provided with any specific information, but it appears that they may have to pay taxes on portfolio income and capital gains. • The degree to which the assets are subject to taxes depends upon the extent to which they are held in tax-sheltered accounts. • Any investment actions must take tax status into consideration.
	Unique Circumstances	**For the Exam:** There are no material unique circumstances. **Discussion:** Other than items addressed at other points in this IPS, there are no unique circumstances that warrant consideration from a financial planning standpoint.

Sample Scoring Key:
2 points for each of the three risk components (ability, willingness, overall).
2 points for each of the return components (real = 3.1%, nominal = 5.1%).
2 points for each constraint.

QUESTION 2

Reference: Book 1, Study Session 3, LOS 7
Book 2, Study Session 5, LOS 20.b,c

Cross-reference to CFA Institute assigned reading: Readings 7 and 20

A. i. **For the Exam:**

Elliot is exhibiting overconfidence.

Discussion:

Elliot's over reliance on his personal belief that there is a high probability of interest rate increases ignores historical evidence that interest rate changes are very difficult if not impossible to predict with that degree of accuracy. Elliot is more than likely overestimating the probability that his analysis will prove correct.

ii. **For the Exam:**

The return objective is excessive, relative to the level of risk that is appropriate for the fund.

Discussion:

Elliot's plan to solve the underfunded status of the plan by investing in high return securities is ill-advised. It requires the plan to invest in high-risk securities to obtain the high returns. Given the current plan funding status, retired to active lives ratio, and the demographic profile of the workforce, the plan's ability to bear risk is below average. Also, Elliot is considering only the present value of the liabilities when interest rates increase, where increasing rates can have a dampening effect on equity returns. Hence, the return objectives are excessive relative to the level of risk that is appropriate for the fund.

iii. **For the Exam:**

The investment of plan assets for the stated purpose of bolstering profitability is inappropriate, and may constitute a violation of Elliot's fiduciary responsibilities under ERISA.

Discussion:

ERISA requires that pension plan assets be invested in the sole interest of plan beneficiaries. Failure to do so most likely constitutes a breach of fiduciary duty. Moreover, the financial implications of such an objective suggest an increase in the uncertainty about the future funding status of the plan. For both reasons, Elliot's investment plan is inappropriate.

Answer for Question 2-B

	Investment Policy Statement for Matrix Corporation
Objectives	Risk tolerance: **For the Exam:** Below average. **Discussion:** There are three relevant pieces of information: • The plan is underfunded. • The age of active employees is high. • The ratio of retired to active lives is high. All of these factors suggest that ability to bear risk is below average. Note: Exam questions do not ordinarily ask for willingness to tolerate risk for an institutional investor.
	Return: **For the Exam:** Return sufficient to meet plan obligations on an inflation-adjusted basis. **Discussion:** The actual return requirement depends on the plan's funded status, the ability of the sponsor to make contributions, characteristics of the workforce, and the accumulation of plan obligations (e.g., growth in firm size with accompanying growth in employment). If the plan is fully funded, the *minimum* return requirement is the discount rate an actuary applies to the plan's obligations (liabilities). The sponsoring firm may wish to set a return requirement above the minimum as insurance against possible future declines in returns or expected increases in pension obligations and to minimize the probability of future firm contributions. For example, if the firm's workforce has an average age that is significantly below the industry average, we would say the plan has a longer than usual time horizon with increased ability to tolerate risk. In that case, management could set a return requirement significantly above the minimum. Likewise, an above-average age translates into a shortened time horizon with accompanying reduced ability to tolerate risk. In that case, the plan would probably only strive to just meet the minimum required return. The bottom line is that the return requirement must be aligned with the plan's ability to tolerate risk. Increasing the required return minimizes the probability that the sponsor will have to make special contributions to the plan, but the higher return requirement could violate the plan's ability to tolerate risk.

Answer for Question 2-C

Time horizon	**For the Exam:** Average employee age > industry average. Time horizon shorter than average. **Discussion:** The principal factor that dictates the time horizon for the pension plan is the average age of active employees. This factor suggests the time horizon is shorter than average. Also, with a low active to retired lives ratio, the firm will probably need to make a special contribution to the plan. This is another indication of a shortened time horizon.
Liquidity	**For the Exam:** Plan liquidity requirements are high. **Discussion:** • The plan funding status and the ratio of active to retired lives suggest that income on plan assets is not far in excess of current benefits, and may be less. • The average age of current employees indicates the income to benefits situation is unlikely to improve dramatically. Plan liquidity requirements are high and will more than likely remain high.
Legal/ Regulatory	**For the Exam:** As a pension plan, significant legal and regulatory requirements apply. **Discussion:** In the vast majority of countries where they exist, pension funds are subject to a legal and regulatory framework. Under U.S. law, Matrix's defined benefit plan must conform to ERISA regulations. • Plan assets must be invested for the sole benefit of plan participants. • Pension fund trustees have fiduciary responsibilities. • Standards of prudence and investment restrictions apply.
Taxes	**For the Exam:** Pension plans in the United States are not subject to taxes on investment income. **Discussion:** • Matrix's defined benefit plan is not taxable under U.S. law, so taxes on securities income and capital gains are not an investment consideration from the plan's perspective. • The benefits received by retirees may be subject to taxes.

Unique circumstances	**For the Exam:** High average employee age; low active to retired lives ratio; significantly underfunded. **Discussion:** Unique circumstances are those that are at least somewhat uncommon but have an impact on the clients' risk and/or return objectives and possibly constraints. For example, a university endowment might have to make a large cash outlay to cover costs of a new building. Even if the outlay isn't significant compared to the size of the fund and, therefore, doesn't affect the funds' required return or risk tolerance, it should be stated under liquidity requirements and unique circumstances. Other examples included an underfunded pension plan or a pension plan with a very low active to retired lives ratio, as in this case.

Sample Scoring Key:
A. 2 points for each critique of Elliot's statement.
B. 6 points for identifying relevant return objectives, 6 points for identifying relevant risk arguments.
C. 2 points for each constraint.

QUESTION 3

Reference: Book 3, Study Session 9, LOS 28.b
Book 3, Study Session 12, LOS 34.a
Book 4, Study Session 13, LOS 36.e

Cross-reference to CFA Institute assigned reading: Readings 28, 34, and 36

Answer for Question 3

Comment	Correct or incorrect? (circle one)	Justification
"The popularity bias can cause problems for measuring value-weighted hedge fund benchmark performance. The popularity bias argues that out-performing hedge funds as well as hedge fund styles tend to attract additional funding, so as they grow in popularity their performance tends to have a greater and greater impact on the value-weighted index's measured performance. This creates a double impact on the value-weighted hedge fund index return; the individual funds have good returns, and their increasing size means they have a greater weight in the index. The result is that the index's return has an upward bias. This bias, however, can be counteracted by utilizing two indices, one long and one short. Since most hedge fund managers attempt to generate alpha through both long and short positions, they can have a net zero weight or even a net negative weight. A single, long-only benchmark will not capture the performance of both strategies."	Incorrect	**For the Exam:** Solution to popularity bias is an equally-weighted index. **Discussion:** The discussions of popularity bias and long-short investing and indices are correct, but they are not related. Popularity bias can lead one or a few funds or styles to dominate a value-weighted hedge fund index, and investors must be aware of this. One alternative is using an equally-weighted index, but equally-weighted indices are not usually rebalanced often and are, therefore, not considered investable. It is also true that hedge fund managers often utilize both long and short trading to generate alpha. One possible solution, since the managers often have zero or even negative net weights, is using two separate indices.

"If an investor is averse to market value risk, the bond benchmark used should have a long maturity so they can lock in a yield to maturity."	Incorrect	**For the Exam:** Long maturity bond portfolios have more market value risk. Should use short maturity. **Discussion:** The market values of long maturity (i.e., long duration) portfolios have more interest rate risk than shorter maturity portfolios. Therefore, the greater the investor's aversion to market risk, the shorter the appropriate maturity of the portfolio and the selected benchmark.
"The recommended solution to the 'free float' problem in international markets is to determine the amount of shares to be floated by an issuer in the upcoming year and use that to recalculate the issuer's weight in market capitalization weighted indices."	Incorrect	**For the Exam:** The free float problem refers to the fact that many firms have shares that are closely held or otherwise not available for public trading. Only the values of firms' freely traded shares should be included in an index. **Discussion:** The "free float" problem refers to the fact that many firms have shares that are closely held and not available for public trading. When calculating the capitalization of firms in a cap-weighted index, only those shares that are freely traded should be included. However, the determination of the free float is often difficult. This problem is particularly acute in emerging markets.
"For bond investors such as foundations who desire a stable stream of income, long-term bond benchmarks should be used."	Correct	**For the Exam:** No explanation required. **Discussion:** If the client is dependent on cash flows from the portfolio, those cash flows should be dependable. Long term bonds offer the investor a longer and more certain income stream. Investors desiring a stable, long-term cash flow should invest in longer-term bonds and utilize long-term benchmarks.

Sample Scoring Key:
1 point for identifying each statement as correct or incorrect.
2 points for justifying why the statement is incorrect.
0 points possible if the correct/incorrect decision is wrong.

QUESTION 4

Reference: Book 2, Study Session 6, LOS 23.b,c

Cross-reference to CFA Institute assigned reading: Reading 23

Answer for Question 4-A

Comment	Is the statement susceptible to problems in using economic data to forecast? (circle one)	If yes, identify and describe the problem
"The stock returns in emerging markets are quite impressive. The mean returns are quite high and the risk is lower than many investors expect. Consider the example of the country of Yalewian. An index of Yalewian stocks had high returns for the period January 1, 1995, to December 31, 2006. This includes the period of crisis for emerging market stocks in 1997 and 1998. Yalewian stocks escaped from this crisis unscathed as their returns were positive during these years."	Yes	**For the Exam:** Using ex post data to make statements about ex ante performance—he is underestimating the risk faced by investors during the emerging market crisis of 97 and 98. This results in an overestimation of their potential future performance. **Discussion:** Barkley is using ex post (past) data to make statements regarding the ex ante (future) risk and return of emerging market stocks. In 1997 and 1998, the stock prices of Yalewian stocks were probably depressed because investors feared that the emerging market crisis would extend to Yalewian stocks. When the country escaped unscathed from the crisis, stock prices and returns increased. In this case, Barkley has underestimated the risk that investors faced in 1997 and 1998 and perhaps overestimated the future returns that could be expected from Yalewian stocks.
"After extensive research on stock price patterns in 30 developed and emerging markets, I have uncovered a turn of the month effect in the U.S. Specifically, the returns for U.S. stocks are higher in the first half of every month compared to the returns during the latter part of the month. The reason why this pattern is found in the United States and not in the other countries is because U.S. investors tend to invest after they have been paid their wages at the end of the month."	Yes	**For the Exam:** Data mining—if one examines enough data, return patterns will appear due to random chance. **Discussion:** Barkley's research findings are probably due to data mining. He has studied the returns for 30 countries and finds one that has a pattern in returns. If he is using a 5% significance level, just by random chance, one out of 20 countries will demonstrate a pattern in returns. In this case $(1 / 20) \times 30 = 1.5$ countries are expected to demonstrate a pattern in returns just by random chance. Although his explanation may have some basis in fact, the analyst must determine whether the observed pattern is just a statistical artifact or if it is real and likely to occur again in the future.

"Using data for U.S. inflation from 1960 to 2006, the average rate was 3.4%. Accordingly, I expect U.S. inflation for the next year to be equal to this historical rate."	Yes	**For the Exam:** Overreliance on historical data and failure to account for conditioning information. **Discussion:** Although historical data can be used as one input to forecasts, there are at least three potential problems here. First, there are limitations to using historical data when data definitions and methodologies have changed over time. For example, the basket of goods in the U.S. CPI (consumer price index) has changed over time. Second, there are limitations to using historical estimates if the data are no longer relevant. For example, the U.S. Federal Reserve has changed its objectives over time and this might impact the future path of inflation such that historical data are no longer relevant. Third, when forecasts fail to account for conditioning information, they may be inaccurate. Conditioning means that the statistical relationships were determined over a given historical time period and are naturally based on economic conditions at that time, and economic conditions can change over time. For example, perhaps the price of oil is expected to increase due to increased demand from developing economies. This information should be used to help form inflation forecasts. Historical data should not be the sole basis of forecasts.
"After evaluating the historical data for the U.S. and European stock markets, I have found that when the central bank is increasing the growth of the money supply, stock returns are higher. When they are restricting the growth, stock returns are lower. In fact, the correlation between the central bank discount rate and stock returns is 0.74 on average, indicating that central bank monetary policy is very influential on stock returns."	Yes	**For the Exam:** Misinterpretation of the correlation statistic—correlation does not imply causation. **Discussion:** Barkley is misusing the correlation statistic. He is assuming that central bank policies drive stock returns, when in fact there are likely other variables influencing the relationship. For example, perhaps economic activity drives both central bank policy and stock returns. The correlation statistic does not indicate causality.

Sample Scoring Key:
1 point each for correctly identifying whether there is a potential problem.
2 points for each description of the problem.
0 points possible if yes/no decision is wrong.

B.   **For the Exam:**

Your objective in this type of question would be to provide the calculations as shown below (without our accompanying verbiage). You should show your work on the exam in case you make a mathematical mistake. This provides you with the potential for receiving partial credit if your process for calculating the answer is correct, but you make a mathematical error.

Discussion:

In the following equations, we denote Airedale as country A, Bermiese as country B, and the MSCI World index as the global market portfolio, M. To solve for the expected returns, we must first calculate the equity risk premium for both markets assuming full integration. Note that for the emerging market, the illiquidity risk premium is included:

$$ERP_i = \rho_{i,M}\sigma_i \left(\frac{ERP_M}{\sigma_M} \right)$$

$$ERP_A = 0.79(0.11)0.26 = 2.26\%$$

$$ERP_B = 0.58(0.21)0.26 + 0.0260 = 5.77\%$$

Next, we calculate the equity risk premium for both markets assuming full segmentation:

$$ERP_i = \sigma_i \left(\frac{ERP_M}{\sigma_M} \right)$$
$$ERP_A = (0.11)0.26 = 2.86\%$$
$$ERP_B = (0.21)0.26 + 0.0260 = 8.06\%$$

We then weight the integrated and segmented risk premiums by the degree of integration and segmentation in each market:

$$ERP_A = (0.85 \times 0.0226) + [(1-0.85) \times 0.0286] = 2.35\%$$
$$ERP_B = (0.65 \times 0.0577) + [(1-0.65) \times 0.0806] = 6.57\%$$

The expected return in each market figures in the risk-free rate:

$$\hat{R}_A = 3.5\% + 2.35\% = 5.85\%$$
$$\hat{R}_B = 3.5\% + 6.57\% = 10.07\%$$

The betas for the markets, which are needed to calculate the covariance of the two markets, are calculated as:

$$\beta_i = \rho_{i,M}\sigma_i / \sigma_M$$
$$\beta_A = (0.79)(0.11) / 0.10 = 0.87$$
$$\beta_B = (0.58)(0.21) / 0.10 = 1.22$$

Lastly, we calculate the covariance:

$$\text{cov}_{i,j} = \beta_i \beta_j \sigma_M^2$$
$$\text{cov}_{A,B} = (0.87)1.22(10.0^2) = 106.14$$

Your answer may be slightly different depending on the number of digits you used for intermediate calculations.

Sample Scoring Key:
6 points for the calculation of the expected returns (3 points each).
6 points for the calculation of the betas (3 points each).
4 points for the calculation of the covariance.

QUESTION 5

Reference: Book 3, Study Session 11, LOS 32.f, i

Cross-reference to CFA Institute assigned reading: Reading 32

A.   **For the Exam:**
- Examine manager's portfolio and divide investments into categories.
- Disadvantage: Subjective classification of categories.
- Advantage over returns-based: Detects style drift faster.

Discussion:

Holdings-based style analysis (HB), as its name implies, involves actually examining the portfolio and classifying securities based on characteristics such as capitalization, value, growth, industry, etc. HB requires access to the portfolio, so it is not applicable to hedge funds and other managers who consider their holdings proprietary. Also, the classifications themselves are subjective, as different analysts might consider the same stock as value and growth, for example, so they might not be the same classifications employed by the portfolio manager in constructing the portfolio. HB requires more data than returns-based analysis but picks up style drift faster.

> Sample Scoring Key:
> 4 points possible: 2 points for describing HB; 1 point each for disadvantage and advantage over returns-based style analysis.

B.   **For the Exam:**

Regress portfolio returns against style indices' returns:

$$R_P = b_0 + b_1 I_1 + b_2 I_2 + b_3 I_3 + b_4 I_4 + ... + b_n I_n + e$$

$$\sum_{i=1}^{n} b_i = 1.0$$

R^2 = degree to which the model explains portfolio returns
b_i = portfolio sensitivity to index i
R_P = portfolio returns
I_i = returns on index i
e = returns to active management
n = number of indices used

Disadvantage: Determining number of and which indices to use.

Advantage over HB: Doesn't require looking at portfolio holdings.

Discussion:

To perform a returns-based style analysis (RB) the analyst regresses the returns on the portfolio against the returns on several style indices. The coefficients are constrained to sum to one, so each coefficient shows the portfolio's proportional exposure (sensitivity) to the respective style index. If a returns-based analysis indicates a coefficient of 0.30 to a large cap growth index, for example, the portfolio is assumed to consist of 30% large cap growth stocks. The analysis requires a significant number of consecutive returns for each index and the portfolio. Rolling regressions can be used to determine style drift over time, but RB does not generally detect style drift as quickly as HB. RB is subject to all the potential difficulties associated with multiple regression analysis, such as asynchronous data, misspecification, multi-colinearity, spurious correlation, etc. A particular limitation of RB is the need to select indices. It is difficult to identify the exact number of indices necessary to describe the returns on the portfolio. R-square identifies the proportion of the variability in the portfolio returns that can be attributed to the model (indices selected), and (1 – R-square) is considered to be the return from active management.

Sample Scoring Key:
10 points possible: 2 points for describing RB; 2 points for writing the equation; 1 point each for identifying index returns, betas (sensitivities), and error term; 1 point for constraint $\left(\sum_{i=1}^{n} b_i = 1.0 \right)$; 1 point for disadvantage; 1 point for advantage over HB.

C.   **For the Exam:**

Full replication: Hold all securities in index and in same proportions. Use to minimize tracking error.

Stratified sampling: Select sample based on cap, value, or growth, etc. Use when cost is important and some tracking error is OK.

Optimization: Factor model replicates factor sensitivities. Use when factor sensitivities are more important than actual holdings.

Discussion:

Full replication (FR) is the most costly to employ, as every security in the index must be purchased in the same proportion as in the index. FR produces the lowest tracking error but its return is somewhat lower than that of the index due to initial trading costs. FR can be inappropriate if the index is frequently rebalanced, as it might require many frequent, small trades to rebalance to the index. FR picks up style drift quickly, but it requires regular access to the portfolio.

Stratified sampling (SS) involves dividing the securities in the portfolio into groups by style, market cap, etc. A sample from each group is selected to represent that group by its weight in the index. For example, if 25% of the securities in the index fall into a group classified as small cap growth, a sample of the group is selected and purchased in an amount equal to 25% of the manager's portfolio. In that way the portfolio and index have the same 25% sensitivity to small cap growth stocks. Benefits to SS include less cost than FR, but increased tracking error. Also, since the manager selects a representative sample from each group of stocks, he can potentially generate alpha by selecting only the best stocks in the group. Note that SS produces the same factor sensitivities as the index and actually holds many of the same securities.

Optimization involves constructing a factor model that replicates the factor sensitivities of the index. The model can be complex and difficult to construct. Optimization usually produces less tracking error than SS but the portfolio can contain different securities than the index. Unlike SS, the factor model method implicitly considers the covariances of the risk factors, but sensitivities are determined from historical data and are subject to change.

Sample Scoring Key:
9 points possible: 1 point for each definition; 2 points for properly identifying when each should be used.

QUESTION 6

Reference: Book 2, Study Session 8, LOS 26.g,n

Cross-reference to CFA Institute assigned reading: Reading 26

For the Exam:

For the calculation part of questions A through C, your objective would be to provide the calculations as shown below. You should show your work on the exam in case you make a mathematical mistake. This provides you with the potential for receiving partial credit if your process for calculating the answer is correct.

A.   **Discussion:**

Since the $750,000 must be paid in one year, the conservative approach is to place the appropriate amount in T-bills and not consider it part of the portfolio.

PV of donation = $750,000 / 1.04 = $721,154

Subtract from the asset base = $5,000,000 − $721,154 = $4,278,846

As a percent of investable assets, the required **spending rate** is then 150,000 / 4,278,846 = 3.51%.

To calculate the investor's return objective, we factor in the spending rate and expected inflation:

r = required after-tax nominal rate of return

r = (1 + s)(1 + i) − 1 = (1.0351)(1.035) − 1 = 0.0713 = 7.13%

The grossed up required before tax nominal rate of return:

7.13 / (1−.25) = 9.51%

Note: If you are not provided with a risk-free rate or exact date for the donation, subtract the total amount. In this case, subtracting the entire $750,000 would leave the portfolio at $4,250,000. The spending rate would be 3.53%; the after-tax nominal rate would be 7.15%; and the before-tax return would be 9.53%.

To obtain Beitia's utility for each of the corner portfolios, use the expected portfolio return, his risk aversion value of 5.0, the variance of the portfolio, and the following formula:

$$U_p = \hat{R}_p - 0.5(A)(\sigma_p^2)$$

Corner Portfolio	Calculation	Utility of Corner Portfolio
1	$0.065 - 0.5(5)0.041^2$	0.0608
2	$0.085 - 0.5(5)0.058^2$	0.0766
3	$0.097 - 0.5(5)0.078^2$	0.0818
4	$0.135 - 0.5(5)0.106^2$	0.1069

Professor's Note: The question does not ask you to identify the portfolio with highest utility-adjusted return, but it is Portfolio 4 at 0.1069. Essentially, the utility-adjusted return for a portfolio is the return for the portfolio minus a deduction for risk. The deduction gets larger as risk aversion increases.

B.   **Discussion:**

Given his required return of 9.5% and no borrowing or short selling, we combine corner portfolios 2 and 3. To solve for their weights, we use:

$0.095 = w_2(0.085) + (1 - w_2)(0.097)$

$w_2 = 0.167 = 16.7\%$; $w_3 = 1 - w_2 = 83.3\%$

$\sigma_p = 0.167(5.8\%) + 0.833(7.8\%) = 7.47\%$

Professor's Note: We can check our weight calculations by calculating the expected return from this portfolio:

$0.167(8.5\%) + 0.833(9.7\%) = 9.5\%$

Also, the approximate expected portfolio standard deviation is a weighted average of the standard deviations of corner portfolios 2 and 3. We assume that the standard deviation is a linear combination of the corner portfolios' standard deviations (we don't use the correlation between them).

As such, the calculated standard deviation represents the maximum standard deviation for the combination of the two corner portfolios in the calculated proportions. If the correlations between the corner portfolios are given, be sure to incorporate them into the standard deviation calculation.

You might be asked on the exam to calculate the resulting weights in assets 1 to 5, given calculated weights for corner portfolios 2 and 3. For example, in our resulting portfolio:

$\text{weight}_{\text{asset 1}} = 0.167(0\%) + 0.833(60\%) = 50\%$
$\text{weight}_{\text{asset 2}} = 0.167(15\%) + 0.833(10\%) = 11\%$
$\text{weight}_{\text{asset 3}} = 0.167(85\%) + 0.833(30\%) = 39\%$
$\text{weight}_{\text{asset 4}} = \text{weight}_{\text{asset 5}} = 0\%$

C. **For the Exam:**

$$0.095 = w_4(0.135) + (1 - w_4)(0.04)$$

$$w_4 = \frac{(0.095 - 0.04)}{(0.135 - 0.04)} = 58\%$$

$$w_{RF} = 1 - w_4 = 42\%$$

standard deviation $= 0.58(10.6\%) + 0.42(0\%) = 6.1\%$

Discussion:

When there is a risk free asset (RF), the investor is always better off combining it with the tangency portfolio, which is the portfolio with the highest Sharpe ratio. Combining the risk free asset with the tangency portfolio creates a capital asset line (CAL), and the CAL always provides the highest available reward to risk, whether or not the investor borrows (negative weight for RF). The portfolio with the highest Sharpe ratio is portfolio 4 (0.896). Since portfolio 4 has the highest Sharpe ratio and its expected return is higher than Beitia's return requirement, we know we will end up with positive weights for both the risk free asset and portfolio 4.

In this case, the restriction on borrowing turned out not to be a constraint, because the expected return for portfolio 4 is higher than the required return. If you were prohibited from borrowing (i.e., shorting the risk-free asset) and the return on portfolio 4 wasn't sufficient, you would not have been asked to combine the risk free asset with one of the corner portfolios. If the return to portfolio 4 had not been sufficient to cover the required return, the only way to stay on the CAL would be to borrow at the risk free rate and invest more than 100% of your assets in portfolio 4 (leverage the return to portfolio 4). This would move the final portfolio to the right of portfolio 4 on the CAL but would still provide the same reward to risk (Sharpe ratio) as portfolio 4. Remember, the slope of the CAL is the Sharpe ratio of the tangency portfolio, so any portfolio that falls on the CAL provides the same Sharpe ratio. Any portfolio not on the CAL will provide less return per unit of risk (i.e., will have a lower Sharpe ratio), so the investor will always try to select a portfolio on the CAL. Exam questions generally follow the form of this practice exam question; combine two corner portfolios or combine the tangency portfolio with the risk-free asset.

> **Sample Scoring Key:**
> A. (9 points maximum) 1 point for deducting present value or full value of $750,000 donation; 2 points for correct portfolio required return; 2 points for correct risk-adjusted utility equation; 1 point for each correct utility adjusted return.
> B. (7 points maximum) 1 point for correctly identifying the two corner portfolios to combine; 4 points for correctly determining the corner portfolio weights; 2 points for resulting standard deviation.
> C. (6 points maximum) 2 points for selecting portfolio 4; 2 points for weights of RF and portfolio 4; 2 points for the portfolio standard deviation.

QUESTION 7

Reference: Book 2, Study Session 5, LOS 20.i

Cross-reference to CFA Institute assigned reading: Reading 20

Answer for Question 7

<table>
<tr><td colspan="3" align="center">*Investment Policy Statement for A1 Casualty*</td></tr>
<tr>
<td rowspan="2">Objectives</td>
<td>Return</td>
<td>

For the Exam:
A1 should follow a total return investment objective that maximizes their ability to maintain a competitive policy pricing, reduce volatility in overall profitability, and achieve a reasonable growth in surplus. (This is a "canned answer" that you can use for most casualty insurance companies' return requirements.)

Discussion:
Casualty companies are plagued by the uncertainties associated with their underlying business. The potential for increasing claims may require shifting some of the asset portfolio into instruments that better match higher liability outflows, but attention to maintaining a reasonable surplus is also required. The overall objective should be to maximize total after-tax return within a prudent asset/liability (ALM) framework that also pays attention to surplus growth.

</td>
</tr>
<tr>
<td>Risk</td>
<td>

For the Exam:
There are two important factors affecting the risk tolerance of A1 in this case: the uncertain cash flow characteristics of their claims and the stock-to-surplus ratio. The primary objective is to meet policyholder claims, and the overall level of risk tolerance is low.

Discussion:
Not only is A1 apparently near the end of a typical 3-year period of an intensely competitive market environment, the current underwriting cycle also appears coincident with a downturn in the general business cycle. In addition, the recent hurricane may generate substantial claims in the near future due to the "long tail" characteristic of claims submissions. If A1 has approximately 50% of overall homeowner exposure to the region impacted by the hurricane, they should be prepared to see substantially more claims in the near future.
The proportion of A1's investment portfolio in equity instruments seems rather high in an environment where the financial stability required to meet the demands of current policyholders should be increasing. Most casualty companies restrict equity investments to no more than 75% of surplus. Although the willingness of A1 to take risk seems apparent, combining all the above with the general quasi-fiduciary role perceived of casualty insurance companies indicates a limited ability to take risks at this stage.

Professor's Note: The underwriting cycle is also known as the profitability cycle. The typical cycle lasts three to five years for casualty insurance companies. The bottom of the cycle usually coincides with an economic recession and/or a competitive pricing environment during which investments are liquidated to meet claims.

</td>
</tr>
</table>

Constraints	Time Horizon	**For the Exam:** The duration of A1's liabilities is relatively short. **Discussion:** The uncertainty associated with A1's liability payments, especially at the end of an underwriting cycle, and the potential for hurricane claims substantially reduces the time horizon pertinent to A1's investment portfolio. Note that the time horizon for casualty insurance companies is usually less than that for life companies.
	Liquidity	**For the Exam:** The timing of the underwriting cycle, combined with the prospect of hurricane-related claims, suggests that liquidity needs are high. **Discussion:** Liquidity is always a concern for casualty companies. The end of the underwriting cycle (which implies fewer new policies and inflows), potential increase in claims due to the hurricane, and a downturn in the general business cycle indicate that a greater than usual level of attention to liquidity is required. A1's portfolio should be positioned to meet higher liquidity demands over the near term.
	Legal/ Regulatory	**For the Exam:** A1 is subject to legal and regulatory requirements that vary from state to state. **Discussion:** Casualty companies are subject to the regulations of the states in which they operate. One specific area of concern is the various state regulations affecting investment and allowable asset classes. Risk-based capital regulations also apply.
	Taxes	**For the Exam:** Casualty companies, such as A1, are taxable entities. **Discussion:** Because investment income is subject to taxes, the portfolio management process should focus on maximizing after-tax returns, consistent with the overall level of risk-tolerance. The use of specialist tax advisers is likely to be required.
	Unique Circumstances	**For the Exam:** Significant claims outstanding and geographical concentration of policies. **Discussion:** A1's location in the underwriting cycle, the potential overhang of hurricane-related claims, the general business cycle, and the common stock to surplus ratio are the main distinguishing factors. These have all been addressed previously in the IPS, but the business cycle is experienced by all firms, so large amount of outstanding claims, geographically concentrated policies, and high stock to surplus ratio are all suitable answers.

Sample Scoring Key:
4 points each for the return and risk components.
2 points for the liquidity component.
1 point each for all other components of the IPS.

©2009 Kaplan, Inc.

QUESTION 8

Reference: Book 5, Study Session 18, LOS 48.c,d,e,f,g,l

Cross-reference to CFA Institute assigned reading: Reading 48

Answer for Question 8

Maximum 12 points for any four of the following non-compliant items.
1. For the Exam: Only four years presented. Must present at least five years or since inception if less than 5 years. **Discussion:** Firms claiming GIPS® compliance must present at least five years' data or since inception if less than five years. If less than five years presented, the firm must add an additional year each year until ten years are presented. Since Bailey was in existence for all of 2004, they should have presented all 5 years.
2. For the Exam: Assets in the composite. Must present the amount of assets in the composite and either total firm assets or the percentage of firm assets represented by the composite. **Discussion:** Firms must present not only the number of portfolios in the composite but also the total assets in the composite.
3. For the Exam: Incorrect dispersion measure. Must present the measure used to calculate internal dispersion. **Discussion:** Firms must present the internal dispersion of the composite (i.e., the dispersion of individual portfolio returns around the composite return) and the measurement method used. The following are allowed methods: range of annual returns; high and low annual returns; inter-quartile range; standard deviation of equal-weighted returns; and asset-weighted standard deviation of annual returns.
4. For the Exam: Incomplete disclosure of fees. Must disclose the presence of and access to a complete fee schedule.
5. For the Exam: Composite information. Disclose the presence of and access to a complete list and description of all the firm's composites.

> **6. For the Exam:**
> Discretionary and non-discretionary portfolios included.
>
> Non-discretionary portfolios should not be included.
>
> **Discussion:**
> All fee-paying discretionary portfolios must be included in at least one composite, but non-discretionary portfolios may not be included. Non-fee paying discretionary portfolios may be included with a disclosure.

> Sample Scoring Key: (12 points maximum)
> 1 point for stating each non-compliant item.
> 2 points for each correct recommended change.

For the Exam:

Any of the GIPS® 26 required disclosures that are relevant to the firm itself or to the presentation should be included in the footnotes. Any omitted disclosures would qualify as errors in the presentation. Be sure you know the required disclosures as well as all GIPS requirements for the exam. Remember, they are all provided for your review in the Level 3 Standards Pack in the back of SchweserNotes Book 5.

These 26 disclosures are found in the footnotes to a GIPS presentation. Firms must disclose:

1. Definition of "firm" in determining assets and compliance.
2. Availability of list and description of composites.
3. Min. size (if any) for portfolio to be included in composite.
4. Currency used to express performance.
5. Presence, use, and extent of leverage or derivatives (if material).
6. Whether returns are gross- or net-of-fees.
7. Treatment of withholding taxes.
8. Inconsistencies in exchange rates.
9. How (if) local laws and reg's conflict with GIPS.
10. How any presentation prior to 1/1/2000 is non-compliant.
11. Prior to 1/1/2010, how cash was allocated to the carve-outs (if any).
12. Existence of total fee schedule.
13. Percentage of composite assets in bundled-fee portfolios (if any).
14. Types of fees included in bundled fees.
15. If returns gross-of-fees, fees in addition to the direct trading expenses (DTE).
16. If net-of-fees, fees in addition to management fees and DTE.
17. Additional information on calculating and reporting returns is available.
18. From 1/1/2006 the use of any sub-advisor(s) and the periods.
19. Significant events that would help interpret performance.
20. Composite description.
21. If firm redefined, date and reason. (Cannot be applied retroactively).
22. If composite redefined, date and nature of change. (Cannot be applied retroactively).
23. Change in name of composite.
24. Composite creation date.
25. Prior to 1/1/2010, whether month-end or last business day of month valuations are used.
26. Composite internal dispersion and measure used.

QUESTION 9

Reference: Book 5, Study Session 17, LOS 46.p

Cross-reference to CFA Institute assigned reading: Reading 46

A.   **For the Exam:**

$$\text{Sharpe Ratio} = \frac{\overline{R_P} - \overline{R_F}}{\sigma_P}$$

$$\text{HNW} = \frac{28.2 - 4.4}{45.0} = 0.53$$

$$\text{S\&P 500} = \frac{22.4 - 4.4}{20.0} = 0.90$$

Sharpe → The HNW portfolio has significantly underperformed the S&P 500.

$$\text{Treynor Measure} = \frac{\overline{R_P} - \overline{R_F}}{\beta_P}$$

$$\text{HNW} = \frac{28.2 - 4.4}{1.35} = 17.6$$

$$\text{S\&P 500} = \frac{22.4 - 4.4}{1.0} = 18.0$$

Treynor → The HNW portfolio has modestly underperformed the S&P 500.

Discussion:

The Sharpe ratio is the portfolio's excess return over the risk-free rate (R_F) divided by the portfolio standard deviation (σ_P):

$$\text{Sharpe Ratio} = \frac{\overline{R_P} - \overline{R_F}}{\sigma_P}$$

$$\text{HNW} = \frac{28.2 - 4.4}{45.0} = 0.53$$

$$\text{S\&P 500} = \frac{22.4 - 4.4}{20.0} = 0.90$$

The greater the Sharpe Ratio, the greater the excess return received per unit of total risk assumed. The HNW portfolio has significantly underperformed the S&P 500 on this basis.

The Treynor Measure is the portfolio's excess return over the risk-free rate (R_F) divided by the portfolio's systematic risk as measured by beta (β_P):

$$\text{Treynor Measure} = \frac{\overline{R_P} - \overline{R_F}}{\beta_P}$$

$$\text{HNW} = \frac{28.2 - 4.4}{1.35} = 17.6$$

$$\text{S\&P 500} = \frac{22.4 - 4.4}{1.0} = 18.0$$

The greater the Treynor Measure, the greater the excess return received per unit of systematic risk assumed. The HNW portfolio has modestly underperformed the S&P 500 on this basis.

> Sample Scoring Key:
> 2 points for computing each of the measures.

B. **For the Exam:**

The Treynor measure uses beta (systematic risk) as a measure of risk, so it underestimates true risk exposure when the portfolio is under-diversified. If investor is also exposed to unsystematic risk, Treynor will rank the portfolio higher than Sharpe will.

Discussion:

The standard deviation of the portfolio's returns is caused by systematic and unsystematic risk factors or only systematic risk factors, depending on whether it is diversified or not. Whether we use Sharpe or Treynor to measure its risk-adjusted excess return depends on the structure of the portfolio as well as its place in the investor's total holdings. In any case, we want to account for the all of the risk faced by the investor, no more and no less.

Consider:

The portfolio comprises a *large part* of the investor's wealth: (i.e., not enough other assets to diversify away any unsystematic risk)
- If it is fully diversified, we can use Sharpe and/or Treynor to measure and rank its risk-adjusted performance.
  - Since the portfolio is fully diversified, its total risk (standard deviation) is comprised of systematic risk only.
  - Both measures accurately capture the risk to which the investor is exposed.
- If it is *not* fully diversified, we should only use *Sharpe*.
  - Treynor captures the systematic risk component only, so it underestimates the risk to which the investor is exposed.
  - Treynor over-states its risk-adjusted performance relative to other portfolios.

The portfolio is only a *small part* of the investor's total wealth: (i.e., plenty of other assets to diversify away any unsystematic risk).
- If it is fully diversified, we can use Sharpe and/or Treynor to measure and rank its risk-adjusted performance.
  - Since the portfolio is fully diversified, its total risk (standard deviation) is comprised of systematic risk only.
  - Both measures accurately capture the risk to which the investor is exposed.
- If it is *not* fully diversified, we should only use *Treynor*.
  - The portfolio's unsystematic risk is diversified away by the investor's other assets.
  - Treynor measures only the systematic risk component, which is the only risk faced by the investor.
  - Sharpe, which uses standard deviation, will in this case measure both systematic and unsystematic risk.
    - Overstates the risk to which the investor is exposed and depresses the portfolio's ranking relative to other portfolios.

Sample Scoring Key:
1 point for differentiating between systematic and unsystematic risk.
1 point for explaining which type of risk is relevant to each measure.
1 point for explaining when each measure is most appropriate.

C. **For the Exam:**

$$M^2 \text{ Measure} = R_F + (R_P - R_F)\frac{\sigma_M}{\sigma_P}$$

$$HNW = 4.4 + (28.2 - 4.4)\frac{20}{45} = 15.0\%$$

The M^2 for any asset will only equal the M^2 for the market if it has the same level of excess return per total risk. That is, they will be the same if the Sharpe ratios are the same.

Discussion:

The M^2 measure evaluates portfolio performance by computing what the portfolio's excess return would have been if the level of total risk was exactly the same as the market. This excess return can be directly compared with the market's excess return in order to determine relative performance for the portfolio.

$$M^2 \text{ Measure} = R_F + (R_P - R_F)\frac{\sigma_M}{\sigma_P}$$

$$M^2_{HNW} = 4.4 + (28.2 - 4.4)\frac{20}{45} = 15.0\%$$

Since the M^2 for the market is its return, 22.4%, we can see that HNW has underperformed the market based on this measure. Since the M^2 ranking will always agree with the Sharpe ratio ranking, we already knew that the portfolio had underperformed from our work in parts A and B.

A portfolio will have an M^2 that is exactly the same as the market if it has the same level of excess return per unit of total risk assumed as the market. That is, they will have identical M^2 if the Sharpe ratios are also the same.

Sample Scoring Key:
1 point for computing the measure.
1 point for explaining the relative performance.
1 point for demonstrating the requirements for the portfolio's measure to equal the market.

QUESTION 10

Reference: Book 2, Study Session 5, LOS 20.i
Book 3, Study Session 11, LOS 32.u

Cross-reference to CFA Institute assigned reading: Readings 20 and 32

 Professor's Note: Recall that the bank's security portfolio is a residual use of funds. That is, the bank's primary business is to take deposits and make loans. Any funds left over are invested in the bank's security portfolio, which can be used to manage the bank's risk, duration, liquidity, and income requirements. The objective and constraints of the bank's security portfolio will be affected by its particular circumstances. The effect on Opportunity's investment objectives, constraints, and investment policies in the described scenarios (when viewing each separately from the others) is as follows.

Answer for Question 10-A

Scenario	*Affect on bank's policies*
1. Due to pressure from local activists, Opportunity has stepped up lending in low-income areas. Groh expects the default rate on these loans to be higher than the loans currently in their portfolio.	**For the Exam:** • Reduce risk tolerance of security portfolio. • Risk of assets in security portfolio should be reduced. • Note in unique circumstances about new loans with increased default rate. **Discussion:** Because Groh expects the default rate on these loans will be higher than the loans in their current portfolio, Opportunity should set the risk objective of its security portfolio at lower risk tolerance. Opportunity should invest in less risky securities in its security portfolio to offset the increased risk in its loan portfolio. Although it does not directly pertain to the bank's security portfolio, the increased lending to low-income areas could be noted in the bank's unique circumstances section of its investment policy statement.
2. Opportunity has bought a regional bank with operations in North Carolina, South Carolina, and Georgia. The acquired bank's loan portfolio consists mostly of commercial loans to small, local businesses.	**For the Exam:** • Loan portfolio has better geographical diversification. • Operating assets have less risk, so risk objective of security portfolio can be increased. **Discussion:** Opportunity has bought banks in a different region of the country and with products that differ from their current loan portfolio. Opportunity's loan portfolio is now better diversified. With the acquisition of banks in other geographical and product areas, Opportunity's security portfolio could allow its risk objective to reflect a greater ability to tolerate risk.

3. A recent downturn in interest rates has caused many of Opportunity's variable-rate mortgages to be refinanced to 15- and 30-year fixed rate mortgages. Opportunity has retained the business of most of its customers who have refinanced.	**For the Exam:** • Increased asset duration. • Increase return objective for security portfolio to compensate for reduced returns on assets. • Reduce liquidity constraint for security portfolio. **Discussion:** The refinancing of Opportunity's variable-rate mortgages to fixed-rate mortgages has several effects. First, it extends the duration of Opportunity's assets, which results in a positive leverage-adjusted duration gap. To counterbalance this increase in duration, Opportunity should decrease the duration of its securities portfolio by investing in shorter duration assets. Second, although Opportunity has retained the business of most of its customers that have refinanced, it will have the cash from those who have not. This increased liquidity decreases the need for the security portfolio to provide liquidity. Third, the new mortgages that Opportunity makes may have a lower return than Opportunity had forecasted. This may put increased pressure on the security portfolio to generate a higher return.

B.   **For the Exam:**

Advantage: Compensation will be more performance based and should better motivate the manager.

Disadvantages:
- Manager has an incentive to take bigger risks when lagging the benchmark.
- Performance-based fee structures are more complicated to administer.

Discussion:

The advantage of the new fee structure is that the manager's compensation is more heavily dependent on performance. Hence, the trust will not pay as much for poor performance as they would if the compensation was based solely on the amount of assets managed (as was the case for the previous manager). The primary disadvantage of performance-based fees is that they create an incentive for the manager to take bigger risks. If the manager's performance is lagging their benchmark, they have an incentive to take greater risk in order to generate higher returns and compensation. Secondly, performance-based fee structures are more complicated to administer.

Sample Scoring Key:
A.   2 points for correctly identifying the influence of *each* scenario.
B.   1 point for identifying the advantage of performance-based fee structures and 1 point for identifying *each* disadvantage of performance-based fee structures.

Exam 2
Afternoon Session Answers

To get detailed answer explanations with references to specific LOS and SchweserNotes content, and to get valuable feedback on how your score compares to those of other Level 3 candidates, use your Username and Password to gain Online Access at *www.schweser.com* and choose the left-hand menu item "Practice Exams Vol. 1."

11.1.	B	15.1.	A	19.1.	B		
11.2.	A	15.2.	C	19.2.	C		
11.3.	B	15.3.	B	19.3.	C		
11.4.	C	15.4.	B	19.4.	B		
11.5.	C	15.5.	C	19.5.	A		
11.6.	A	15.6.	C	19.6.	A		
12.1.	C	16.1.	C	20.1.	C		
12.2.	C	16.2.	B	20.2.	C		
12.3.	A	16.3.	C	20.3.	C		
12.4.	C	16.4.	A	20.4.	A		
12.5.	A	16.5.	C	20.5.	C		
12.6.	B	16.6.	B	20.6.	C		
13.1.	B	17.1.	C				
13.2.	B	17.2.	A				
13.3.	B	17.3.	B				
13.4.	A	17.4.	A				
13.5.	C	17.5.	C				
13.6.	B	17.6.	A				
14.1.	A	18.1.	C				
14.2.	B	18.2.	C				
14.3.	B	18.3.	A				
14.4.	C	18.4.	A				
14.5.	B	18.5.	B				
14.6.	B	18.6.	A				

Exam 2
Afternoon Session Answers

QUESTION 11

Reference: Book 1, Study Session 1

Cross-reference to CFA Institute assigned reading: Readings 1 and 2

11.1. **B** In the meeting with Pavlica's children, King disclosed Pavlica's medical condition. Since King learned this information as a result of his professional relationship with the client, he has a duty to keep it confidential, even from her children. By breaking the confidentiality, King has violated Standard III(E) Preservation of Confidentiality. (Study Session 1, LOS 1.b)

11.2. **A** Since the annual meeting between Pavlica and King was only three months before the meeting between King and Pavlica's children, it is safe to assume the portfolio allocation represented Pavlica's investment policy statement. King reallocated the portfolio before meeting with Pavlica to discuss the suggested strategy and then withheld information that he had met with her children. The reallocation (after meeting with the children) was according to the wishes of Pavlica's children, who are not beneficiaries of the trust. King has a responsibility under Standard III(A) Loyalty, Prudence, and Care to act solely in the best interest of his client and maintain loyalty to Pavlica, not her children. He has thus violated the Standard. (Study Session 1, LOS 1.b)

11.3. **B** King has essentially guaranteed a certain level of portfolio performance by stating that Pavlica's spending requirements will definitely be met by the new strategy. This is a violation of Standard I(C) Misrepresentation, which prohibits misrepresentations in dealing with clients. The investment strategy has some inherent level of uncertainty and by implicitly guaranteeing performance, King has misrepresented the strategy. (Study Session 1, LOS 1.b)

11.4. **C** Private placement shares are likely to be illiquid and have more risk than publicly traded equity. By not taking any shares for himself and only allocating shares to accounts for which the investment is appropriate, King has complied with the Standards. However, King has violated Standard VI(B) Priority of Transactions by trading his shares ahead of his client's shares. It doesn't matter that in this situation it benefited the client. King must always take investment action first for his clients and act in their best interests. (Study Session 1, LOS 1.b)

11.5. **C** King may accept the directorship even though it may create a potential conflict of interest as long as the conflict is prominently disclosed in understandable language to all clients and prospects as well as to his employer. According to Standard VI(A) Disclosure of Conflicts, such disclosure is necessary so that all related parties can assess the impact the potential conflict will have on King's professional activities. Additionally, the directorship will provide additional compensation that must be approved ahead of his assuming the position. (Study Session 1, LOS 1.b)

11.6   **A**   Standard VI(A) Disclosure of Conflicts. Performance compensation such as the one in effect at Rowan Brothers encourages portfolio managers to act in their own interests instead of their clients' best interest (a potential conflict of interest) and encourages them to take additional risks to attain the 10% goal. Therefore, this compensation scheme must be totally disclosed to all clients and prospects. By not disclosing the fees to current clients (he only discloses the new fee structure to prospective clients), King has violated the Standard. It is not a violation to have such a compensation program, however, as long as it is disclosed. (Study Session 1, LOS 1.b)

> Sample Scoring Key: 3 points for each correct response.

QUESTION 12

Reference: Book 1, Study Session 1

Cross-reference to CFA Institute assigned reading: *Standards of Practice Handbook*, 9th edition (CFA Institute, 2005).

12.1. **C** Bracco has not violated any soft dollar standards. This is an example of *client-directed brokerage* where the client, in this case Stephen Carobilo, is allowed to direct the investment manager to use a specific broker to execute trades. Moreover, one could take the view that the client benefits in the sense that Stephen Carobilo knows he is helping his friend at First Trades Brokerage by utilizing them as the broker. A commingled fund is a fund that is comprised of different client's funds. (Study Session 1, LOS 1.b)

12.2. **C** Bracco is in violation of Standard II(A) Material Nonpublic Information, which states that members and candidates cannot trade or cause others to trade based on material nonpublic information that could affect the value of an investment. Even though Bracco has performed his own research and the information he acquired from McNulty and his colleague was an accident, it was nonetheless material nonpublic information and therefore cannot be traded upon. (Study Session 1, LOS 1.b)

12.3. **A** This is not a violation of an effective corporate governance system. Effective corporate governance requires that a majority of board members are independent. For effective corporate governance, boards should comprise a balance of independent members and others with relevant expertise. Clearly, James would not be considered an independent board member because she is paid as a consultant to the firm. The fact that James's husband also performs consulting work for Stiles Corporation is not a violation of effective corporate governance because he is not considered part of management. Board members are allowed to hire outside consultants without management's interference or approval, but James's husband was hired as a consultant to the firm and not the board. (Study Session 1, LOS 1.b)

12.4. **C** Short-term interest should not be taken away from accounts who should have received the original shares, making Gun's statement incorrect. Accounts that do not meet the minimum transaction amount as described in the company's policies and procedures should not receive shares of the IPO, making Bracco's statement incorrect. (Study Session 1, LOS 1.b)

12.5. **A** McNulty has violated both the Code of Ethics and the Standards of Professional Conduct. The Code of Ethics states in part that members of CFA Institute must act with integrity, competence, diligence, respect, and in an ethical manner with employees and colleagues in the investment profession. The inappropriate behavior has violated the Code. The unethical behavior also violates Standard I(D) Misconduct. The Standard states in part that members and candidates must not commit any act that reflects adversely on their professional reputation, integrity, or competence. His inappropriate behavior, especially drinking heavily with Stiles' management, has violated this Standard. (Study Session 1, LOS 1.b)

12.6. **B** The information in the notebook is clearly material and non-public, as its public release will affect Stiles' stock price. As such, McNulty should have taken steps to protect it. His drinking and behavior at the party are the obvious blame for his accidentally losing the notebook, but the reasons for losing it are not the point here. Whether he intentionally or accidentally lost the notebook, McNulty has violated Standard III(E), Duties to Clients, by not taking steps to preserve the confidentiality of his client's planned offering. Sampson violated Standard II(A) by sharing material, non-public information with others and trading on it. (Study Session 1, LOS 1.b)

> Sample Scoring Key: 3 points for each correct response.

QUESTION 13

Reference: Book 3, Study Sessions 9 and 10
Book 4, Study Session 15

Cross-reference to CFA Institute assigned reading: Readings 29, 30, and 43

13.1. **B** When evaluating bond investment alternatives based on mean reversion analysis only, the bond that is most attractive is the one whose current spread is the largest positive number of standard deviations above the mean.

Bond issue YY has a current spread that is below its mean so it is not an attractive candidate. For the spread to revert to its mean, it must widen and the bond will depreciate in value.

The number of standard deviations above the mean is computed as follows:

Bond Issue VV: (125 − 98) / 28 = 0.96;   Bond Issue XX: (100 − 75) / 15 = 1.67

Morrison should purchase Bond Issue XX, since the current spread exceeds its mean spread by the greatest number of standard deviations. (Study Session 9, LOS 29.e)

13.2. **B** Implication of cyclical and secular changes in the corporate bond market include:

Securities with embedded options will command a premium due to their scarcity, and the percentage of long-term issues will decline. Thus, Morrison is incorrect. Effective duration and aggregate interest rate risk sensitivity will decline. Asset/liability managers with long horizons may be willing to pay premiums for long-term bonds.

Tabler's statement is correct. Credit-based derivatives will be used increasingly to achieve desired exposures to credit sectors, issuers, and structures. (Study Session 9, LOS 29.b)

13.3. **B** To answer this question you have to bring to mind the price-yield graph for a callable bond. You will remember that the price-yield graph for a callable bond is concave below the coupon rate (i.e., the callable bond experiences negative convexity at very low interest rates). While a non-callable bond will continually increase in value as its required return falls, the value of the option in the callable bond increases as the required return falls and places a cap on the maximum value of the callable bond. Therefore, as rates fall below the coupon rate, the non-callable bond will outperform a comparable callable bond.

When rates are already below the coupon rate but are increasing, the callable bond will not fall in value as quickly, so it will outperform the non-callable bond. The difference between the values of the callable and comparable non-callable bond is the value of the embedded call option. Thus, as rates fall below the coupon rate, the value of the call option increases in value, consuming an increasing amount of the total value of the bond. When the required return is significantly higher than the coupon rate, the value of the call option goes to zero and both bonds behave as if they are non-callable. (Study Session 9, LOS 29.e)

13.4. **A** Morrison is correct. Corporate spread curves, which measure the yield spreads between higher and lower rated bonds, tend to change with the economic cycle, so in order to properly conduct this analysis the analyst must carefully examine credit and yield curves. Tabler is also correct. Corporate spread curves narrow during upturns and widen during downturns. The reason for this is that default becomes more likely during a recession and yields on risky corporate bonds increase. Yield spreads decrease during an expansion because default is generally less likely. (Study Session 9, LOS 29.e)

13.5 **C** Both Morrison and Tabler are correct. There is a positive relationship between the federal funds rate and the repo rate. The use of collateral with limited ability decreases the repo rate. Furthermore, as credit quality and liquidity increase, the repo rate declines. As the term decreases, the repo rate decreases. Lastly, the repo rate will be lower if the collateral is delivered to the lender, rather than to the borrower's bank. (Study Session 10, LOS 30.b)

13.6. **B** The net interest paid is determined as follows:

Pay in the loan	–(LIBOR + 120 bp)
– Pay fixed in swap (5.20% + 100 bp)	–6.20%
+ Receive in swap	+LIBOR
Net =	–7.40%

LIBOR paid in the loan is cancelled by the LIBOR received in the swap. In net, the client will pay a fixed rate of 6.20% + 1.20% = 7.40%. (Study Session 15, LOS 43.a)

Sample Scoring Key: 3 points for each correct response.

QUESTION 14

Reference: Book 3, Study Session 10
Book 4, Study Session 14

Cross-reference to CFA Institute assigned reading: Readings 30 and 39

14.1. **A** The provision responsible for Cramer's difficulty is the cross-default provision. A cross-default provision specifies that the borrower is in default of that agreement if it defaults on any of its borrowing/credit agreements. Jump-to-default risk is another name for current credit risk. (Study Session 14, LOS 39.i)

14.2. **B** Cramer is incorrect because current credit risk is not always a reliable indicator of potential credit risk. Firms currently having credit problems may be able to correct their situations, which will reduce potential credit risk. Alternatively, firms presently having no apparent current credit difficulties may lack the ability to honor obligations in the future.

McNally is correct. Current credit risk relates to the possibility of default on current obligations, whereas future credit risk relates to potential default on future obligations. (Study Session 14, LOS 39.i)

14.3. **B** Current credit risk refers to the amount due now and there is none. However, the forward contract has positive value to the long of $50 minus the present value of $50, so there is potential credit risk (of future default) in that amount. Any position that has a positive value under the forward contract has potential credit risk because there is a risk that the counterparty will not pay. (Study Session 14, LOS 39.i)

14.4. **C** Cramer is incorrect. Although it is true that firms can control their credit risk by making use of netting arrangements, requiring collateral from counterparties, and requiring a periodic mark to market of asset positions, they should do business with an SPV, not create one. Doing business with SPVs can lower the probability of credit losses. Special purpose vehicles are created by dealer banks to offer higher credit-rated swaps that are protected from non-derivative claims against the parent company. SPVs are usually well capitalized and hedge their derivative risk. The parent is also liable for the SPV's debt up to the parent's equity investment.

McNally is incorrect. In a total return swap, the purchaser receives cash flows over the life of the swap determined by a floating rate plus a spread. (Study Session 14, LOS 39.k)

14.5. **B** A credit spread call option will provide protection if the reference asset's spread (at option maturity) over the relevant risk-free benchmark increases beyond the strike spread (here 3%). The increase in the spread beyond the strike spread (i.e., the option being in the money) constitutes an identifiable credit event, in and of itself. These contracts may specify for the payoff to be delivery of a physical or a cash settlement.

Credit spread puts are analogous to protective puts. If the credit spread on an asset exceeds the reference spread, the put holder has the right to sell the asset to the put writer at the price determined by the reference spread.

In a credit default swap, the protection buyer (i.e., the asset holder) makes regular payments to the dealer and receives a payment when a specified credit event occurs. (Study Session 10, LOS 30.g)

14.6. **B** Since the spread has widened, the credit spread forward results in a payoff to the **buyer** of $300,000:

FV = (actual spread − contract spread) × notional principal × risk factor

FV = (0.045 − 0.03) × $2 million × 10 = $300,000

(Study Session 10, LOS 30.g)

Sample Scoring Key: 3 points for each correct response.

QUESTION 15

Reference: Book 3, Study Sessions 9 and 10

Cross-reference to CFA Institute assigned reading: Readings 29 and 30

15.1. **A** In a cross hedge the manager enters into a forward contract to deliver the original foreign currency (the baht) for a second foreign currency (the won), which is predicted to appreciate against the domestic currency. The currency risk is changed from an exposure in the baht to one in the won.

In a proxy hedge the manager enters into a forward contract between the domestic currency and a second foreign currency highly correlated with the first foreign currency. Proxy hedges are typically employed when forward contracts are thinly traded or not available on the original foreign currency.

In the forward hedge, the baht would be delivered for the dollar. (Study Session 10, LOS 30.j)

15.2. **C** In the case of all three foreign countries, the cash rate is lower than the cash rate in the United States, which means that all three currencies will trade at a forward premium to the U.S. dollar.

The forward differential for each foreign currency relative to the dollar is approximated as the difference between the domestic and the foreign interest rates. Assume the U.S. dollar is currency d, the Thai baht is currency i, the Korean won is currency j, and the Japanese yen is currency k. Forward rates are denoted f, and the cash rates in each currency are denoted c.

$$f_{d,i} = c_d - c_i = 6.50 - 2.50 \ = +4.00$$

$$f_{d,j} = c_d - c_j = 6.50 - 3.20 \ = +3.30$$

$$f_{d,k} = c_d - c_k = 6.50 - 4.20 = +2.30 \text{ (Study Session 10, LOS 30.j)}$$

15.3. **B** In breakeven rate analysis, the analyst determines the yield change that makes the returns on bonds equivalent. Recall that we hold the short duration bond constant and examine the yield change in the longer duration bond that would make the returns equivalent.

To determine the yield change at which the investor would be indifferent between purchasing two bonds, we must first compare the bonds' yields over the holding period. Over the 1-year time horizon, the Nakhon Metals bond has a yield advantage of 0.70% (5.2% – 4.5%). For the returns to be equivalent over the 1-year time horizon (assuming the bonds are purchased at their current prices), the price for the Nakhon Metals bond must fall by 0.70%. For its price to fall, its yield must increase. The magnitude of the yield change is provided by rearranging the modified duration formula:

$$\%\Delta\text{price} = -\text{modified duration} \times \Delta\text{yield}$$

$$\frac{\%\Delta\text{price}}{-\text{modified duration}} = \Delta\text{yield}$$

$$\frac{-0.70\%}{-7.30} = 0.0959\% \text{ or } 9.59 \text{ basis points}$$

So if the yield for the Nakhon Metals bond increases by 9.59 basis points and the yield for the Powhatan Industries bond remains constant, the returns for the two bonds will be equivalent over the next year. Given that the Nakhon Metals bond has an initial yield advantage of 0.70%, its return will be higher as long as its yield does not increase by more than 9.59 basis points over the next year. In this case, the yield on the Nakhon Metals bond is expected to increase by 15 basis points, so the Powhatan Industries bond is more attractive. (Study Session 10, LOS 30.k)

15.4. **B** Thomas is correct and Bentley's friend is incorrect. To determine whether a foreign currency-denominated investment should be hedged or not, the manager must compare the expected currency gain or loss implied by the respective cash rates to his expectations. Using the cash rates for the United States and Japan, the expected forward premium for the Yen is 6.5% – 4.20% = 2.3%. In other words, the market predicts the Yen will appreciate 2.3% against the dollar. According to Thomas's and Bentley's expectations, however, the yen should appreciate 3.5% against the dollar. The conclusion is that the forward Yen is too cheap; it is not priced high enough relative to the dollar. Bentley's friend's statement is correct only if the forward differential implied by the cash rates is the same as Thomas's and Bentley's expectations. Since Thomas and Bentley expect the yen to appreciate more than predicted by the market, Thomas's U.S. managers would be better off not hedging. (Study Session 10, LOS 30.j)

15.5. **C** Both Thomas and Bentley are correct. Both callable bonds and bonds with long durations trade at a premium due to their scarcity. (Study Session 9, LOS 29.b)

15.6. **C** When interest rates are near coupon rates and fall for callables and non-callables, non-callables will increase in value more than callables. This is because the price of a callable is depressed as the value of the embedded option increases with the drop in interest rates. Under scenario A, therefore, non-callables outperform callables.

When interest rates are historically very low and rise for both callables and non-callables, the value of the non-callable will fall faster than the value of the callable bond. Therefore, under scenario B the callable will outperform the non-callable. (Study Session 9, LOS 29.e)

Sample Scoring Key: 3 points for each correct response.

QUESTION 16

Reference: Book 4, Study Session 13

Cross-reference to CFA Institute assigned reading: Readings 36 and 37

16.1.   **C**   The only possible answer from the given reasons is a high water mark provision. Since the firm had experienced losses for two years before increasing in value in the previous year, it is likely that the value of the fund had yet to achieve a previous "high water mark" that it must exceed in order for there to be an earned incentive fee. (Study Session 13, LOS 36.q)

16.2.   **B**   Since futures are a zero-sum game, a fully hedged and passively managed futures portfolio should only earn the risk-free rate. (Study Session 13, LOS 36.t)

16.3.   **C**   Similar to a term structure of interest rates, the term structure of futures prices shows the relationship at a point in time between futures prices and time to maturity. When the term structure is negative, longer-term contracts have lower prices than shorter-term contracts, so the curve has a negative slope. With the passage of time, the maturity of a long-term contract shortens and its price rises to that of a shorter-term contract. Thus, an investor can go long a long-term contract and profit as time passes, and the steeper the curve (the greater the backwardation), the greater the potential returns. (Study Session 13, LOS 36.n)

16.4.   **A**   Kanter says he will research companies who do business in commodities. He feels that using the indirect method of buying the stock of those companies to gain commodity exposure is an efficient and effective method for gaining exposure to commodities. This is not necessarily true because those companies often hedge their exposure to commodities. The other statements are true. Agricultural commodities are negatively correlated with inflation, but the broad commodity indices have been positively correlated with inflation. Also, commodities have not generally outperformed stocks and bonds. They are attractive in that they can provide a comparable return while diversifying the portfolio. (Study Session 13, LOS 36.o)

16.5.   **C**   Like interest rate swaps, the fixed value is a weighted average of the futures or forward values where the weights are slightly heavier for the contracts with a shorter maturity. Thus, the swap price is probably slightly more than $53. It is probably not much higher than $53 since the risk-free rate is so low. (Study Session 13, LOS 37.a)

16.6.   **B**   Commodity swaps can have both seasonal prices and notional principals. This should not be surprising since swaps are OTC contracts that the participants can design any way they choose. (Study Session 13, LOS 37.a)

> Sample Scoring Key: 3 points for each correct response.

QUESTION 17

Reference: Book 3, Study Session 10
Book 3, Study Session 12
Book 4, Study Session 15

Cross-reference to CFA Institute assigned reading: Readings 30, 35, 41, and 43

17.1. **C** Edwards is incorrect. The value of the note goes down if interest rates increase. An interest rate call seller provides a payment to the buyer of the call when interest rates increase. If interest rates increase, a short position in interest rate calls would decrease in value, so this will not hedge the risk of the note.

Palmer is correct. The swap can effectively turn the fixed-rate note into a floating-rate note and reduce the duration of the position. If interest rates rise, Anderson receives the higher floating rate in the swap. (Study Session 15, LOS 43.a)

17.2. **A** In order to calculate how much Anderson will receive in dollars as a result of the swap, first calculate the implied notional principal (NP) from the quarterly cash flows of CHF12,000,000:

$$NP\left(\frac{0.066}{4}\right) = CHF12,000,000$$

$$NP = \frac{CHF12,000,000}{\left(\frac{0.066}{4}\right)} = CHF727,272,727$$

Next, calculate the dollar implied principal at the current exchange rate and then calculate a dollar cash flow using the dollar interest rate:

$$CHF727,272,727 \times (\$ / CHF1.24) = \$586,510,264$$
$$\$586,510,264 \times (2.80\% / 4) = \$4,105,572 \qquad \text{(Study Session 15, LOS 43.f)}$$

17.3. **B** The statement is accurate. Transaction exposure is from transactions already entered into and the amount to hedge is thus known. Transaction exposures are the most commonly hedged exposures of a firm. Economic risk, the relationship between changing exchange rates and asset values, is not contractual and the amount to hedge is thus less certain, making it harder to hedge. Translation risk refers to the effect of exchange rate changes on the income statement and balance sheet and is often not hedged. (Study Session 15, LOS 41.f)

17.4. **A** Edwards is correct. If management predicts that interest rates will fall, they will not want to be stuck paying a high, fixed rate. To take advantage of falling rates, they can enter a pay-floating swap (or swaption). The fixed receipt from the swap will at least partially offset the fixed payment on the bonds, while the firm ends up paying a lower floating rate. If desired, management could enter a second pay fixed swap after rates have fallen to lock in the lower fixed rate. The net duration on the first swap can be calculated as the duration of the fixed arm minus the duration of the floating arm, which is 3.75 − 0.25 = 3.5. The notional principal for the swap can be calculated as follows:

$$NP = \$10,000,000\left(\frac{4}{3.5}\right) = \$11,428,571$$

Note: Anderson will assume the receive-fixed arm of the swap, so its duration to Anderson is positive. Also, Anderson is not hedging price risk. That is, they are not trying to change the duration of the bond, so we enter the duration, as it is, in the equation.

Palmer is incorrect. Anderson is paying out a fixed rate, so to take advantage of falling rates, they should receive a fixed rate and pay out a floating rate in the swap. Because the fixed side of the swap has a greater duration than the floating side, Anderson's position in the swap will have a net positive duration. (Study Session 15, LOS 43.f)

17.5. **C** If $275,000 is invested in the U.S. bond and $155,000 is invested in the British bond, the total value of the portfolio is $430,000. The duration contribution of the U.S. bond is $(275,000 / 430,000) \times 4.0 = 2.56$.

To obtain the duration contribution of the British bond, we must first adjust its duration by its yield beta. The yield beta tells us how much British bond yields will change, if U.S. bond yields change by 1%. Using the yield beta of 1.40, the duration contribution of the British bond is $(155,000 / 430,000) \times 8.5 \times 1.40 = 4.29$.

The duration of the entire bond portfolio from a U.S. perspective is then $2.56 + 4.29 = 6.85$. (Study Session 10, LOS 30.i)

17.6. **A** Comment 1 is correct. Emerging market debt has been shown to have increased resiliency over time. When emerging debt markets are hit by some event, they tend to bounce back offering the potential for high returns. (Study Session 10, LOS 30.l)

Comment 2 is incorrect. It is true that emerging market debt is quite volatile due in part to political risk and that analysts should monitor the risk of these markets. However, the standard deviation would be a poor measure of risk because the returns for emerging market debt are often negatively skewed. This non-normal return distribution makes the standard deviation a poor measure of risk because it assumes normality. (Study Session 12, LOS 35.c)

> Sample Scoring Key: 3 points for each correct response.

QUESTION 18

Reference: Book 3, Study Session 9
Book 4, Study Session 14
Book 4, Study Session 15

Cross-reference to CFA Institute assigned reading: Readings 28, 39, 42, and 43

18.1. **C** To hedge their Treasury bond position, Washington Capital should sell:

(1 / 0.4) × (5,000,000 / 100,000) = 125 calls. (Study Session 15, LOS 42.e)

18.2. **C** Thomas is correct. When the option is at-the-money or near expiration, it becomes more important for the portfolio manager to incorporate both gamma and delta into their option hedge analysis so as to increase the precision of the hedge.

Bentley is correct. An increase in the price of the underlying increases delta, so the size of a delta hedge call position should be decreased. (Study Session 15, LOS 42.e,f)

18.3. **A** To return the portfolio to its original dollar duration, the manager could purchase additional amounts of each bond. Alternatively, the manager could select one of the bonds to use as a control-ling position. Since the dollar duration has fallen and Bond 1 has the longest duration, the manager could use the least amount of additional cash by increasing only the holding in Bond 1 (i.e., using Bond 1 as the controlling position):

$$\text{desired increase in DD} = \text{target DD} - \text{current DD}$$
$$= \$157,200 - \$142,095 = \$15,105$$

$$\text{increase in Bond 1: new DD of Bond 1} = \$35,100 + \$15,105$$
$$= \$50,205$$

$$\text{required new value of Bond 1} = \frac{\$50,205}{\$35,100} \times \$780,000 = \$1,115,667$$

Thus, the manager could purchase another $335,667 (= $1,115,667 − $780.000) of Bond 1. The new portfolio total value will be $4,217,000 + $335,667 = $4,552,667, and the portfolio dollar duration will be back to its original level:

$$DD_{new} = [\$1,115,667(4.5) + \$2,500,000(3.4) + \$524,000(2.7) + \$413,000(1.9)](0.01)$$
$$= [\$5,020,501.50 + \$8,500,000 + \$1,414,800 + \$784,700](0.01)$$
$$= \$15,720,002(0.01) = \$157,200 = DD_{Original}$$

(Study Session 9, LOS 28.g)

18.4. **A** Given that LIBOR is projected to be above the FRA rate of 4.4%, Canopy will receive a payment and bears the risk that the counterparty will default. If LIBOR is above the FRA rate at inception of the loan, Canopy will receive a payment based on the notional principal ($5,000,000), the term of the loan (nine months), a discount factor, and the difference between the LIBOR (4.60%) and the FRA rate (4.40%). The discount factor will be based on the LIBOR at the inception of the loan. The amount received is calculated as:

$$\text{payment from the FRA} = \$5,000,000 \times \frac{(0.046 - 0.044) \times (270/360)}{1 + (0.046 \times (270/360))}$$

©2009 Kaplan, Inc.

To find the current value of the credit risk, we calculate the present value of the expected proceeds from the FRA discounted at the risk-free rate:

$$PV = \frac{\$7,250}{(1.038)^{0.25}} = \$7,183$$ (Study Session 14, LOS 39.i)

18.5. **B** Thomas is incorrect. If they use bonds with high yields, it is true that the cost of immunization will be cheaper. Expected returns are higher so they will have to purchase fewer bonds. However, such bonds will also have higher credit risk and contingent immunization assumes no default. If one of the bonds defaults, the immunization strategy will not provide the terminal value required.

Bentley is correct. The risk from nonparallel shifts in the yield curve (immunization risk) can be minimized by concentrating the cash flows around the horizon date. (Study Session 9, LOS 28.f)

18.6. **A** If LIBOR does increase, the cost of Kershaw Ross's floating rate loan will increase. In this case the firm will want to pay a fixed rate and receive a floating rate in a swap. The payer swaption will allow them to pay a predetermined, lower fixed rate in a swap.

If interest rates increase and the fixed rate on swaps in one year (projected at 9.3%) exceeds the swaption fixed rate, the firm will exercise the swaption and pay 8.5%. They receive LIBOR from the swaption and pay in total 8.5% + 1.5% = 10% in the swap and the loan. The firm's first quarterly payment in net will be:

10% × £5,000,000 × 90 / 360 = £125,000.

Note that if swap fixed rates are less than 8.5% in one year, the firm would not exercise the swaption. The firm could either (a) enter a swap at that time and pay the lower fixed rate or (b) not enter a swap and just pay the floating rate in the loan. (Study Session 15, LOS 43.h)

Sample Scoring Key: 3 points for each correct response.

QUESTION 19

Reference: Book 5, Study Session 16

Cross-reference to CFA Institute assigned reading: Reading 44

19.1. **B** Gleeson is correct concerning the nature of uncertainty. Market orders have price uncertainty but no execution uncertainty, while limit orders eliminate price uncertainty but have execution uncertainty. However, he is incorrect concerning when these order types should be used. In most cases, information-motivated and liquidity-motivated trades should use market orders to ensure that execution takes place, while value-motivated and rebalancing trades should use limit orders because price is typically more important than the speed of execution. (Study Session 16, LOS 44.a)

19.2. **C** The quoted spread for the first trade = $22.36 - 22.18 = 0.18$. The quoted spreads for the remaining three trades are 0.20, 0.19, and 0.26, so the **average quoted spread** = $(0.18 + 0.20 + 0.19 + 0.26) / 4 = 0.2075$.

The mid-quote for the first trade = $(22.36 + 22.18) / 2 = 22.27$, and the effective spread = $(22.33 - 22.27) \times 2 = 0.12$. The effective spreads for the remaining three trades are 0.20, 0.17, and 0.30, so the **average effective spread** = $(0.12 + 0.20 + 0.17 + 0.30) / 4 = 0.1975$.

The **weighted average effective spread** = $(900 / 3,000) \times 0.12 + (600 / 3,000) \times 0.20 + (700 / 3,000) \times 0.17 + (800 / 3,000) \times 0.30 = 0.1957$. (Study Session 16, LOS 44.b)

19.3. **C** The VWAP for the day = $(900 / 3,000) \times 22.33 + (600 / 3,000) \times 22.43 + (700 / 3,000) \times 22.47 + (800 / 3,000) \times 22.65 = 22.468$, and the trader's goal would be to have an average cost that is less than the VWAP if they are buying. (Study Session 16, LOS 44.f)

19.4. **B** The benchmark price is 22.36, and the benchmark quantity is 5,000, so the benchmark investment = $22.36 \times 5,000 = \$111,800$. The terminal benchmark value = $22.65 \times 5,000 = \$113,250$, and the benchmark gain = $113,250 - 111,800 = \$1,450$.

The actual portfolio cost = $(900 \times 22.33) + (600 \times 22.43) + (700 \times 22.47) + (800 \times 22.65) = 67,404 + 210 = \$67,614$. The actual portfolio terminal value = $22.65 \times 3,000 = \$67,950$, and the actual gain = $67,950 - 67,614 = \$336$.

The implementation shortfall = $(1,450 - 336) / 111,800 = 0.00996$ or 0.996%. (Study Session 16, LOS 44.g)

19.5. **A** In general, implementation shortfall will be positive (i.e., profits will be foregone) if prices are rising when the trader is attempting to buy, or if prices are falling when the trader is attempting to sell, and all of the order is not completed. Cancellation of a buy order prior to a fall in price, or cancellation of a sell order prior to a rise in price will give rise to a negative implementation shortfall (i.e., the trader will be made better off by the cancellation). (Study Session 16, LOS 44.f)

19.6. **A** Because an algorithmic trading strategy involves mechanical rules to guide trading, one of the concerns is that the portfolio can become over-concentrated. For example, the portfolio could become over-concentrated in sectors that are more liquid and easier to trade when buying, and the opposite problem could occur when selling (i.e., the most liquid assets are sold first, leaving the portfolio over-concentrated in illiquid securities). (Study Session 16, LOS 44.m)

> Sample Scoring Key: 3 points for each correct response.

QUESTION 20

Reference: Book 4, Study Session 14
Book 5, Study Session 17

Cross-reference to CFA Institute assigned reading: Readings 39 and 46

20.1. C   The time-weighted return is approximately 11.4% and money-weighted return is 6.8%. To calculate the time-weighted return, first calculate the returns for each period:

Sub-period 1 (Days 1–16):

$$r_{t,1} = \frac{(\$17,800,000 - \$4,000,000) - \$11,200,000}{\$11,200,000} = 0.2321 = 23.21\%$$

Sub-period 2 (Days 17–31):

$$r_{t,2} = \frac{\$16,100,000 - \$17,800,000}{\$17,800,000} = -0.0955 = -9.55\%$$

Compounding the returns together to calculate a monthly return:

$$r_{twr} = (1 + 0.2321)(1 - 0.0955) - 1 = 0.1144 = 11.44\%$$

To obtain the money weighted-return, we can use our financial calculator. We assume compounding every 15 days because the cash flow comes exactly in the middle of the month, such that it is 15 days from the beginning of the period and 15 days from the end of the period. Using the IRR function on the TI BAII Plus®:

$$MV_1 = MV_0(1 + R)^2 + CF_1(1 + R)$$
$$\$16,100,000 = \$11,200,000(1 + R)^2 + \$4,000,000(1 + R)$$
$$R = 3.36\%$$

Keystrokes on the TI BAII Plus®:

CF 2nd	CLR WORK
–11,200,000	ENTER ↓
–4,000,000	ENTER ↓↓
16,100,000	ENTER
IRR	CPT → 3.36

To convert this half-month return to a monthly return, we compound it over two periods:

$$MWR = (1.0336)^2 - 1 = 0.0683 = 6.8\% \text{ (Study Session 17, LOS 46.c)}$$

20.2. **C** Mercer is incorrect, because although time-weighted return may be easy to calculate, it is not easy to administer. Accounts must be valued every time a significant cash inflow or outflow occurs. For most accounts this would mean daily valuations. Marking to market daily can be expensive to administer and potentially introduces more errors.

Seagram is incorrect because the money-weighted return is influenced by the timing of external cash flows, over which the manager may have no control. In this example, the manager received a cash flow in the middle of the month. Thus, the return during the second half of the month was weighted more heavily than the return during the first half of the month. The manager's return during the first half of the month was quite impressive but the return during the second half of the month was negative. Consequently, the time-weighted return was 11.44% and money-weighted return was lower at 6.8%. The money-weighted return penalizes the manager, because the contribution was not received until later in the month and the manager had no control over this. (Study Session 17, LOS 46.c)

20.3. **C** The M-squared measure for the Bison fund is 11.2%.

To calculate the M-squared ratio for Bison, use the following formula:

$$M_P^2 = \bar{R}_F + \left(\frac{\bar{R}_P - \bar{R}_F}{\hat{\sigma}_P} \right) \hat{\sigma}_M$$

$$M_P^2 = 0.035 + \left(\frac{0.141 - 0.035}{0.315} \right) 0.23 = 0.112 = 11.2\%$$

We compare the M^2 of 11.2% to the return on the market of 9% and conclude that, compared to the market, the Bison Fund had superior risk-adjusted performance over the period. (Study Session 17, LOS 46.f)

20.4. **A** To evaluate the diversification of the two funds, we calculate the Jensen's alpha, Treynor, Sharpe, and M-squared measures for each fund. Using the Bison fund as an example, you would have obtained a Jensen's alpha of:

$$\hat{R}_{Bison} = R_F + \beta_{Bison} \left(\hat{R}_M - R_F \right) = 0.035 + 0.9(0.09 - 0.035) = 8.45\%$$

$$\alpha_{Bison} = R_{Bison,t} - \hat{R}_{Bison}$$

$$\alpha_{Bison} = 0.141 - 0.0845 = 5.7\%$$

The Treynor ratio for Bison is calculated as:

$$T_{Bison} = \frac{\bar{R}_A - \bar{R}_F}{\beta_{Bison}}$$

$$T_{Bison} = \frac{14.1 - 3.5}{0.9} = 11.8$$

The Sharpe ratio for Bison would be calculated as:

$$S_{Bison} = \frac{\bar{R}_A - \bar{R}_F}{\hat{\sigma}_{Bison}}$$

$$S_{Bison} = \frac{14.1 - 3.5}{31.5} = 0.34$$

The M-squared measure is calculated in the answer for question 20.3. If we repeat these calculations for the Lunar fund, we arrive at the following:

	Bison	*Lunar*
Jensen's alpha	5.70%	5.20%
Treynor ratio	11.80	9.50
Sharpe	0.34	0.35
M-squared	11.20%	11.70%

The Bison fund ranks higher by Jensen's alpha and the Treynor ratio, but the Lunar fund ranks higher by the Sharpe and M-squared measures. Jensen's alpha and the Treynor ratio account only for systematic risk as measured by beta. The Sharpe and M-squared measures account for total risk. Thus, since the rankings using alpha and Treynor versus Sharpe and M^2 are reversed, it must be the case that Bison has more unsystematic risk than Lunar and that Lunar is better diversified.

To evaluate the relative performance considering downside risk only, we employ the Sortino ratio, which measures risk relative to the downside risk of returns. It is calculated as the portfolio return minus the minimum acceptable return (MAR) divided by a standard deviation that uses only returns below the MAR. The calculation for Bison is:

$$Sortino_{Bison} = \frac{14.1 - 4.5}{15.1} = 0.64$$

For Lunar, the Sortino ratio is 0.71. Thus, Lunar provides better performance according to the Sortino ratio. Sortino is similar to the Sharpe ratio in that an excess return is divided by a standard deviation. Note however that the Sharpe ratio (which uses the standard deviation in the denominator) examines all returns, whether they correspond to positive or negative alphas. The use of the Sharpe ratio could result in a measurement that is unfair to managers who have consistently outperformed their benchmark and whose variability of returns is primarily on the upside. (Study Session 14, LOS 39.l and Study Session 17, LOS 46.p)

20.5. **C** Mercer is correct because, although manager universes are measurable (after the fact), they are subject to survivor bias. Survivor bias refers to the tendency to include only those managers currently in existence in the benchmark, thereby ignoring those who have left the business or stopped reporting. The poorer performers' records are left out, creating an upward bias in the benchmark performance.

Seagram is correct because manager universes possess only one quality of a valid benchmark, which is measurability. A valid benchmark should meet the following criteria: (1) specified in advance, (2) appropriate, (3) measurable, (4) unambiguous, (5) reflect current investment opinions, (6) accountable, and (7) investable. The median manager cannot be identified in advance and is therefore also ambiguous. The benchmark will differ from one period to another and is therefore not investable. It is impossible to determine its appropriateness and whether it is reflective of current opinion due to its ambiguity. It is also difficult to determine its accountability because fund sponsors must rely on the compiler's representations. (Study Session 17, LOS 46.e, f, h)

20.6. **C** Operations risk is not explicitly mentioned. The risk exposures an analyst should report as part of an enterprise risk management system include liquidity risk, settlement risk, credit risk, operations risk, model risk, sovereign risk, and regulatory risk. In this question, of the responses listed, operations risk is not explicitly mentioned. Operations risk is the potential for failures in the firm's operating systems due to personal or technological, mechanical, or other problems. Although Jaguar is sure to have exposure to operations risk, it is not explicitly described in these transactions. Credit risk is the potential for default, which is certainly a possibility in Jaguar's forward contract. Herstatt risk or settlement risk is the possibility that one party could default on a contract while the other is settling. This has been a problem in foreign exchange markets due to time differences and is certainly possible in Jaguar's currency swap.

Note also that Jaguar's sale of the Mexican pesos is subject to liquidity risk. Liquidity risk refers to the potential for sustaining losses due to the inability to sell or buy a position quickly. (Study Session 14, LOS 39.b)

Sample Scoring Key: 3 points for each correct response.

Exam 3
Morning Session Answers

QUESTION 1

Reference: Book 1, Study Session 4, LOS 14.j,k

Cross-reference to CFA Institute assigned reading: Reading 14

Answer for Question 1

For the Exam:

Investment Policy Statement for Middendorf		
Objectives	Risk Tolerance	**Ability:** Middendorf's situation indicates an above average risk tolerance. **Willingness:** Her statements indicate average to below average willingness to tolerate risk. **Overall:** Middendorf's overall risk tolerance is average to below average.
	Return Objectives	There is no numerical return objective. The goal is to maximize her after-tax return within her risk objectives.
Constraints	Time Horizon	Long-term, 2-stage (pre-retirement and retirement)
	Liquidity	Her liquidity needs, in light of the $750,000 payment pending, are minimal.
	Legal/Regulatory	There are no special legal or regulatory issues.
	Taxes	She is taxed as an individual, and her tax situation is straightforward. Taxes related to diversifying the portfolio must be considered.
	Unique Circumstances	She is single with no dependents. Her portfolio is concentrated, and this matter should be addressed.

Discussion:

		Investment Policy Statement for Middendorf
Objectives	Risk Tolerance	**Ability:** Middendorf's ability is a function of her assets, income, and personal characteristics which form the basis for the constraints section of the IPS. *Assets:* significant net worth. Argues for an above average level of risk tolerance. *Income:* substantial. Above average level of risk tolerance. *Personal characteristics:* long time horizon, manageable liquidity needs, no special legal/regulatory issues, straightforward tax situation, single with no dependents. All argue for above average risk tolerance. **Willingness:** Middendorf's willingness is a function of her personality traits, which we must infer from her statements. She states that she is concerned about the recent volatility exhibited by her portfolio, though we do not have statistical information from which we can assess whether or not this was excessive. She also indicates a desire for a lower volatility portfolio going forward. Both of these statements indicate an average to below average willingness to bear risk. **Overall:** If ability is less than willingness, the level dictated by ability should be the binding constraint. If ability is greater than willingness, the investor should be counseled with a view toward increasing the level of willingness to match ability. The resulting level of willingness becomes the binding constraint. Since we have no information that would lead us to believe that the level of willingness has been increased, her overall risk tolerance is average to below average.
	Return Objectives	Since there is no portfolio income requirement for the foreseeable future, there is no numerical return target. Her objective is simply to maximize total after-tax return, subject to the portfolio meeting her risk objectives.

Constraints	Time Horizon	Middendorf is 52, with no plans to retire in the foreseeable future, so her overall time horizon is at least 25–35 years. She has a 2-stage time horizon: employment and retirement.
	Liquidity	She does not require income from her portfolio. She needs liquidity to fund her planned travel and for emergency situations. The $750,000 severance payment, net of taxes, will be more than sufficient to meet her liquidity needs for the foreseeable future. Her portfolio liquidity requirement is low.
	Legal/ Regulatory	There are no special legal or regulatory issues.
	Taxes	Middendorf is taxed as an individual. She may have to pay taxes on portfolio income and capital gains, depending upon the extent to which her assets are held in tax-sheltered accounts. Any investment actions must take tax status into consideration, including those relating to the diversification of the concentrated stock position.
	Unique Circumstances	She is single with no dependents. Her portfolio is concentrated, and this matter should be addressed (i.e., diversified) as soon as possible.

Sample Scoring Key:
1 point for each of the three risk components (ability, willingness, overall).
2 points for each of the return components (no numerical target, maximize subject to risk objectives).
2 points for each constraint.

QUESTION 2

Reference: Book 1, Study Session 4, LOS 16.c, d

Cross-reference to CFA Institute assigned reading: Reading 16

Answer for Question 2-A

Combined Probability	Real Annual Spending	Expected Real Spending	Present Value
0.9980 = (0.9248 + 0.9736) − 0.9248 × 0.9736	$150,000	**$149,700** = $150,000 × 0.9980	**$146,765** = $149,700 / (1.02)
0.9912 = (0.8418 + 0.9446) − 0.8418 × 0.9446	$150,000	**$148,680** = $150,000 × 0.9912	**$142,907** = $148,680 / $(1.02)^2$
0.9781 = (0.7501 + 0.9125) − 0.7501 × 0.9125	$150,000	**$146,715** = $150,000 × 0.9781	**$138,253** = $146,715 / $(1.02)^3$
0.9569 = (0.6489 + 0.8771) − 0.6489 × 0.8771	$150,000	**$143,535** = $150,000 × 0.9569	**$132,604** = $143,535 / $(1.02)^4$
0.9251 = (0.5371 + 0.8381) − 0.5371 × 0.8381	$150,000	**$138,765** = $150,000 × 0.9251	**$125,684** = $138,765 / $(1.02)^5$
Core Capital			**$686,213** = $146,765 + $142,907 + $138,253 + $132,604 + $125,684
Excess Capital			**$313,787** = $200,000 + $500,000 + $300,000 − $686,213

Sample Scoring Key: (Maximum 24 points)
2 points for each correctly calculated combined probability. (10 points max)
1 point for each correctly calculated expected real spending amount. (5 points max)
1 point for each correctly calculated present value. (5 points max)
2 points for correct core capital.
2 points for correct excess capital.

Professor's Note: If you see an essay question with this many calculations and extra space to perform them, be sure to identify each calculation and circle the answer, so that the grader can compare the calculation to the answer you entered in the template.

Answer for Question 2-B

More beneficial to gift or bequest the fund?	Gift	Bequest
Value as Tax-Free Gift	PV = $300,000; N = 5; Tax rate: 35%; Expected return: 7% FV(tax-free gift) = **$374,750** $= \$300,000[1 + 0.07(1 - 0.35)]^5$ $= \$300,000(1.0455)^5$	
Value as Bequest	PV = $300,000; N = 5; Tax rate: 25%; Expected return: 7% Inheritance tax-rate = 20% FV(bequest) = **$309,972** $= \$300,000[1 + 0.07(1 - 0.25)]^5(1 - 0.2)$ $= \$300,000[(1.0525)^5](0.8)$	
Relative Value	**1.2090** = $374,750 / $309,972	

Sample Scoring Key: (Maximum 8 points)
3 points for FV gift.
3 points for FV bequest.
1 point each for correct relative value and correctly identifying gift as best alternative.

QUESTION 3

Reference: Book 3, Study Session 11, LOS 32.e,i,s
Book 3, Study Session 11, LOS 33.b,d,e

Cross-reference to CFA Institute assigned reading: Readings 32 and 33

A.   **For the Exam:**
(Note: From the information provided we know we will have to use the Fundamental Law of Active Management to assess the performance of the two managers.)

true active return = active return − normal portfolio return

Sycamore: 12 − 15 = −3%
Malta: 16 − 14 = +2%

$$\text{total active risk} = \sqrt{\left(\text{true active risk}\right)^2 + \left(\text{misfit active risk}\right)^2}$$

Sycamore: 2.86%
Malta: 2.14%

$$\text{true information ratio} = \frac{\text{true active return}}{\text{true active risk}}$$

Sycamore: −1.05
Malta: 0.94

Performance evaluation:

Sycamore:

Compared to the fund manager's benchmark, the Sycamore manager outperformed the benchmark and generated a positive alpha. However, based on the normal benchmark portfolio, the Sycamore manager underperformed the Malta fund manager (i.e., negative active return).

Malta:

Compared to the fund manager's benchmark, the Malta manager underperformed the benchmark and generated a negative alpha. However, based on the normal benchmark portfolio, the Malta manager outperformed the Sycamore fund manager (i.e., positive active return).

Discussion:

The manager's total active return can be decomposed into "true" and "misfit" components. The true return is the manager's return minus the appropriate benchmark, the normal portfolio. The normal portfolio has a level of systematic risk exposure that is typical of the manager's portfolio. Thus, the true active return is "true" in the sense that it measures what the manager earned relative to the level of risk normally assumed.

true active return = active return − normal portfolio return

Sycamore: 12 − 15 = −3%
Malta: 16 − 14 = +2%

The misfit return is the normal portfolio return minus the investor's benchmark. The misfit active return is "misfit" to the extent that the benchmark is not consistent with the manager's style.

misfit active return = normal portfolio return − investor's benchmark return

Sycamore: 15 − 11 = +4%
Malta: 14 − 18 = −4%

To derive the true active risk, we need to know the total active risk and misfit risk:

$$\text{total active risk} = \sqrt{(\text{true active risk})^2 + (\text{misfit active risk})^2}$$

Sycamore: $4.0\% = \sqrt{(\text{true active risk})^2 + (2.8\%)^2} = 2.86\%$

Malta: $4.1\% = \sqrt{(\text{true active risk})^2 + (3.5\%)^2} = 2.14\%$

The true information ratio is simply a reward to risk measure:

$$\text{true information ratio} = \frac{\text{true active return}}{\text{true active risk}}$$

Sycamore: $\dfrac{-3.0}{2.86} = -1.05$

Malta: $\dfrac{2.0}{2.14} = 0.94$

If the information ratio is positive, the manager has generated positive risk-adjusted returns, and the larger the ratio, the better the portfolio manager's performance.

Performance evaluation:

Sycamore's performance relative to its benchmark suggests that the portfolio has generated positive alpha. Conversely, Malta's performance suggests that it has generated negative alpha.

However, the benchmarks are misspecified. Judged against the appropriate benchmark— one that has the same level of systematic risk typically assumed by the portfolio—we can see that the Sycamore has actually underperformed, while Malta has outperformed.

Here's a **key point** to make on the exam: The true information ratio provides a more accurate measure of the manager's performance, and by this measure, Malta has outperformed.

Sample Scoring Key:
2 points for the calculations of each firm's true information ratio.
2 points for the discussion of each firm's performance.

B. i. **For the Exam:**

Kishwaukee appears to be a large-cap value fund, while Rockford appears to be a small-cap growth fund. Value stocks tend to have higher earnings volatility than growth stocks.

Discussion:

It appears that Kishwaukee is a large-cap value fund. Relative to the broad market, its holdings have a high dividend yield, low earnings growth, high median market cap, low P/B ratio, and low P/E ratio, which are all characteristics of a large-cap value fund. Additionally, it also has greater representation in the financial and utility industries. It appears that Rockford is a small-cap growth fund. Relative to the broad market, its holdings have a low dividend yield, high earnings growth, low median market cap, high P/B ratio, and high P/E ratio, which are all characteristics of a small-cap growth fund. Additionally, it also has greater representation in the technology and healthcare industries. Relative to growth stocks, value stocks tend to have higher earnings volatility. Thus, we would expect Kishwaukee's holdings to have higher earnings volatility.

ii. **For the Exam:**

Jensen is using holdings-based style analysis, and Miller is using returns-based style analysis. Holdings-based analysis will detect changes in style more quickly than returns-based style analysis.

Discussion:

Jensen is using holdings-based style analysis because she characterizes the holdings of the manager's portfolio by examining its contents. Miller is using returns-based style analysis because she uses a regression approach where the manager's returns are regressed against various security indices. Holdings-based analysis will detect changes in style (style drift) more quickly than returns-based style analysis. The reason is that returns-based analysis typically uses monthly returns over the past several years. Thus, a portion of the analysis is based on data that may no longer reflect the manager's emphasis. Holdings-based style analysis uses the portfolio's current contents to characterize the portfolio and provides a more up-to-date picture of the portfolio's contents.

iii. **For the Exam:**

Kishwaukee is a mutual fund and mutual funds are generally less tax efficient than an ETF such as Rockford.

Discussion:

Kishwaukee is a mutual fund and mutual funds are generally less tax efficient than an ETF such as Rockford. When an investor wants to liquidate their ETF shares, they sell to another investor, which is not a taxable event for the ETF. Additionally, when an ETF redeems a large number of ETF shares for an institutional investor, the ETF may exchange the ETF shares for the basket of stocks underlying the ETF. This also is not a taxable event for the ETF. In an index mutual fund, redemptions typically involve a sale of the underlying securities for cash, which is a taxable event that is passed onto shareholders. Thus, an ETF is more tax efficient for the investor than a mutual fund.

> Sample Scoring Key:
> 3 points for the discussion of each issue.

Answer for Question 3-C

Comment	Correct or incorrect? (circle one)	Explanation
"I am encouraged that PharmaScreen has institutions that hold their stock. The institutions will help monitor management and will use their influence to effect the change needed with PharmaScreen's management."	Incorrect	**For the Exam:** The amount of PharmaScreen stock held by a single institution is likely too small for there to be an incentive to monitor management. **Discussion:** Although Jensen is correct that, in general, institutions help monitor management, the amount of PharmaScreen stock held by a single institution is likely too small and liquid for there to be an incentive to monitor management. PharmaScreen's largest investor is Cape Fear, which holds a small amount of this small-cap stock. Given that Cape Fear is a large hedge fund, their small holding in PharmaScreen would be insignificant to them. The fact that Cape Fear has sold their publicly traded shares indicates that they might sell more shares rather than pushing for change. If the holdings of Cape Fear or another institution were larger or less liquid, they would be more likely to force change at the firm.
"PharmaScreen's management needs a compensation structure that more closely aligns the interests of management and shareholders. One possible solution would be to weight management's compensation more heavily toward out-of-the-money stock options so that they have a strong incentive to increase the stock price. The drawback of this form of compensation is that management would have an incentive to undertake too much risk."	Correct	**For the Exam:** Stock options align the interests of management with shareholders, but out-of-the-money options may induce management to undertake too much risk in an attempt to increase the stock price. **Discussion:** An appropriately structured grant of stock options should work to align the interests of management with those of the shareholders (i.e., that the value of the equity be increased). However, if the options are sufficiently far out of the money, it may appear to management that it is unlikely the options will be in the money prior to expiration under normal circumstances. Thus, management may have an incentive to seek projects that have large potential returns but are excessively risky, in the hope that the options come into the money. In essence, the options have given managers an incentive to gamble with shareholder capital.

Sample Scoring Key:
1 point for identifying whether the statement is correct or incorrect.
2 points for the explanation of why each is correct or incorrect.
0 points possible if correct/incorrect decision is wrong.

D. i. **For the Exam:** (note the question only asks for two reasons)
- Debt eliminates excess cash which managers may waste.
- Debt requires that managers ensure firm liquidity to repay debt.
- Debt motivates managers to keep the firm's control out of the debt-holders' hands in a bankruptcy.
- Debt allows manager-owners to more clearly see the end result of their efforts.

Discussion:

1. Debt motivates management because it takes excess cash out of management hands. With the pressure to make periodic interest and principal payments, management does not have the luxury of spending cash on frivolous projects and perks.

2. To ensure that the firm has cash flow for future investments after repaying its debt, the managers must assure the firm's liquidity. The risk of insufficient liquidity provides an incentive effect for management.

3. If the firm lacks liquidity to the degree where debtholders force the firm into bankruptcy, the managers lose control of the firm and possibly their jobs.

4. If managers hold the majority of the firm's equity, then the issuance of debt, rather than equity, means they don't have to share their residual claim on profits. If equity had been issued instead, the managers-owners would be sharing residual profits with other equity holders.

ii. **For the Exam:** (note the question only asks for one limitation)
- Illiquidity can prevent the firm from investing in new projects.
- Bankruptcy is more likely with more debt and bankruptcy is costly.

Discussion:

1. The threat of illiquidity that motivates management can also deny the firm investment in new projects. The illiquidity may be due to circumstances beyond management's control.

2. If the firm is severely liquidity constrained and cannot pay the interest on its debt, it might be forced into bankruptcy. Bankruptcy costs can be substantial.

Sample Scoring Key:
2 points for the discussion of each reason why debt is an effective mechanism.
2 points for the discussion of the limitation of debt as an effective mechanism.

QUESTION 4

Reference: Book 3, Study Session 9, LOS 28.d
Book 4, Study Session 14, LOS 39.a,f,h,l
Book 4, Study Session 15, LOS 42.f

Cross-reference to CFA Institute assigned reading: Readings 28, 39, and 42

Answer for Question 4-A

Comment	Correct or incorrect? (circle one)	Explanation
"Antelope must evaluate the risk of its bond positions and equity index option positions carefully because of recent volatility in interest rates and in the stock markets. For bonds and options, standard deviation is not the preferred risk management tool. Necessary and sufficient risk measures for bonds and options are the duration of bonds and delta of options."	Incorrect	**For the Exam:** The durations and deltas are not sufficient; convexity and gamma should also be used. **Discussion:** Although it is true that standard deviation is not preferred as a measure of bond and option risk, the durations of bonds and the deltas of options are not sufficient by themselves. Second-order effects should also be used. For bonds, this would be convexity; for options it would be gamma.
"One risk management tool Antelope should consider is maximum loss optimization. This tool involves recognizing those factors with the greatest potential to damage the value of Antelope's portfolio. Antelope could then take steps to limit the damage from these factors."	Correct	**For the Exam:** Maximum loss optimization can model the non-normal events arising from Antelope's options and nontraditional assets. **Discussion:** In maximum loss optimization, the risk factors that have the greatest potential impact on the portfolio are identified. Once the factors are identified, procedures are put in place to limit their impact. This tool is especially valuable for assets with non-normal return distributions because this method does not assume normally distributed returns.

Sample Scoring Key:
1 point for identifying whether the statement is correct or incorrect.
1 point for the explanation of why each is correct or incorrect.
0 points possible if correct/incorrect decision is wrong.

B.   i.   **For the Exam:**

In Antelope's case, a centralized system should be used. The critical flaw, in a multi-manager setting, is that a decentralized risk management system will not account for interactions between manager positions.

Discussion:

Although a decentralized risk management system makes those individuals with the most knowledge (those closest to the action) responsible for risk, a centralized system allows upper management to view risk for the firm as a whole so that the interactions (i.e., correlations) between manager positions can be accounted for. This is especially true in Antelope's case, because the firm has positions in many alternative assets that are likely to have low correlations with traditional assets. A centralized system also allows senior management to monitor for "rogue" managers.

ii.   **For the Exam:**

In Antelope's case, the variance-covariance or analytical VAR should not be used because Antelope holds assets with non-normal returns. The variance-covariance VAR assumes returns are normally distributed.

Discussion:

Although the variance-covariance VAR allows for the correlations of risks across portfolios, the presence of options and nontraditional assets with non-normal return distributions suggests that Antelope should use the historical method or the Monte Carlo method. These methods do not assume a normal distribution of returns.

> Sample Scoring Key:
> 2 points for the discussion of each issue.

C.   The three ratios to use in your answer are the Sharpe ratio (total risk), the Sortino ratio (downside risk), and the RoMAD (maximum drawdown). Note that although the M-squared measure also uses total risk (standard deviation) to evaluate risk-adjusted return, the required data (i.e., market return, market risk, risk-free rate) are not provided in Figure 1. Jensen's alpha and the Treynor measure evaluate performance based on systematic risk (not total risk) using beta, which is also not provided.

For the Exam:

$$\text{Sharpe ratio} = \frac{\overline{R_P} - \overline{R_F}}{\sigma_P}$$

$$\text{Davis} = \frac{20.6 - 4.5}{33.2} = 0.48$$

$$\text{Brooks} = \frac{21.3 - 4.5}{31.2} = 0.54$$

Sharpe: Brooks has outperformed Davis.

$$\text{Sortino ratio} = \frac{\overline{R_P} - \text{MAR}}{\text{downside deviation}}$$

$$\text{Davis} = \frac{20.6 - 5.3}{15.05} = 1.02$$

$$\text{Brooks} = \frac{21.3 - 5.3}{16.5} = 0.97$$

Sortino: Davis has outperformed Brooks.

$$\text{RoMAD} = \frac{\overline{R_P}}{\text{maximum drawdown}}$$

$$\text{Davis} = \frac{20.6}{15.2} = 1.36$$

$$\text{Brooks} = \frac{21.3}{13.7} = 1.55$$

RoMAD: Brooks has outperformed Davis.

Discussion:

The Sharpe ratio is the portfolio's excess return over the risk-free rate ($R_P - R_F$) divided by the portfolio total risk as measured by standard deviation (σ_P):

$$\text{Sharpe ratio} = \frac{\bar{R}_P - \bar{R}_F}{\sigma_P}$$

$$\text{Davis} = \frac{20.6 - 4.5}{33.2} = 0.48$$

$$\text{Brooks} = \frac{21.3 - 4.5}{31.2} = 0.54$$

The greater the Sharpe ratio, the greater the excess return received per unit of total risk assumed. Since Brook's value is larger (0.54 > 0.48), he has outperformed Davis on the basis of this measure.

The Sortino ratio is the portfolio's excess return over some minimum acceptable return (MAR) divided by the downside deviation (the standard deviation of the returns falling below the MAR):

$$\text{Sortino ratio} = \frac{\bar{R}_P - \text{MAR}}{\text{downside deviation}}$$

$$\text{Davis} = \frac{20.6 - 5.3}{15.05} = 1.02$$

$$\text{Brooks} = \frac{21.3 - 5.3}{16.5} = 0.97$$

The idea behind the Sortino ratio is that volatility is only "bad" when the deviation is below the target return, that the manager should not be penalized for the volatility of returns exceeding the MAR. Thus, only the downside deviation is used in its calculation. The greater the Sortino ratio, the greater the excess return per unit of downside risk assumed. Since Davis's value is larger (1.02 > 0.97), he has outperformed Brooks on the basis of this measure.

The return over maximum drawdown (RoMAD) is the portfolio's return divided by the maximum drawdown (i.e., the largest percentage loss, peak to trough, over some specified period of time):

$$\text{RoMAD} = \frac{\bar{R}_P}{\text{maximum drawdown}}$$

$$\text{Davis} = \frac{20.6}{15.2} = 1.36$$

$$\text{Brooks} = \frac{21.3}{13.7} = 1.55$$

The RoMAD is a reward to risk ratio, so the greater the RoMAD, the better the performance. Since the RoMAD for Brooks is greater (1.55 > 1.36), he has outperformed Davis on the basis of this measure.

Sample Scoring Key:
1 point for the calculation of each measure for each manager and 1 point for each evaluation (1 point for each ratio). Total: 9 points

For the Exam:

The Sortino Ratio is most appropriate. Since Davis has beaten his benchmark every year, his volatility is on the upside; standard deviation and maximum drawdown overstate his true risk.

Discussion:

The vignette states that Davis has had tremendous success and has beaten his benchmark every year. Using standard deviation or maximum drawdown as a risk measure would penalize Davis because his volatility is derived exclusively from returns in excess of his benchmark. Therefore, the most appropriate measure is the Sortino ratio because it assumes that the relevant risk is failure to achieve the minimum acceptable return or MAR. (Note that Davis could exceed his benchmark in a given period but still fail to achieve the MAR.)

Sample Scoring Key:
1 point for identification of the correct measure and 2 points for the justification. Total: 3 points

QUESTION 5

Reference: Book 2, Study Session 5, LOS 20.i
Book 3, Study Session 11, LOS 32.t

Cross-reference to CFA Institute assigned reading: Readings 20 and 32

Answer for Question 5-A

Comment	Correct or incorrect? (circle one)	Explanation
"The trust officers at the bank may want to suggest an alpha-beta separation approach. This approach is particularly useful in less efficient markets such as small cap markets."	Incorrect	**For the Exam:** Alpha-beta separation approach works best in efficient markets. -OR- It may be difficult or costly to implement in small-cap markets. **Discussion:** In an alpha and beta separation approach, the investor may gain a systematic risk exposure (beta) through a low-cost index fund or ETF while adding an alpha through a long-short strategy. This strategy may be particularly suitable for those markets that are highly efficient and difficult to generate an alpha from. A limitation of the alpha and beta separation approach is that it may be difficult or costly to implement short positions in markets such as emerging markets or small-cap markets.

"Portfolio managers should be aware, however, that some institutions may not be able to use an alpha-beta separation approach because of institutional constraints."	Correct	**For the Exam:** An alpha-beta separation approach requires a short position, which some investors may be restricted from using. **Discussion:** Some investors, such as institutions, may not be able to use an alpha and beta separation approach because the strategy typically obtains an alpha through a long-short strategy. These investors, however, could create a similar exposure as the alpha and beta separation approach if they can trade equity futures. For example, suppose the investor wanted a beta from large-cap U.S. stocks and an alpha from European equities. The investor could take a long position in the S&P 500 index futures contract and invest with a European equity manager to generate the alpha. To become market neutral in the European equity market, the investor would then short a futures contract based on European equities.

Sample Scoring Key:
1 point for identifying whether the statement is correct or incorrect.
1 point for the explanation of why each is correct or incorrect.
0 points possible if correct/incorrect decision is wrong.

B. i. **For the Exam:**

Most bank liabilities are of shorter term than its loans.

The time horizon for securities portfolio assets must balance the difference and usually has a maturity of three to seven years.

Discussion:

The time horizon for the bank's securities portfolio is determined by the bank's need to manage interest rate risk (duration) and the need to earn a positive spread. A bank's liabilities are usually of shorter term than its loans. The securities portfolio must balance the difference and usually has a maturity of three to seven years.

ii. **For the Exam:**

Liquidity is needed for liabilities and new loans.

Bank liabilities are uncertain, so the securities portfolio must be fairly liquid.

Discussion:

Banks must maintain liquidity in their securities portfolios to help meet demand for new loans. Furthermore, the bank cannot be certain when its liabilities will "mature." If interest rates rise, then bank depositors may withdraw cash from their accounts and move their money into higher yielding accounts.

iii. **For the Exam:**

Banks are highly regulated and face capital requirements, reserve requirements, and regulations on asset risk.

Discussion:

Banks in industrialized nations are highly regulated. For example, banks may not be able to hold sub-investment quality securities, and there may be specified minimum amounts of common equity. In addition, risk-based capital guidelines require banks to establish capital reserves of 100% against most loan categories. Because of reserve requirements, banks also have to pledge collateral (usually short-term treasuries) against certain uninsured public deposits.

> Sample Scoring Key:
> 3 points for the discussion of each issue.

QUESTION 6

Reference: Book 5, Study Session 18, LOS 48.d,e,k,l

Cross-reference to CFA Institute assigned reading: Reading 48

Answer for Question 6-A

Comment	Does statement comply with GIPS® requirements? (circle one)	Explanation
"Since most of our investments are made in fixed income securities, our performance reflects accrual accounting for bond interest, but not for the interest income of non-fixed income securities."	**No**	**For the Exam:** Accrual accounting must be used for all assets that accrue interest income. **Discussion:** When a fixed-income security or other asset that accrues interest is sold, the accrued interest is paid by the purchaser to the seller on settlement date. As a result, for accurate performance measurement, the accrued interest must be accounted for in all portfolio valuations.
"As you can see from all the various countries in which we invest, we have to pay much attention to exchange rate effects. Since some of our investments are in countries where exchange rate information is difficult to retrieve, we use a multitude of sources to calculate the exchange rate effects for our composites and benchmarks. These differential sources of information allow us to find the most accurate exchange rate data and are disclosed in performance presentations."	**Yes**	**For the Exam:** No explanation required. **Discussion:** GIPS® requires that the firm must disclose and describe any known inconsistencies in the exchange rates used among portfolios contained within a composite and also any inconsistencies between a composite and its benchmark.

"Return performance is presented gross of all fees, expenses, and loads."	No	**For the Exam:** Return performance may be presented gross of fees but must be net of all direct trading expenses. **Discussion:** When presenting gross-of-fees returns, firms must disclose if there are any other deductions beyond the direct trading expenses. When presenting net-of-fees returns, firms must disclose if there are any other deductions beyond the investment management fee and direct trading expenses.

Sample Scoring Key:
1 point each for consistent/inconsistent decision.
2 points each for correct explanation, where required.
0 points possible if consistent/inconsistent decision is wrong.

B.   There are a total of six items not in compliance:

1. **For the Exam:**

    Cannot display noncompliant data after January 1, 2000.

    Discussion:

    To claim compliance with GIPS, performance presentations after January 1, 2000 must be GIPS compliant. Any non-compliant performance data presented for periods prior to 2000 must disclose not only the period but also how the presentation is not in compliance. This is true, even if the non-compliant data is consistent with existing local laws and regulations.

2. **For the Exam:**

    Performance of portfolios and composites for periods of less than one year cannot be presented on an annualized basis.

    Discussion:

    Annualizing returns that were realized over some fraction of a year is tantamount to the simulation of returns over the periods required to complete the full year. This violates the spirit of GIPS® and is not allowed.

3. **For the Exam:**

   Footnote 8 regarding the return calculations is not in compliance.

   Discussion:

   The firm can claim compliance on the overall basis of its performance presentation. It cannot flatly state that a specific aspect of the presentation, such as the return calculation, is "performed as prescribed" by the GIPS®.

4. **For the Exam:**

   Footnote 6 concerning non-fee-paying portfolios is not adequate.

   Discussion:

   Although the presence of non-fee paying portfolios is acknowledged, the firm must also disclose the percentage of the composite they represent.

5. **For the Exam:**

   Footnote 9 concerning the percentage of firm assets represented by discretionary accounts is not in compliance.

   Discussion:

   Total firm assets must include the market values of all discretionary and non-discretionary accounts under management.

6. **For the Exam:**

   The use of estimated trading expenses as mentioned in footnote 3 is not in compliance.

   Discussion:

   Actual direct trading expenses are known when an investment is bought/sold and must be included in return calculations. Using estimated trading expenses is prohibited.

Sample Scoring Key:
2 points for each of four correctly identified non-compliant component.

QUESTION 7

Reference: Book 2, Study Sessions 5, LOS 20.c,i
Book 2, Study Session 8, LOS 26.c,o
Book 5, Study Session 16, LOS 45.a,b,c

Cross-reference to CFA Institute assigned reading: Readings 20, 26, and 45

A. **For the Exam:**

The characteristics that help to determine pension plan risk tolerance:
- Plan surplus.
- Sponsor financial status and profitability.
- Sponsor and pension fund common risk exposures.
- Plan features.
- Workforce characteristics.

Discussion:

There are at least five characteristics of any defined pension plan that determine the appropriate level of risk tolerance. These are:
- Plan surplus—the amount by which the present value of the plan assets exceeds the present value of plan liabilities. In general, the greater the surplus, the greater the risk tolerance.
- Sponsor financial status and profitability—if the sponsor is in strong financial health and is profitable, this implies a greater likelihood that the sponsor will be in position to cover any funding shortfall. Thus, there is a positive relationship between sponsor financial status and profitability and the plan's ability to tolerate risk.
- Sponsor and plan common exposures—this concern is that certain macroeconomic factors can have a simultaneous negative impact on plan funded status and the plan's sponsor. The greater the degree of common exposure, especially on the downside with regard to pension plan asset values, the lower the level of risk tolerance.
- Plan features—plans that allow participants to elect for early retirement and other features that can accelerate fund payouts generally reduce risk tolerance.
- Workforce characteristics—the principal issue here is average age of the participants. The greater the average age, the shorter the average time horizon to payout and the lower the plan's risk tolerance. There is also a positive relationship between the active to retired lives rates and risk tolerance.

> Sample Scoring Key:
> 1 point for each characteristic listed, up to a maximum of 3 points total.

B. **For the Exam:**

The constraints:
- Liquidity.
- Time horizon.
- Legal regulatory.
- Taxes.
- Unique needs.

The return objectives:
- The pension plan must focus on meeting or exceeding its actuarial required rate of return.
- The endowment focuses on a total return approach.

Discussion:

The factors that determine investment policy for institutional investors are the objectives and constraints. The objectives are concerned with risk tolerance and return. The constraints are limiting factors that often help to define the appropriate level of risk tolerance. These include the level of liquidity that must be maintained, the time horizon(s) until liabilities must be satisfied, any legal and regulatory issues such as the need to meet ERISA standards or diversification rules, the tax status of the fund, and any unique issues relating to the investment fund.

The pension fund's objective is to meet the promised pension payments. These are determined by various actuarial assumptions embedded in the present value calculations. Its return objective will be to meet or exceed the specified actuarial rate. An endowment's funding commitments are more flexible and can be adjusted to meet changes in the endowment's circumstances. Consequently, its focus will normally be on total return.

> Sample Scoring Key:
> 1 point for each constraint listed, up to 3 in total.
> 1 point for correctly describing each return objective, for 2 in total.

C.   **For the Exam:**

Role of the strategic allocation:
- The strategic asset allocation provides an observable measure of the level of systematic risk that is believed to be appropriate given the investor's risk tolerance and the manager's capital market expectations.
- The empirical evidence indicates that, on average, more than 90% of a portfolio's returns are determined by the asset allocation.

Discussion:

The strategic allocation reflects the confluence of the investor's risk and return objectives and the expectations for the capital market expectations. The market expectations are formally expressed in the form of the efficient frontier, representing the set of optimal trade-offs for risk and return that are available to the investor. From this optimal set, the portfolio manager recommends a specific point that is best suited to satisfy the investor's risk and return objectives. As such, the point selected provides an observable measure of what has been deemed an appropriate level of risk tolerance for the investor.

Empirical evidence suggests that, on average, more than 90% of portfolio returns are determined by the strategic allocation and less than 10% by other factors, including active management. This suggests that determining the appropriate strategic allocation is the most important single decision to be made by the portfolio manager.

> Sample Scoring Key:
> 2 points for noting that the allocation provides an observable measure of appropriate risk tolerance.
> 1 point for relating the allocation to capital market expectations.
> 1 point for noting that more than 90% of portfolio returns are determined by asset allocation.

D.   **For the Exam:**
- Institutions, such as defined pension funds, are primarily concerned with satisfying liabilities.
- Individuals are usually interested in accumulating wealth that can be used to achieve their required and, if possible, their desired lifestyle objectives.

Discussion:

Institutional investment pools are normally created to fund some liability structure, such as pension payouts, life insurance claims, the ability to fund charitable causes, etc. Consequently, the primary concern is the fund's ability to meet these liabilities.

Individuals typically accumulate funds to meet a series of lifestyle objectives, which are often classified into required and desired objectives. A required objective might be to fund a minimally acceptable standard of living in retirement. A desired objective might be to take a vacation in Europe every year. Because individual liabilities are usually not fixed, as are many institutional liabilities, the focus is usually on wealth accumulation.

> Sample Scoring Key: 1 point for correctly stating each objective.

E.   **For the Exam:**
The portfolio manager has a duty to:
- Construct a portfolio that meets the needs of the client.
- Monitor the portfolio to be sure it continues to meet the client's needs.

Two basic factors indicate the potential need for monitoring, rebalancing, and review of the strategic allocation. These are:
- Changes in market/economic conditions and expectations.
- Changes in the investor's circumstances.

Discussion:

The institutional portfolio manager is in a position of managing the assets that belong to others. As such, they are in a position of fiduciary responsibility and have a duty of loyalty and prudence to the client.
- The first of the manager's fundamental responsibilities is to construct a portfolio that meets the needs of the client. The first test of appropriateness is with respect to risk tolerance.
- The second of the manager's fundamental responsibilities is to monitor the portfolio to be sure it continues to meet the client's needs. At minimum, this means the portfolio should be reviewed once per year—more often if circumstances dictate.

The main factors that will determine when monitoring should occur and action potentially be taken are changes in market conditions or investor circumstances.
- Changes in market conditions can include large changes in market value or significant events that have an impact upon market expectations for the future.
- Changes in client circumstances include a change in the terms of the pension plan agreement, the bankruptcy of the sponsor, or any other material matter affecting the plan's financial outlook.

> Sample Scoring Key:
> 1 point each for listing each of the portfolio manager's key responsibilities.
> 1 point each for listing each basic factor (market changes, changes in client circumstances).

QUESTION 8

Reference: Book 1, Study Session 4, LOS 19.b,c,d,g

Cross-reference to CFA Institute assigned reading: Reading 19

A. i. **For the Exam:**

Fisher: Human capital is low risk ⇒ Portfolio can be more aggressive and favor equity.

Pollard: Human capital is high risk ⇒ Portfolio must be conservative and favor bonds.

Discussion

Fisher: The asset allocation should be weighted towards equity. Her government job is secure; thus, her human capital has low earnings risk (i.e., it is bond-like). Because her human capital is secure, her financial capital (her portfolio) can be invested more aggressively and should be weighted towards equity.

Pollard: The asset allocation should be weighted towards bonds. His commissioned sales job has high risk; thus, his human capital has high earnings risk (i.e., it is equity-like). Because his human capital is risky, his financial capital (his portfolio) must be invested conservatively and should be weighted towards bonds.

Although the question does not ask for sector allocations, Easterling should recommend an asset allocation for Pollard that excludes the health care industry. Easterling would structure a completion portfolio (described in Reading 17) that has a low correlation with the health industry. In other words, he would minimize the correlation between Pollard's human and financial capital to mitigate Pollard's earnings risk.

 Professor's Note: You could also justify a bias towards equity for Fisher using her long time horizon and a bias towards bonds for Pollard using his potentially short time horizon (as discussed in Reading 14). Hers is long because of good health and his is potentially short due to a poor family health history.

> Sample Scoring Key: 12 points maximum.
> 1 point for each investor's correct asset allocation.
> 1 point for the justification of each investor's asset allocation.
> 0 points possible if the investor's asset allocation is incorrect.

B. i. **For the Exam:**

Fisher: Probability of death is low ⇒ Low demand for insurance.

Pollard: Probability of death is relatively high ⇒ High demand for insurance.

Discussion

Fisher: She is in good health and expects a long life, so her mortality risk is low. Given a low probability of death, her demand for life insurance would be low.

Pollard: He has a poor family health history, so his mortality risk is potentially high. Given a relatively high probability of death, his demand for life insurance would be high.

ii. **For the Exam:**

Fisher: Human capital is low risk $\Rightarrow$ High demand for insurance.

Pollard: Human capital is high risk $\Rightarrow$ Low demand for insurance.

Discussion

Fisher: Her government job is secure and is bond-like. Insurance acts as a substitute for human capital. Because the human capital is of low risk, a low discount rate is applied to it. Its present value is thus high, and more insurance would be needed to replace it. So her demand for life insurance would be high.

Pollard: His commissioned sales job has high risk and is equity-like. Because the human capital is risky, a high discount rate is applied to it. Its present value is thus low and less insurance would be needed to replace it. So his demand for life insurance would be low.

iii. **For the Exam:**

Fisher: Bequest preference is rather low $\Rightarrow$ Low demand for insurance.

Pollard: Bequest preference is high $\Rightarrow$ High demand for insurance.

Discussion

Fisher: Her desire to leave an estate is fairly low. Although she states a desire to leave a modest amount to charity and enough for the care of her pets, she has no human heirs. So her desire for a bequest is rather low and, hence, her demand for life insurance would be low.

Pollard: His desire to leave an estate is high. He states that his wife has few job prospects and he fears leaving his family destitute. So his desire for a bequest is high and, hence, his demand for life insurance would be high.

Sample Scoring Key: 12 points maximum.
1 point for the insurance decision for each factor for each investor.
1 point for the justification for each factor for each investor.
0 points possible if the investor's insurance demand is incorrect.

QUESTION 9

Reference: Book 3, Study Session 10, LOS 30.h,i,j,k

Cross-reference to CFA Institute assigned reading: Reading 30

A.   **For the Exam:**

1.   Market selection.

2.   Currency selection.

3.   Duration management.

4.   Sector selection.

5.   Credit analysis.

6.   Investing outside the relevant benchmark.

Discussion:

Market selection refers to the country in which the investment is to be made.

Currency selection (or management) involves the decision of which currency exposures to hedge.

Duration management concerns the selection of maturities that are likely to benefit from changes in the yield curve.

Sector selection concerns industry, ratings categories, and other classifications.

Credit analysis can generate excess returns if the manager is able to purchase securities with improving credit quality.

Investing outside the benchmark means that the manager selects bonds that are similar in risk to those in the benchmark but are anticipated to perform better than those contained in the benchmark.

Sample Scoring Key: 1 point for each correct item listed.

B.   **For the Exam:**

Estimated yield change for Bond X = 1.30 × 80 = 104 bps = 1.04%.

Estimated change in value of Bond X = −7 × 0.0104 × 100 = −7.28%.

Discussion:

The relationship between domestic and foreign yields can be estimated with the following regression equation:

$$\Delta \text{yield}_{\text{foreign}} = \beta(\Delta \text{yield}_{\text{domestic}}) + e$$

In the regression, β is the country beta, and e is the error term $(\hat{e} = 0)$. The country beta estimates the relative change in the foreign interest rate for a given change in domestic rates.

The change in the value of the foreign bond can then be estimated using the forecast change in the domestic rate, the resulting change in the bond's yield (i.e., the foreign interest rate) and the bond's duration:

$$\Delta P = -D \times \Delta y \times 100$$

Since the change in yield was positive, the estimated change in value is negative.

> Sample Scoring Key:
> 3 points for the estimated change in yield.
> 2 points for the estimated change in value.

C. **For the Exam:**

Forward discount for Currency Y = $C_d - C_y$ = 4.55 − 5.65 = −1.10%.

Expected depreciation for Currency Y = −0.95.

−0.95 > −1.10 → Do not hedge.

Discussion:

The foreign currency forward discount (−) or premium (+) is approximated by the differential in the cash rates for the two currencies (domestic cash rate minus foreign). In this case, the differential is −1.10, so the foreign currency is trading at a discount of 1.10% in the forward market. This is the forward currency differential that is locked in if the position is hedged by selling the foreign currency forward at current forward prices.

Since the portfolio manager expects Currency Y to depreciate by only 0.95%, they expect the currency to outperform the expectations that are embedded in the forward rates. If this turns out to be the case, the spot value of the currency one year from today will be greater than the current forward rate, and the manager will be better off by not hedging.

> Sample Scoring Key:
> 3 points for calculating the forward discount.
> 2 points for recommending not to hedge if the rationale is provided correctly (i.e., that −0.95 > −1.10).

D.   **For the Exam:**

Bond X's yield disadvantage not considering the change in currency value = 4.55 – 7.05 = –2.50%.

The forward discount or premium: 5.65 – 3.05 = 2.60% forward premium for currency X.

Taking into consideration the appreciation of currency X:

2.60 – 2.50 = 0.10% overall yield advantage for bond X or 0.10 / 2 = 0.05% over the 6-month time horizon.

Breakeven yield change for Bond X = (–0.05 / –7) × 100 = 0.71 bps.

The two bonds will break even if the yield on Bond X increases 0.71 bps. Since Greystone expects X's yield to increase 15 bps, the expected capital loss on Bond X will make Bond Y the better investment.

Discussion:

Breakeven analysis is used by portfolio managers to measure the stability of the yield advantage/disadvantage between two bonds. Once the breakeven change in rates has been determined, the manager can compare it to his interest rate expectations.

Bond Y's yield advantage over Bond X is 250 basis points per year, not taking into consideration the change in value of the currencies. Once the appreciation of currency X is taken into consideration, Bond X is at a yield *advantage* of 0.1% or 0.05% over the 6-month investment horizon. Thus, if Bond X decreases in value by 0.05%, the yield advantage will be offset and the two bonds will break even over the period.

Note that we calculate the breakeven change in yield for Bond X because it is the bond with the greater duration. Performing the calculation using the bond with the greater duration is a conservative approach because that bond's value is relatively more sensitive to changes in interest rates.

Since Greystone expects the yield on X to increase (15 bps) more than the breakeven yield change of 0.71 bps, Bond X should experience a capital loss sufficient to make Bond Y the better investment.

Sample Scoring Key:
1 point for stating 0.5% yield advantage for Bond X or 0.5% disadvantage for Bond Y.
3 points for breakeven calculation of 0.71 bps increase in yield for Bond X.
0 points if stated in terms of Bond Y.

Exam 3
Afternoon Session Answers

To get detailed answer explanations with references to specific LOS and SchweserNotes content, and to get valuable feedback on how your score compares to those of other Level 3 candidates, use your Username and Password to gain Online Access at *www.schweser.com* and choose the left-hand menu item "Practice Exams Vol. 1."

10.1.	A	14.1.	B	18.1.	C
10.2.	A	14.2.	A	18.2.	A
10.3.	A	14.3.	C	18.3.	B
10.4.	A	14.4.	B	18.4.	B
10.5.	C	14.5.	A	18.5.	C
10.6.	B	14.6.	C	18.6.	C
11.1.	A	15.1.	C	19.1.	B
11.2.	C	15.2.	B	19.2.	B
11.3.	A	15.3.	C	19.3.	A
11.4.	A	15.4.	B	19.4.	C
11.5.	C	15.5.	A	19.5.	B
11.6.	B	15.6.	C	19.6.	A
12.1.	C	16.1.	B		
12.2.	B	16.2.	C		
12.3.	C	16.3.	B		
12.4.	B	16.4.	A		
12.5.	B	16.5.	A		
12.6.	C	16.6.	C		
13.1.	B	17.1.	C		
13.2.	A	17.2.	C		
13.3.	B	17.3.	C		
13.4.	B	17.4.	A		
13.5.	A	17.5.	A		
13.6.	B	17.6.	B		

EXAM 3
AFTERNOON SESSION ANSWERS

QUESTION 10

Reference: Book 5, Study Session 17

Cross-reference to CFA Institute assigned reading: Reading 46

10.1. **A** Harrison is correct. Since the Treynor ratio uses beta, which measures only systematic risk, it is appropriate only for an investor with a well-diversified portfolio. Recall that unsystematic risk is diversified away in a well-diversified portfolio.

Powell is incorrect. The Sharpe ratio uses the standard deviation as the measure of risk. Since the Treynor ratio uses systematic risk as the relevant measure of risk, it may rank portfolios differently than the Sharpe ratio. Consider a portfolio with low systematic risk but high unsystematic and total risk. This portfolio may rank highly using the Treynor ratio but quite low using the Sharpe ratio. (Study Session 17, LOS 46.p)

10.2. **A** The pure allocation effect is calculated by taking the differences between the portfolio and benchmark weights for each sector and multiplying it by the difference between the benchmark return for that sector and the total benchmark return. The products are then summed across the sectors:

benchmark return = (0.6)(0.286) + (0.25)(0.124) + (0.15)(0.0885) = 0.216

The pure allocation effect = (0.5 − 0.6)(0.286 − 0.216) + (0.3 − 0.25)(0.124 − 0.216) + (0.2 − 0.15)(0.0885 − 0.216) = −1.80%.

So TopTech does not demonstrate superior ability to choose sectors, because the allocation effect is negative at −1.80%. (Study Session 17, LOS 46.l)

10.3. **A** The within-sector selection effect measures the manager's ability to select superior securities to represent each sector in the portfolio. It is the sum of the weight for each sector in the benchmark times the difference in that sector's return in the portfolio and in the benchmark.

Within sector selection effect = (0.60)(0.187 − 0.286) + 0.25(0.158 − 0.124) + (0.15)(0.125 − 0.0885) = −0.0594 + 0.0085 + 0.0055 = −0.0454 = −4.54%.

In sum, in the financial and large cap sectors, the manager chose superior stocks, so they show superior ability there. The overall within-sector selection effect is negative (−4.54%), however, so they do not show a consistent overall ability to select stocks.

The remaining component of attribution analysis (the allocation/selection interaction effect) can be calculated as the difference between the portfolio and benchmark weights for each sector multiplied by the difference between the return for the sector in the portfolio and the return for the sector in the benchmark. The total allocation/selection interaction effect is the sum of these products.

Allocation/selection interaction effect = $(0.50 - 0.60)(0.187 - 0.286) + (0.30 - 0.25)$ $(0.158 - 0.124) + (0.20 - 0.15)(0.125 - 0.0885) = 0.0099 + 0.0017 + 0.0018 = 0.0134 = 1.34\%$.

The total excess return for the manager is then $-1.80\% + 1.34\% - 4.54\% = -5.00\%$.

This should be equal to the excess return calculated using the total returns for the benchmark and the portfolio. The total return for the benchmark is calculated above as 21.6%. For the portfolio it is: $= (0.5)(0.187) + (0.3)(0.158) + (0.2)(0.125) = 16.6\%$. Thus, the excess return calculated using the total returns for the portfolio and the benchmark is $16.6\% - 21.6\% = -5.0\%$. (Study Session 17, LOS 46.l)

10.4. **A**   TopTech's benchmark appears to be reflective of current investment opinion, because the managers have knowledge of the securities in the benchmark. It also appears to be unambiguous, because the weights and identities of the securities in the benchmark are clearly identified.

However, a benchmark must satisfy five other criteria to be considered valid. In TopTech's case, the benchmark is not specified in advance and is not investable. By choosing the top 10% of managers after the fact, TopTech's managers have no knowledge of what securities constitute the benchmark before the fact. Thus, their benchmark is also not investable. TopTech's managers cannot replicate the benchmark positions before the fact because they do not know the top ten managers at the beginning of the measurement period. In sum, TopTech's benchmark does not possess all the properties of a valid benchmark. (Study Session 17, LOS 46.f)

10.5. **C**   Harrison is incorrect. The benchmark level examines the difference between the return to custom benchmarks reflecting the managers' styles and the return to a broad asset category. Essentially the benchmark return measures the return to style bets resulting from the policy weighting in various styles.

Powell is incorrect. Although the investment manager's level does reflect the return from active management, it uses the policy weights established for each manager. Returns due to differences between policy weights and the amounts actually allocated to each manager do not show up until the last level of macro attribution analysis (i.e., allocation effects). (Study Session 17, LOS 46.k)

10.6. **B**   Benchmark B is the best benchmark for the small-cap value manager. A good benchmark will have a beta relative to the portfolio that is close to one, so the tracking error (i.e., the standard deviation of the excess return of the portfolio relative to the benchmark) will be low. The benchmark turnover should be low so that it is investable by a passive manager. The correlation between the return to the manager's active management (A) and the return to the manager's style (S) should be low. Otherwise, the benchmark has not adequately captured the manager's style.

Benchmark B is the best benchmark using all four measures. (Study Session 17, LOS 46.i)

Sample Scoring Key: 3 points for each correct response.

QUESTION 11

Reference: Book 1, Study Session 1

Cross-reference to CFA Institute assigned reading: Reading 1

11.1. **A** According to Standard V(B) Communication with Clients and Prospective Clients, he is required to distinguish between fact and opinion in his research reports. He has fully conformed to this requirement. The statement is in accordance with CFA Institute Standards. (Study Session 1, LOS 1.b)

11.2. **C** His action is not supported by reasonable and adequate basis in fact, and thus constitutes a violation of Standard V(A) Diligence and Reasonable Basis. In fact, he totally missed the Reuters report, which would indicate a lack of due diligence. (Study Session 1, LOS 1.b)

11.3. **A** Under CFA Institute Standard V(A) Diligence and Reasonable Basis, Lepage is required to exercise due diligence and thoroughness. His ignorance of information that is of material (disseminated before Lepage's decision to sell the shares of AirCon) is an obvious violation of the Standard. (Study Session 1, LOS 1.b)

11.4. **A** CFA Institute Standard III(B) Fair Dealing requires that members and candidates deal fairly with clients when taking investment actions (including trade allocations). Recommended procedures to comply with this Standard include allocating trades on a pro rata basis when the entire order is being filled over time such that the prices are the same in all accounts. Lepage has conformed with the Standards in his execution and allocation of the shares of Spectra Vision. (Study Session 1, LOS 1.b)

11.5. **C** Shareholders are most often concerned with the long-term prospects for the company. Giving management a large number of options that expire in the current year creates strong incentive for management to engage in behavior that puts the long-term value of the company at risk in favor of short-term gains in the stock price (thus maximizing the value of management's stock options). The base salary should be a small proportion of the overall compensation package and can be supplemented by performance-based bonuses (not a guaranteed bonus structure). Use of company assets for personal use should be restricted, whether or not the manager does a good job for the shareholders. (Study Session 1, LOS 1.b)

11.6. **B** Lepage's first statement is incorrect. While it is a noble goal for a board to structure management compensation packages to align the managers' interests with those of the shareholders, best practices in corporate governance dictate that the board must continue to evaluate the effectiveness of management in managing the firm in accordance with shareholders' interests. Lepage's second statement is correct. Good corporate governance practices provide the audit committee independence from firm management and the authority to hire an auditor and scrutinize the auditor's work, including any financial statements produced internally. (Study Session 1, LOS 1.b)

> Sample Scoring Key: 3 points for each correct response.

QUESTION 12

Reference: Book 2, Study Session 6
Book 3, Study Session 12

Cross-reference to CFA Institute assigned reading: Readings 23 and 35

12.1. **C** Ms. So is referring to psychological traps and model and input uncertainty. Psychological traps are behavioral characteristics such as anchoring, status quo, overconfidence, etc. The main point is that these traps can result in biased capital market expectations. Problems relating to the choice of models and accuracy of data are known as model and input uncertainty. The analyst wants to choose the model that most correctly describes the market valuation process, but any time there is a choice, there is a chance that the incorrect model will be chosen. (Study Session 6, LOS 23.a)

12.2 **B** The required return on the Singapore index can be estimated with the dividend discount model.

$$3,750 = \frac{90(1.06)}{(R_M - 0.06)} \Rightarrow R_M = 8.544\%$$

The market risk premium for Singapore = 8.544 − 2.4 = 6.144%. The market risk premium for Taiwan = 6.144 × 1.10 = 6.76, so the required return on the market in Taiwan is 6.76 + 2.7 = 9.46%. Thus, we can estimate the intrinsic value of the Taiwan index.

$$\frac{450(1.045)}{(0.0946 - 0.045)} = 9,481$$

(Study Session 6, LOS 23.c)

12.3. **C** The presenter is incorrect on both counts. For any pair of freely traded currencies, interest rate parity is governed by arbitrage and must hold in the short run. On the other hand, the relative form of purchasing power parity is not governed by arbitrage, and currency values can deviate widely from their PPP value in the short run. However, the evidence suggests that PPP is a useful forecasting tool for the long run. (Study Session 6, LOS 23.l)

12.4. **B** Although it is true that, in general, emerging market sovereign debt has increased in quality and emerging market governments have the ability to access global capital (e.g., World Bank), these generalities in and of themselves do not present any specific return-enhancing capabilities. Also, it is true that emerging market debt can be highly volatile with negatively-skewed returns distributions. This characteristic, however, presents an increased probability of low or negative returns (increased risk). Expected returns (prices) will compensate for the increased risk, but this again does not in and of itself present any specific return-enhancing capability. It is also true that the EMBI+ index is dominated by the debt securities of Latin American countries. Ordinarily an investor would not want to invest in a concentrated index, due to its lack of diversification. However, with such a concentrated index, the investor is faced with both unsystematic and systematic risk and, hence, an increased return potential. Thus, combining the index with a well-diversified portfolio of fixed income securities presents the global fixed income manager the potential to generate enhanced returns. (Study Session 12, LOS 35.a)

12.5. **B** When an economic crisis, such as that which began in Thailand in 1997, spreads to other countries, this is known as contagion. The fact that emerging market asset returns may exhibit greater non-normality makes it more difficult to apply parametric models (e.g., those based upon the statistical concepts of mean and standard deviation). In such instances, the analyst should consider non-parametric approaches, such as bootstrapping techniques and Monte Carlo simulation to estimate risk. (Study Session 6, LOS 23.k)

12.6. **C** All else being equal, the economic statistics presented favor Russia over Brazil for hard currency bond investment. Russia has a relatively greater level of foreign exchange relative to short-term debt, implying that short-term ability to pay is greater, and the overall indebtedness relative to GDP is lower.

While India and China each have the advantage in two of the four economic growth statistic categories, in aggregate, the statistics presented favor China for equity investment.

estimated long-term growth = population growth + labor force

participation growth + growth in capital spending + growth in total factor productivity

estimated long-term growth for China: 0.8 + 1.8 + 1.3 + 0.9 = 4.8%

estimated long-term growth for India: 1.3 + 0.5 + 1.4 + 0.4 = 3.6%

In addition, China enjoys a relatively more favorable savings to investment balance, implying that the growth may be more sustainable. (Study Session 6, LOS 23.q)

QUESTION 13

Reference: Book 3, Study Session 9

Cross-reference to CFA Institute assigned reading: Reading 28

13.1.   **B**   The cushion spread is the difference between the safety net return (minimum acceptable return) and prevailing immunized rate. In this case, the cushion spread is 8% – 6% = 200 basis points. (Study Session 9, LOS 28.i)

13.2.   **A**   The required terminal value at the initial safety net return of 6% is:

$100 million$(1.03)^{10}$ = $134.39 million

The amount required to achieve the required terminal value at the current immunization rate of 8% over the five remaining years is $134.39 million / $(1.04)^{10}$ = $90.79 million.

So, the dollar safety margin is $100 million – $90.79 million = $9.21 million. (Study Session 9, LOS 28.i)

13.3.   **B**   After one year, the value of the portfolio is the price of the bond plus accumulated interest. The price of the bond is computed as follows:

FV = 100; N = 18; I/Y = 4.5; PMT = 4; CPT → PV = 93.92

The accumulated value of the coupon payments is the compounded value of the first coupon at 4% (= 8% / 2) for one 6-month period plus the value of the second coupon payment received at the end of the first year, or:

4(1.04) + 4 = 4.16 + 4 = $8.16

Thus, the value of the portfolio after one year is 93.92 + 8.16 = 102.08, or $102.08 million.

The required terminal value is $100 million$(1.03)^{10}$ = $134.39 million.

The portfolio value necessary to achieve the required terminal value at the prevailing immunization rate of 9%, compounded semiannually, over the four remaining years, is:

$134.39 million / $(1.045)^{8}$ = $94.50 million

So, the dollar safety margin is: $102.08 million – $94.50 million = $7.58 million. (Study Session 9, LOS 28.i)

13.4. **B**   The dollar safety margin hits zero when the portfolio falls to the minimum value necessary to achieve an immunization strategy, and that value is the present value of the liability at the current immunized rate. The present value of $134.39 million at the immunized rate of 11% (for 5 years) is ($134.39 million)/(1.055)10 = $78.676 million. To answer the question, therefore, we determine the required return that will push the portfolio value ($100 million, 10-year, 8%, semi-annual bonds) to that amount:

FV = 100,000,000; PMT = $8 / 2 = 4,000,000; N = 10 × 2 = 20; PV = –$78,676,000; CPT → I/Y = 5.83 × 2 = 11.67%

If the required return on the portfolio of bonds increases to 11.67%, the present value of the bonds will be exactly the minimum amount necessary to implement an immunization strategy at the current immunized rate. (Study Session 9, LOS 28.i)

13.5. **A**   Price has correctly described cash flow matching but has incorrectly described horizon matching. Cash flow matching involves finding a bond with a maturity date equal to the liability payment date, buying enough in par value of that bond so that the principal and final coupon fully fund the last liability, and continuing this process, using a recursive procedure, until all liabilities are matched. Features of multi-cash flow immunization include ensuring that assets and liabilities have the same present values and durations. Horizon matching (a.k.a. combination matching) is a combination of cash flow matching and multiple liability immunization. (Study Session 9, LOS 28.m)

13.6   **B**   Immunization risk can be totally eliminated by investing in zero-coupon bonds (e.g., Treasury strips) with a maturity and face value equal to that of the liability, so that statement is incorrect. That strategy is rarely followed, however, due to the high asset cost (low return potential). His statement about the dispersion of cash flows around the horizon date is correct, because the greater the dispersion the higher the reinvestment risk; the less the dispersion the lower the reinvestment risk. Note that using zeros is the extreme example of concentrating the asset maturities and cash inflows at the horizon date. (Study Session 9, LOS 28.f)

> Sample Scoring Key: 3 points for each correct response.

QUESTION 14

Reference: Book 2, Study Session 8
Book 3, Study Session 10
Book 4, Study Sessions 14 and 15

Cross-reference to CFA Institute assigned reading: Readings 27, 31, 40, and 41

14.1. **B**   RS is using a balanced mandate approach. In a balanced mandate approach, the manager is allowed discretion for hedging currency risk within the guidelines of the investor's investment policy statement. This approach manages currency risk as an integral part of the portfolio. It allows the manager to view the interaction between the risk of the asset and the currency. The currency overlay approach would assign the currency hedging process to another manager when the portfolio manager does not have the necessary hedging expertise. The overall process is still managed within the guidelines established by the investment policy statement. The currency as a separate asset allocation approach manages currency risk separate from the rest of the portfolio, such that the cash manager decides which currencies to hedge. (Study Session 14, LOS 40.i)

14.2. **A**   The hedging of currency risk with options should focus on buying an option, not writing (selling) them. In this case, the purchase of a put on Japanese yen provides RS with a minimum amount of Canadian dollars they will receive for the sale of Japanese yen. The sale of a call on Japanese yen would provide income enhancement but would not provide a complete hedge against adverse currency movements. The sale of a put on Canadian dollars is the same position as the sale of a call on Japanese yen (RS is giving the counterparty the right to sell them dollars in exchange for the counterparty buying Japanese yen). (Study Session 14, LOS 40.f)

14.3. **C**

$$\text{\# contracts} = \left(\frac{\beta_{target} - \beta_{current}}{\beta_{futures}}\right)\left(\frac{V_P}{V_F}\right)$$

$$= \left(\frac{1.80 - 0.60}{1.02}\right)\left(\frac{2,000,000}{110,000}\right) = 21.39 \ (\text{buy 21 contracts})$$

(Study Session 15, LOS 41.a)

14.4. **B**   RS would be least likely to hedge the currency risk of the British manufacturers. The currency hedging decision should consider the correlation between the asset and the currency. In developed markets, there is often a negative correlation between the currency and the equity. The reasoning is that when the currency depreciates, the foreign firm's exports are more competitive on international markets. Such a scenario is most likely for the developed market manufacturing firm here that exports. Because emerging market currencies are volatile, the Argentine cellular phone firm position would be more likely hedged than the British manufacturer position. (Study Session 8, LOS 27.c)

14.5. **A**   The CWC International mortgage has a higher coupon rate than newly issued mortgages. As such, it is likely to be called (i.e., homeowners will refinance) when interest rates decline and it has negative convexity (just as with any callable bond). If rates decline, the mortgage price rise will be capped at the call price. The price rise in the mortgage will be less than the loss in the short futures position. Thus, the mortgage and hedge combination would have a weak return if interest rates fall. (Study Session 10, LOS 31.a)

14.6. **C** Both Rolle and Sims are correct. Since mortgage securities exhibit negative convexity, two Treasury bond futures contracts are typically used as a hedge. If the volatility of interest rates increases, an investment in an MBS declines in value. The mortgage holder has sold the borrower an interest rate call that allows him to refinance the mortgage. As with any option, an increase in the underlying's volatility increases the value of the option. (Study Session 10, LOS 31.b)

Sample Scoring Key: 3 points for each correct response.

QUESTION 15

Reference: Book 3, Study Sessions 9 and 10

Cross-reference to CFA Institute assigned reading: Readings 28, 29, and 30

15.1. **C** To calculate the number of futures contracts necessary for the hedge, we must first obtain the dollar durations for the CTD and Bond Q:

The dollar duration for a given change in interest rates at time t is expressed as:

DD_t = duration$_t$ × assumed change in interest rates × value of asset at time t

DD_{CTD} is given as $13,245.46 for a 100 bps change in interest rates, which corresponds to a DD_{CTD} of $10,596.36 (= 0.8 × $13,245.46) for an 80 bps change in interest rates.

DD_Q = 10.32 × 0.008 × $104.98 = $8.6671 per $100 of par

The number of futures contracts necessary for the hedge can be computed as:

$$\text{\# contracts} = \left(\frac{DD_T - DD_P}{DD_{CTD} \big/ \text{conversion factor}} \right) (\text{yield beta})$$

The dollar duration of Bond Q:

$$(8.6671)\left(\frac{10,000,000}{100} \right) = \$866,710$$

$$\text{\# contracts} = \left(\frac{0 - \$866,710}{\$10,596.36 \big/ 1.3698} \right)(1.00) = -112.04$$

Therefore, sell 112 contracts.   (Study Session 10, LOS 30.e)

15.2. **B** The portfolio's dollar duration is the sum of the individual bond's dollar durations:

$$DD_P = DD_Q + DD_R + DD_S$$

$$= [(1.0498 \times 10,000,000) \times 0.01 \times 10.32]$$

$$+ [(0.9836 \times 25,000,000) \times 0.01 \times 8.67]$$

$$+ [(1.0121 \times 15,000,000) \times 0.01 \times 7.38]$$

$$= 1,083,394 + 2,131,953 + 1,120,395 = \$4,335,742$$

(Study Session 9, LOS 28.g)

15.3. **C** $$DD_{portfolio} = 0.01\big[(10m \times 1.0498 \times 9.46) + (25m \times 0.9836 \times 7.83) + (15m \times 1.0121 \times 6.51)\big]$$
$$= \$3{,}906{,}822$$

rebalancing ratio $= 4{,}901{,}106 / 3{,}906{,}822 = 1.2545$

We must increase the value of the portfolio by the rebalancing ratio, which assumes a proportionate increase in each bond. To do this, multiply the necessary percentage increase by the total value of the portfolio.

required cash = 0.2545 (Total value of Bond Q, Bond R, and Bond S)

required cash $= 0.2545\big[(10m \times 1.0498) + (25m \times 0.9836) + (15m \times 1.0121)\big] = \$12{,}793{,}588$

(Study Session 9, LOS 28.g)

15.4. **B** Rawlins is incorrect. If the slope coefficient from Tejada's regression was greater than one, the number of futures contracts needed to hedge a position would *increase* because the yield on the underlying bond would be more volatile than the yield on the hedge instrument.

Tejada is correct. The yield beta is obtained from using a regression equation in the following form:

yield on bond to be hedged = a + b(yield on CTD issue) + error

The yield beta, *b*, measures the relationship between changes in yields. If the yield spread between the bond being hedged and the CTD issue is assumed to be constant, the yields must move together and the yield beta must equal one.
(Study Session 10, LOS 30.e)

15.5. **A** Rawlins's basis for trading would most likely be characterized as that of yield pickup. He favors the bond with the higher yield and ignores the potential change in price of either bond. Rawlins should be examining both yield differentials and potential changes in both bonds' prices (a total return approach).

Tejada's basis for trading would most likely be characterized as a total return approach. He correctly evaluates both yield differentials and potential price changes in the bonds under evaluation. (Study Session 9, LOS 29.d)

15.6. **C** To determine which bond would be more attractive using breakeven analysis, we use modified duration. Recall the formula:

$$\%\Delta price = -modified\ duration \times \Delta yield \Rightarrow \Delta yield = \frac{\%\Delta price}{-modified\ duration}$$

For the returns to the two bonds to be equal over the next three months, the price for the Dynacom bond must fall by 0.5% (its yield advantage calculated by Rawlins in the vignette), holding the yield for the Bergamo bond constant. The change in yield that would result in this price change is:

$$\Delta yield = \frac{-0.5\%}{-5.13} = 0.0975\%$$

If the yield on the Dynacom bond rises 0.0975%, the return on the two bonds will be equal. So Tejada is correct because if the yield on the Dynacom bond rises by 0.75%, its price will fall such that its return will be lower than the return on the Bergamo bond over the next three months.

Rawlins is correct as well. Note that breakeven analysis uses the duration relationship, which provides only an approximate price change. Recall that the use of duration ignores any nonlinearity (i.e., convexity) in the bond price/yield relationship. (Study Session 10, LOS 30.k)

Sample Scoring Key: 3 points for each correct response.

QUESTION 16

Reference: Book 2, Study Session 7
Book 3, Study Session 10
Book 4, Study Sessions 14 and 15

Cross-reference to CFA Institute assigned reading: Readings 25, 30, 40, and 41

16.1. **B** All the BRIC countries except Russia are expected to remain below the G6 countries in terms of per capita income. Because developing countries currently utilize relatively low amounts of capital, an increase in investment capital will result in a relatively high level of output. Furthermore, as developing countries adopt technology available in developed countries, their productivity will increase. (Study Session 7, LOS 25.a,b,c)

16.2. **C** Amsler's portfolio is invested in European stocks that are denominated in the euro. She is therefore long European stocks and long the euro. In order to hedge, short positions should be taken in both the European stocks and the euro. If the European equity index or euro decline in value, the short positions in the derivative contracts will rise, therefore offsetting the losses in the underlying equity and currency positions. (Study Session 15, LOS 41.a,f)

16.3. **B** Tavinsky is incorrect. He has ignored the relative betas of the portfolio and futures contract.

The number of futures contracts can be calculated as:

$$N_f = \left(\frac{0-1.15}{0.975}\right)\left(\frac{15,000,000}{120,000}\right) = -147.44 \Rightarrow \text{short 147 contracts}$$

Treblehorn is correct. In a "hedging the principal" strategy, the investor simply sets the principal of the forward contract equal to the beginning principal value of the investment. The reason that the investor uses the beginning value and not some future value is that, especially in equity investments, the future value of the investment is very difficult to predict with accuracy. (Study Sessions 14 and 15, LOS 40.a and 41.a)

16.4. **A** If the local market declined by 12%, the equity position will decline an estimated $(-12\%)(1.15) = -13.8\%$. This would translate into a portfolio worth €15,000,000 × $(1 - 0.138) = €12,930,000$ at the end of the year. The ending position in dollars is worth $(€12,930,000)($1.12 / €) = $14,481,600$. Since the beginning portfolio value was worth $(€15,000,000)($1.05 / €) = $15,750,000$, this translates into a U.S. dollar loss of 8.05%. (Study Session 14, LOS 40.a)

16.5. **A** If the futures position was a perfect hedge, the euro rate of return on the equity portfolio will be the local risk-free rate of 2%. This would translate into an ending portfolio value of €15,300,000. The dollar equivalent of that portfolio would be $(€15,300,000)($1.12 / €) = $17,136,000$, which is an 8.8% return ($17,136,000 / $15,750,000 – 1$).

Professor's Note: Looking at it another way, the investor earns 2% in the local market and 6.67% [(1.12 / 1.05) – 1] on the euro appreciation. [(1.02) × (1.0667)] –1 = 8.8% total return.

(Study Session 14, LOS 40.a)

16.6. C Tavinsky is incorrect. By covered interest rate parity, the forward rate between two currencies must reflect the current spot times one plus the interest rate differentials in the two countries. So the forward rate must be ($1.05 / €) × (1.04 / 1.02) = ($1.0706 / €).

If a perfect hedge took place using equity futures, then the rate of return on the equity portfolio would be the local risk-free rate of 2%. This would translate into an ending portfolio value of €15,300,000.

If the €15,300,000 is sold in one year at the forward rate of ($1.0706 / €), the value of the portfolio in dollars will be $16,380,180. The starting portfolio value in dollars was (€15,000,000)($1.05 / €) = $15,750,000. So the investor's return in dollars, hedging both equity and currency risk, would be 4% ($16,380,180 / $15,750,000 – 1).

 Professor's Note: We could have arrived at this answer more quickly by recognizing that by interest rate parity, the return on a currency-hedged, risk-free foreign investment must equal the return on a domestic risk-free investment. So if interest rate parity holds the return must be 4%.

Treblehorn is incorrect. As noted previously, the forward rate must reflect interest rate differentials between the two countries. In this case, the forecasted spot rate of $1.12 / € does not equal the forward rate dictated by covered interest rate parity (i.e., $1.0706 / €). (Study Session 10, LOS 30.j)

Sample Scoring Key: 3 points for correct response.

QUESTION 17

Reference: Book 4, Study Session 14
Book 5, Study Session 17

Cross-reference to CFA Institute assigned reading: Readings 39 and 46

17.1. **C** The information ratio is calculated as average excess return (alpha) divided by the standard deviation of alpha (a.k.a. tracking error, active risk, or tracking risk). The information ratio shows not only the manager's ability to generate alpha, but his ability to *consistently* generate alpha. The greater the volatility of alpha compared to the average alpha, the less consistent the manager's performance. That is, as the information ratio decreases, the distribution of the manager's alpha increases (i.e., widens) relative to his average alpha. As the distribution of alpha increases, the probability of a zero or negative alpha in any single measurement period increases. A higher information ratio, therefore, generally indicates a superior ability to consistently generate alpha over time. (Study Session 17, LOS 46.p)

17.2. **C** The risk governance and risk budgeting statement (the second statement) is correct. Risk governance is part of the firm's overall corporate governance system and is the process of developing a risk management system and putting it into operation. A decentralized risk governance system puts risk management into the hands of those closest to the risk (e.g., individual managers). The primary drawback to a decentralized system is the inability for individual managers to gain a sense of how their risk affects the firm's overall risk. A centralized system is called an Enterprise Risk Management (ERM) system. ERM systems are overseen by top management who are better positioned to view and analyze the firm's overall risk.

Risk budgeting is the process of determining which risks are acceptable and how total risk is allocated across business units or portfolio managers. Through the ERM system upper management allocates capital across portfolio managers, each with an associated VAR.

The ERM statement (the third statement) is incorrect. Individual managers cannot determine the correlation of their portfolio risk to that of other managers, so only upper management is in a position to measure and monitor firm risk. In an ERM system upper management allocates capital to each manager based on the manager's risk and the desired overall firm risk. (Study Session 14, LOS 39.a)

17.3. **C** Liquidity risk is the possibility of sustaining losses due to the inability to take or liquidate a position quickly at a fair price. It is considered a financial risk. (Study Session 14, LOS 39.d)

17.4. **A** The Monte Carlo statement is correct. The main advantage of the Monte Carlo Method is the ability to incorporate any returns distribution or asset correlation. The historical VAR statement is incorrect. The variance/covariance method, not the historical method, is based on MPT. (Study Session 14, LOS 39.f)

17.5.   **A**   To calculate the daily VAR, we must first calculate a daily expected return and daily standard deviation. Note that to obtain a daily standard deviation from an annual standard deviation, we must divide the annual standard deviation by the square root of 250. We then calculate a daily percent VAR by subtracting 1.65 times the daily standard deviation from the daily expected return. The daily dollar VAR is calculated last using the fund's asset base:

daily expected return = 12.1% / 250 = 0.0484%

daily standard deviation = 18.2% / $(250)^{0.5}$ = 1.1511%

daily percent VAR = 0.0484% − (1.65 × 1.1511%) = −1.8509%

daily dollar VAR = $140 × 1.8509% = $2.59 million

(Study Session 14, LOS 39.e)

17.6.   **B**   Incremental VAR (IVAR) is used to measure the impact of a single asset on the portfolio VAR. By measuring the VAR of the portfolio with and without the asset, IVAR captures the effects of the correlations of the individual assets on the overall portfolio VAR. (Study Session 14, LOS 39.g)

Sample Scoring Key: 3 points for each correct response.

QUESTION 18

Reference: Book 3, Study Session 10
Book 4, Study Session 15

Cross-reference to CFA Institute assigned reading: Readings 30, 41, and 42

18.1. **C** The sale has resulted in transaction exposure; a change in revenues or costs that result from changes in foreign exchange rates. If the size of Smiler's sales to Frexa were to change as a result of a change in the $/€ rate this would be economic exposure. The third type of exposure is translation exposure, and it occurs when financial statements are converted from foreign currency to home currency.

The proceeds from the forward contract = €10m × 1.45$/€ = $14.5 million.
(Study Session 15, LOS 41.f)

18.2. **A** The cost of the call is 0.000943443 × 25 million = $23,586.

The future value of this premium at the beginning of the loan period based on current 90-day LIBOR plus the 150 bp spread is:

23,586 × [1 + (0.048 + 0.015) 90 / 360] = $23,957, making the net loan:

25,000,000 − 23,957 = $24,976,043

The payoff on the call = ($25,000,000)(0.0573 − 0.048)(180 / 360) = $116,250.

The effective dollar interest cost = ($25,000,000)(0.0573 + 0.0150)(180 / 360) − $116,250 = $787,500.

Alternatively, the interest on the loan can also be calculated as the exercise rate plus the spread because the call is in the money at expiration: (0.048 + 0.015) × 180 / 360 × 25,000,000 = $787,500.

The annualized rate on the loan is ($25,787,500 / $24,976,043)$^{365/180}$ − 1 = 6.6982%.
(Study Session 15, LOS 42.c)

18.3. **B** The equation to determine the number of contracts and the direction of the trade (long or short) is:

$$\text{number of contracts} = \left(\frac{\beta_{Target} - \beta_{Current}}{\beta_{Futures}}\right)\left(\frac{\text{portfolio value}}{\text{future contract value}}\right)$$

which in numeric terms is:

$$\text{number of contracts} = \left(\frac{0.9 - 1.25}{0.98}\right)\left(\frac{\$52,750,000}{1,050 \times \$250}\right) = -71.77; \text{ short 72 contracts.}$$

(Study Session 15, LOS 41.a)

18.4. **B** The dollar duration of the $25,000,000 corporate bond issue based on the expected yield to maturity at issuance with a constant spread to Treasuries is:

$25,000,000 \times 0.005 \times 9.90 = \$1,237,500$

$$\text{number of contracts} = \frac{DD_T - DD_P}{DD_{CTD}/\text{conversion factor}}\left(\text{yield beta}\right) \qquad \left[DD_T = 0\right]$$

$$= \frac{-\$1,237,500}{\$6,932.53/1.259}(1.05) = -236$$

(Study Session 10, LOS 30.e)

18.5. **C** The futures contract has an expiration date that coincides with the expected date of the bond issuance, so the basis will be zero and does not have to be estimated. (Study Session 10, LOS 30.e)

18.6. **C** Ng has an investment in British stocks, which he will be converting to U.S. dollars in one year. The problem with hedging the foreign exchange rate risk of an equity investment is that the investor does not know how much to hedge because the investment's value fluctuates. (Study Session 15, LOS 41.f)

Sample Scoring Key: 3 points for each correct response.

QUESTION 19

Reference: Book 1, Study Session 1

Cross-reference to CFA Institute assigned reading: Reading 1

19.1. **B** Olson has failed to exercise due diligence and form a reasonable basis for her statement regarding rayon feedstocks. She has used information from two executives at one company in the industry to draw conclusions about the overall market. This does not reflect the thoroughness required by Standard V(A) Diligence and Reasonable Basis, and, thus, Olson has violated the Standard. In addition, she may have violated Standard V(B) Communication with Clients and Prospective Clients by failing to distinguish between opinion and fact in her research report. (Study Session 1, LOS 1.b)

19.2. **B** According to CFA Institute Standard I(C) Misrepresentation, members and candidates are allowed to utilize factual information and data published by well-known entities that report financial and statistical information or other sources that are similar without providing citations of these sources. Widely published data from S&P and the central bank of the Korean government would fall into this category. (Study Session 1, LOS 1.b)

19.3. **A** Under CFA Institute Standard I(C) Misrepresentation, members and candidates are required to acknowledge the sources of information that they incorporate into their own work that do not originate from a recognized financial/statistical reporting service. Therefore, Olson must properly cite the information obtained from the brokerage reports in order to comply with Standard I(C). (Study Session 1, LOS 1.b)

19.4. **C** Olson's report mischaracterizes the level of risk inherent in the investment. As such, this constitutes a violation of Standard V(B) Communication with Clients and Prospective Clients. Olson has also violated Standard I(C) Misrepresentation by misleading investors as to the true nature of the risk associated with an investment in Han Chemical. (Study Session 1, LOS 1.b)

19.5. **B** In most cases, it would be a violation of CFA Institute Standards to divulge information, which was transmitted in confidence. However, under Standard III(E) Preservation of Confidentiality, an exception is made for information pertaining to an illegal act. Especially since she has issued a research report and buy order for Han, she is compelled under the Standard to divulge such information. She should address the matter with Bern's chief compliance officer as the first step in the process. (Study Session 1, LOS 1.b)

19.6. **A** All of Hundt's actions are consistent with CFA Institute Standard IV(C) Responsibilities of Supervisors. According to this Standard, supervisors exercise reasonable supervision by ensuring that employees follow the written compliance procedures established by their supervisor. Supervisors have a responsibility to disseminate the compliance procedures to employees and it is recommended that they regularly update procedures and continually educate personnel subject to the procedures. If a supervisor knows of a violation, she must promptly begin an investigation into the matter. (Study Session 1, LOS 1.b)

> Sample Scoring Key: 3 points for each correct response.

Notes

Notes

Notes

Notes

Notes